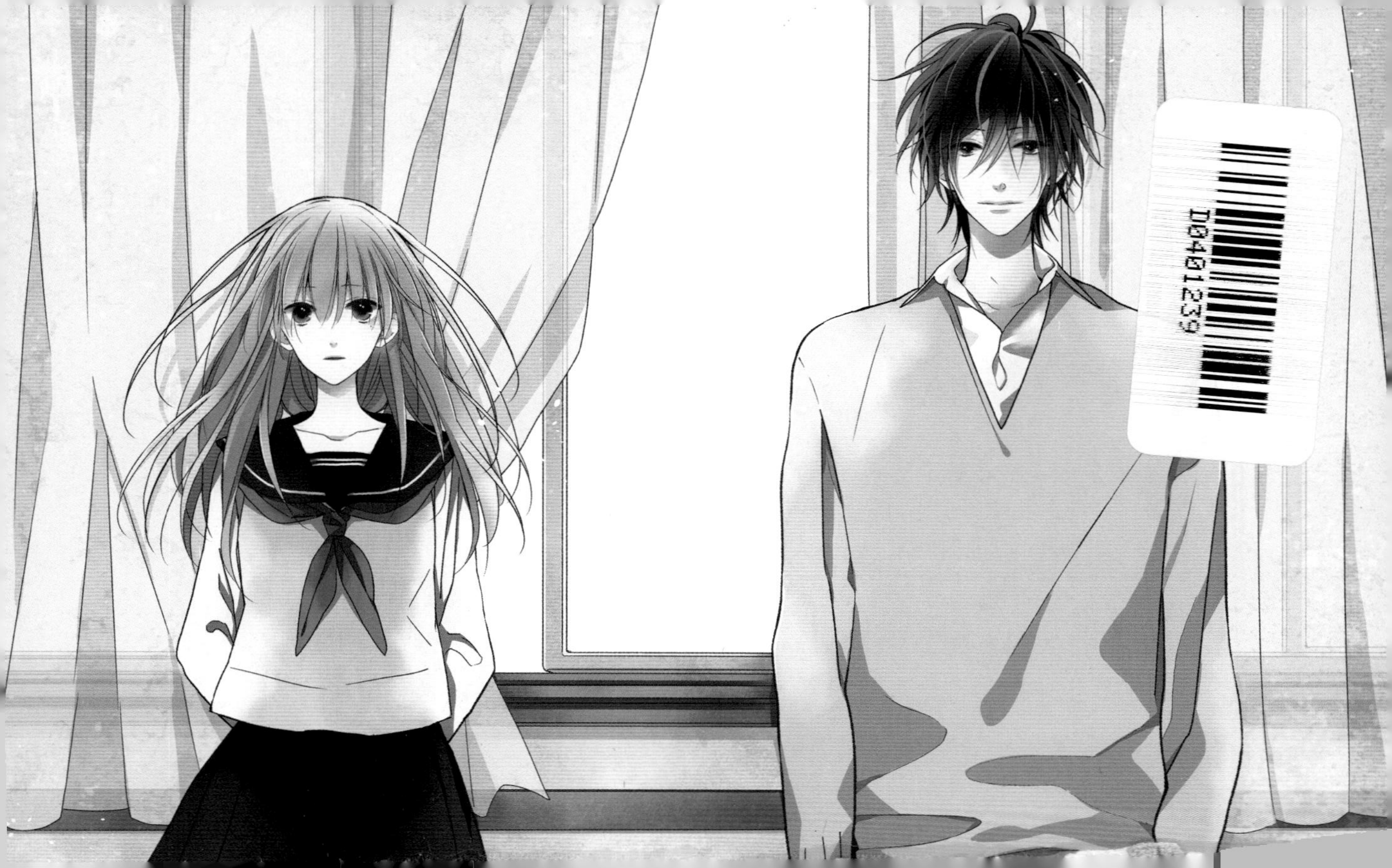

That Wolf-Boy is Mine!

Contents

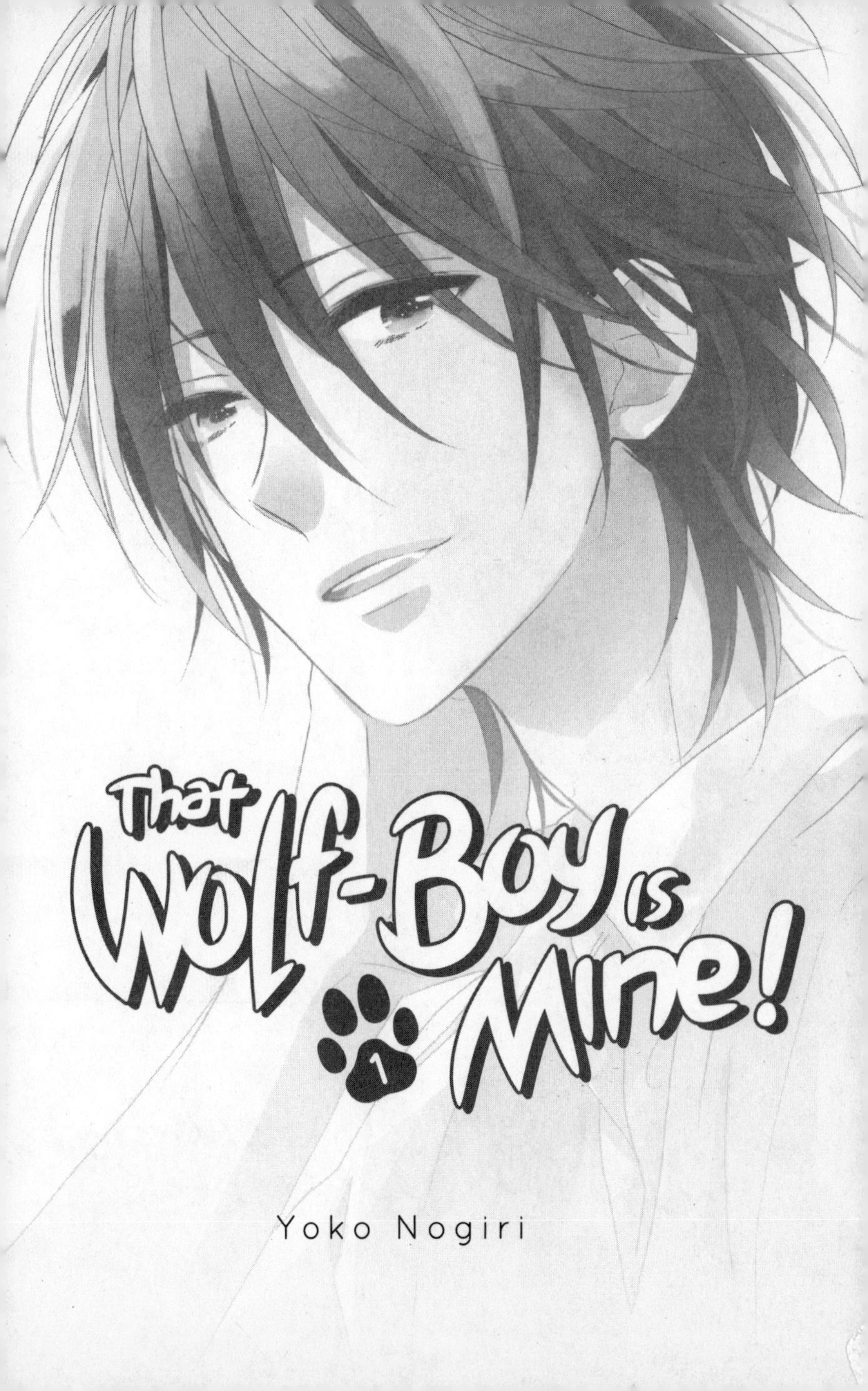
That Wolf-Boy is Mine!
1

Yoko Nogiri

That Wolf-Boy is Mine!

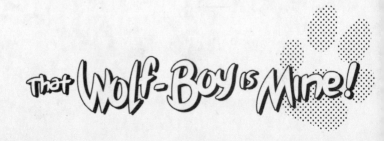

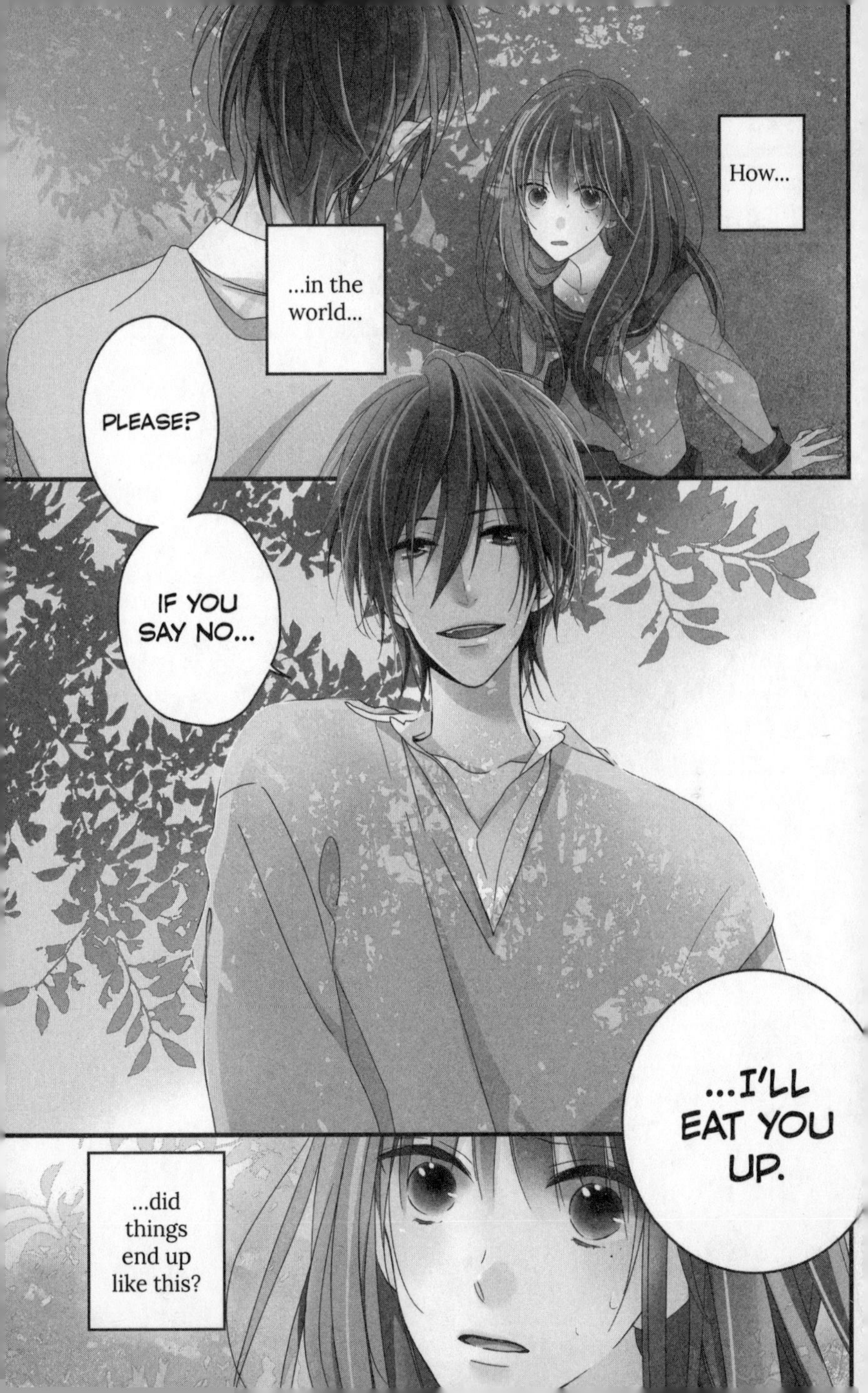
How...
...in the world...
PLEASE?
IF YOU SAY NO...
...I'LL EAT YOU UP.
...did things end up like this?

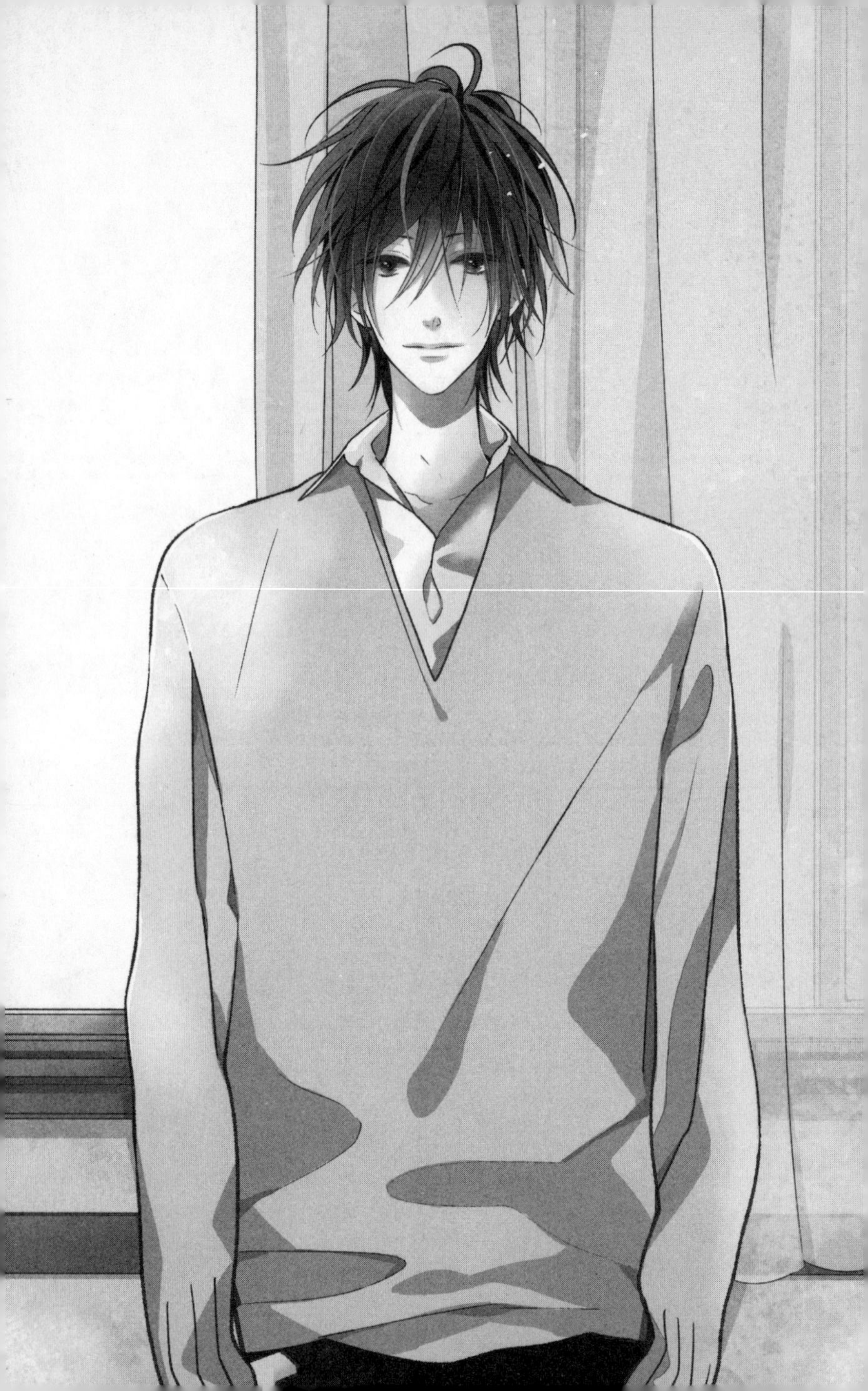

Chapter 1

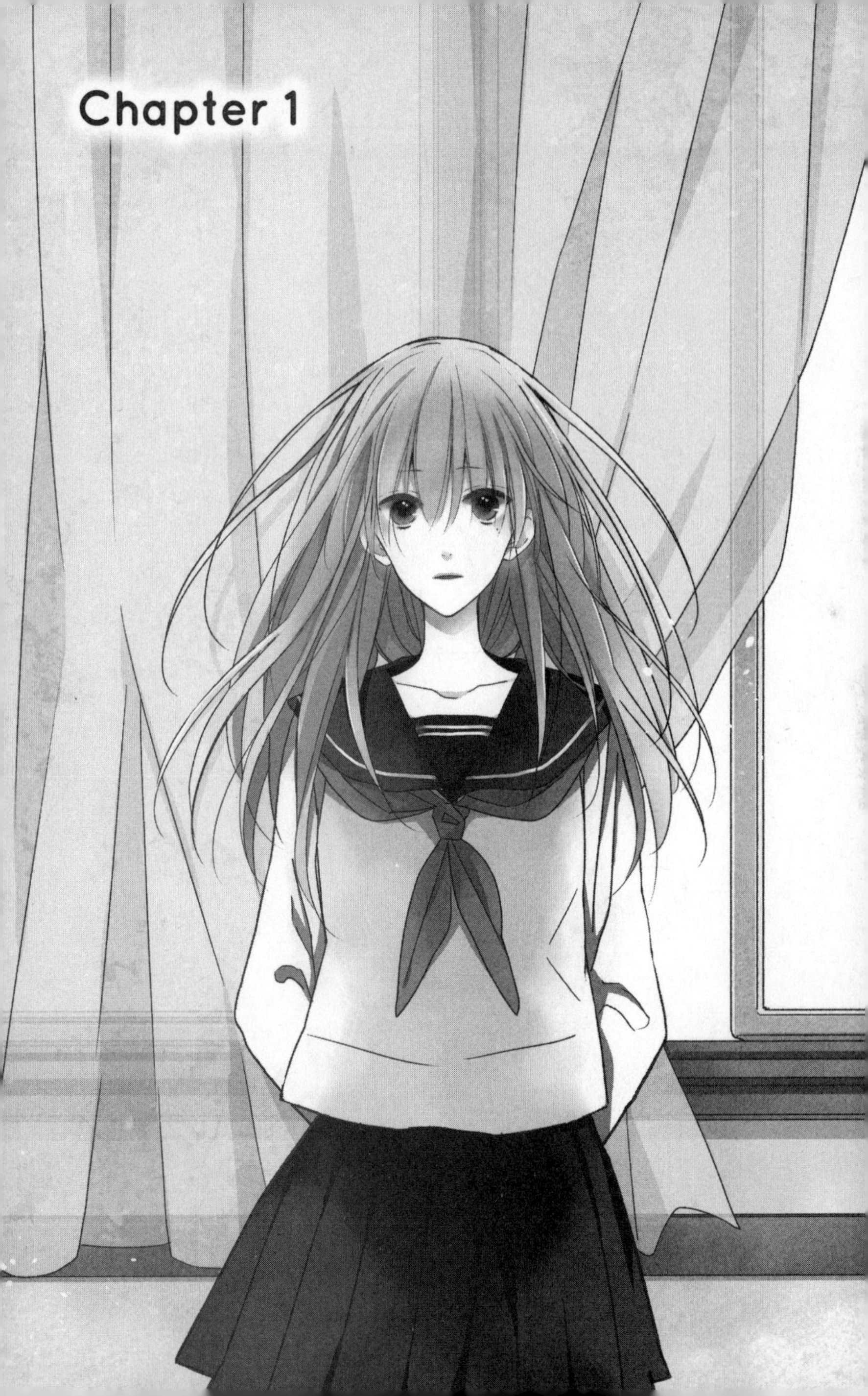

That Wolf-Boy is Mine!

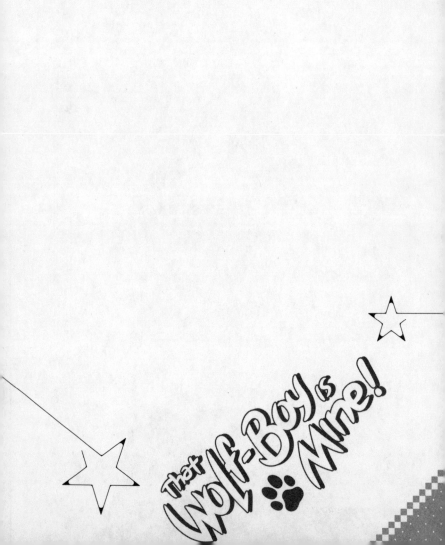

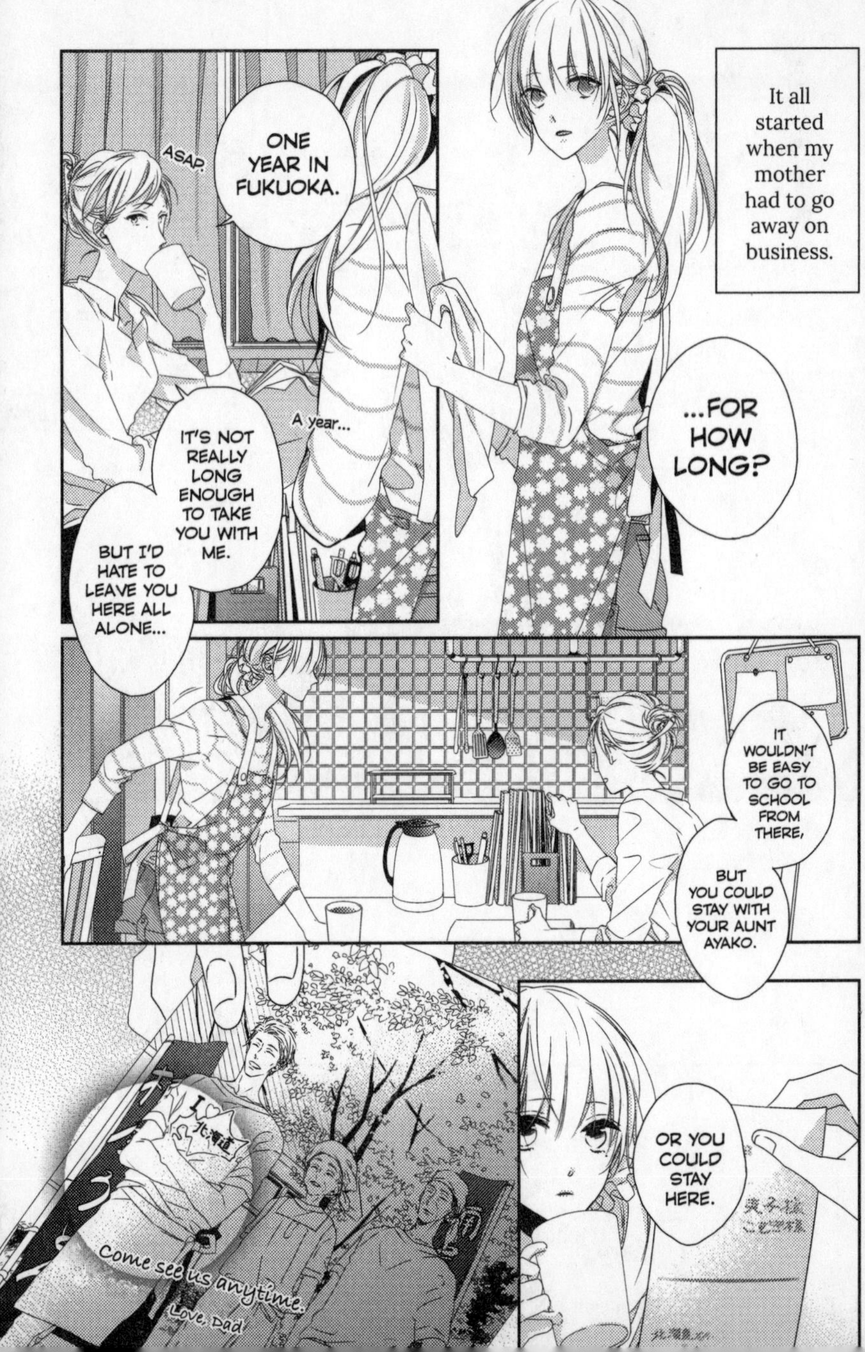
It all started when my mother had to go away on business.
...FOR HOW LONG?
ONE YEAR IN FUKUOKA.
ASAP.
A year...
IT'S NOT REALLY LONG ENOUGH TO TAKE YOU WITH ME.
BUT I'D HATE TO LEAVE YOU HERE ALL ALONE...
IT WOULDN'T BE EASY TO GO TO SCHOOL FROM THERE,
BUT YOU COULD STAY WITH YOUR AUNT AYAKO.
OR YOU COULD STAY HERE.
Come see us anytime.
Love, Dad

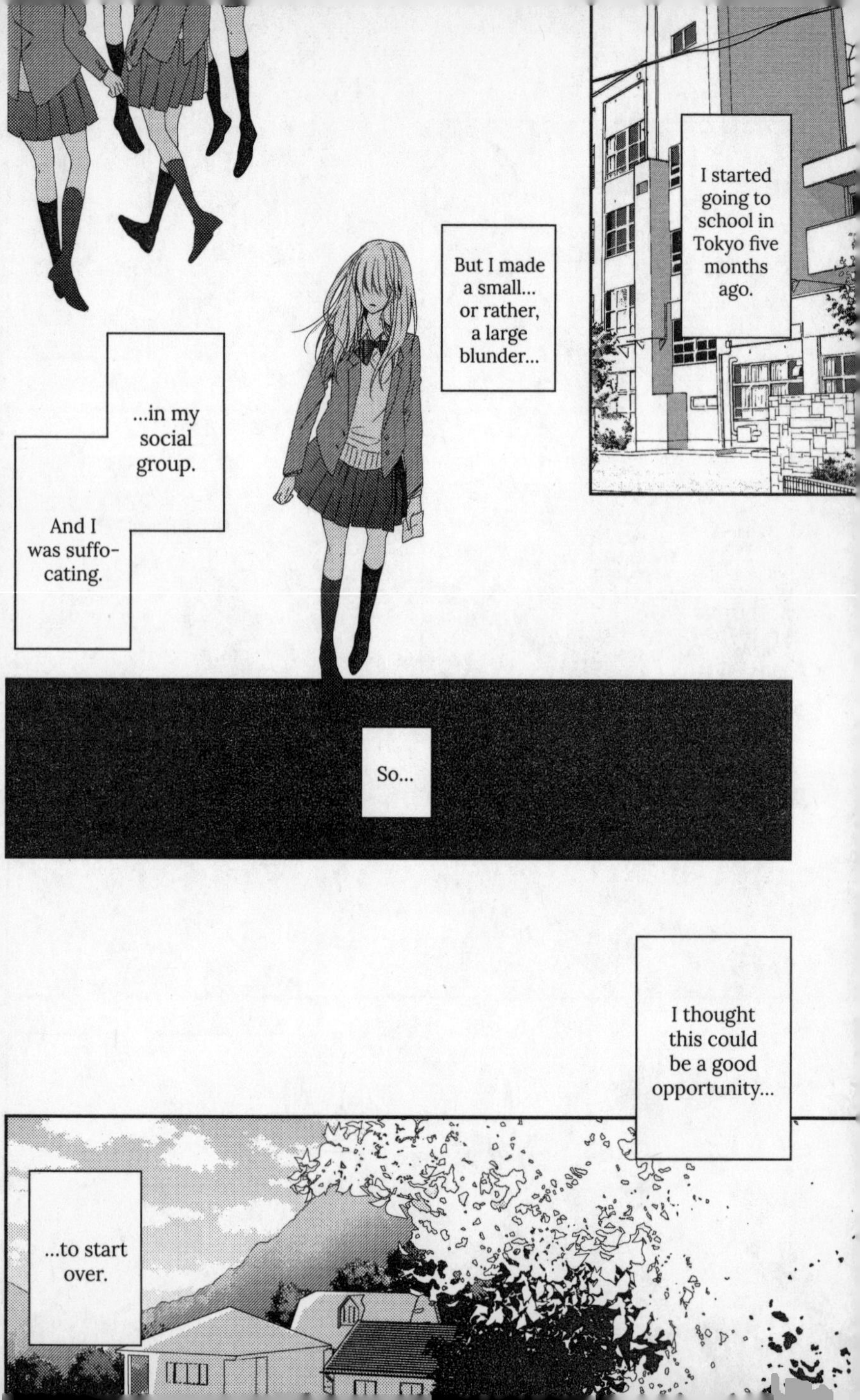
I started going to school in Tokyo five months ago.
But I made a small... or rather, a large blunder...
...in my social group.
And I was suffocating.
So...
I thought this could be a good opportunity...
...to start over.

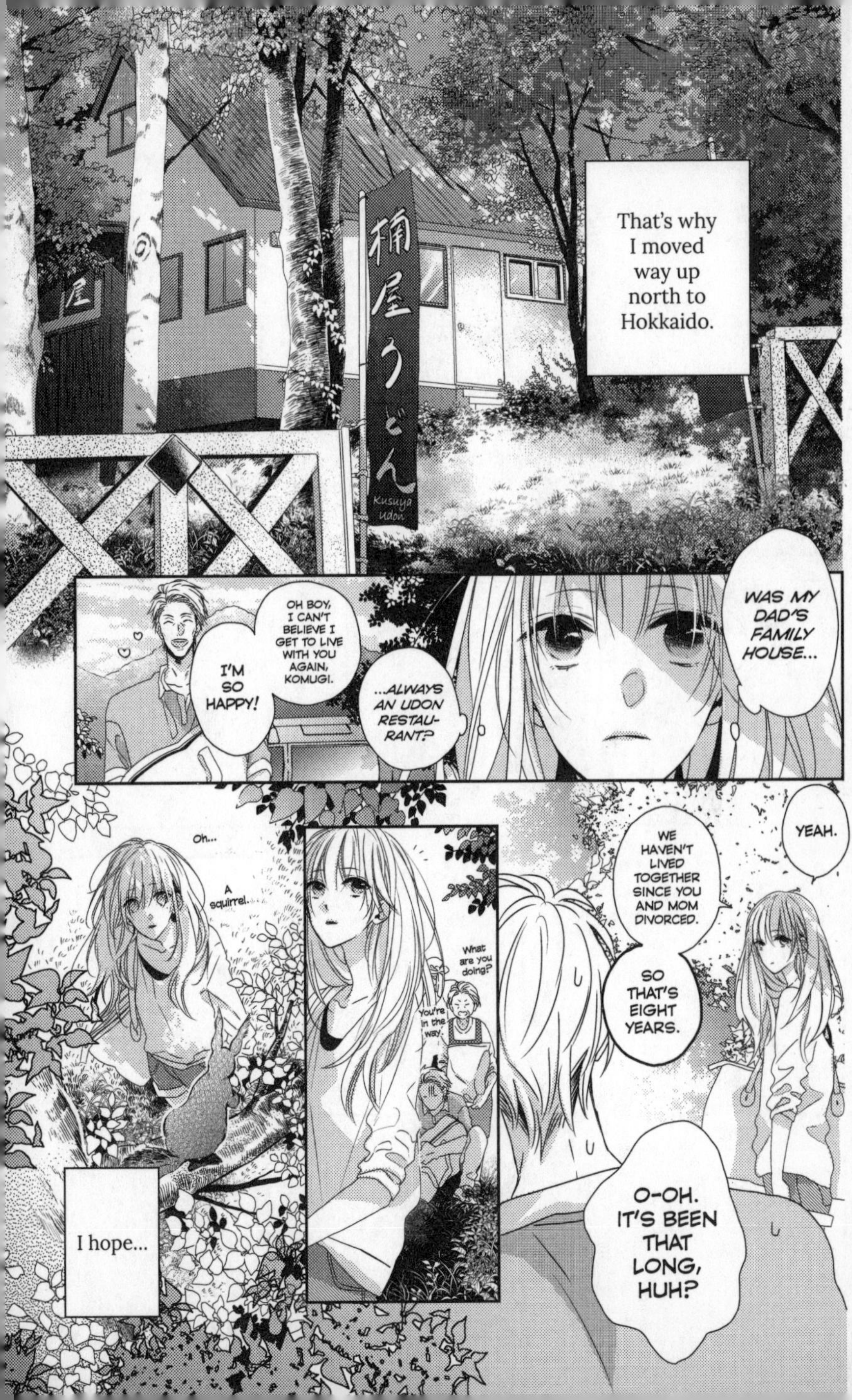

楠屋うどん
Kusuya Udon
That's why I moved way up north to Hokkaido.
WAS MY DAD'S FAMILY HOUSE...
...ALWAYS AN UDON RESTAURANT?
OH BOY, I CAN'T BELIEVE I GET TO LIVE WITH YOU AGAIN, KOMUGI.
I'M SO HAPPY!
YEAH.
WE HAVEN'T LIVED TOGETHER SINCE YOU AND MOM DIVORCED.
SO THAT'S EIGHT YEARS.
O-OH. IT'S BEEN THAT LONG, HUH?
What are you doing?
You're in the way.
Oh...
A squirrel.
I hope...

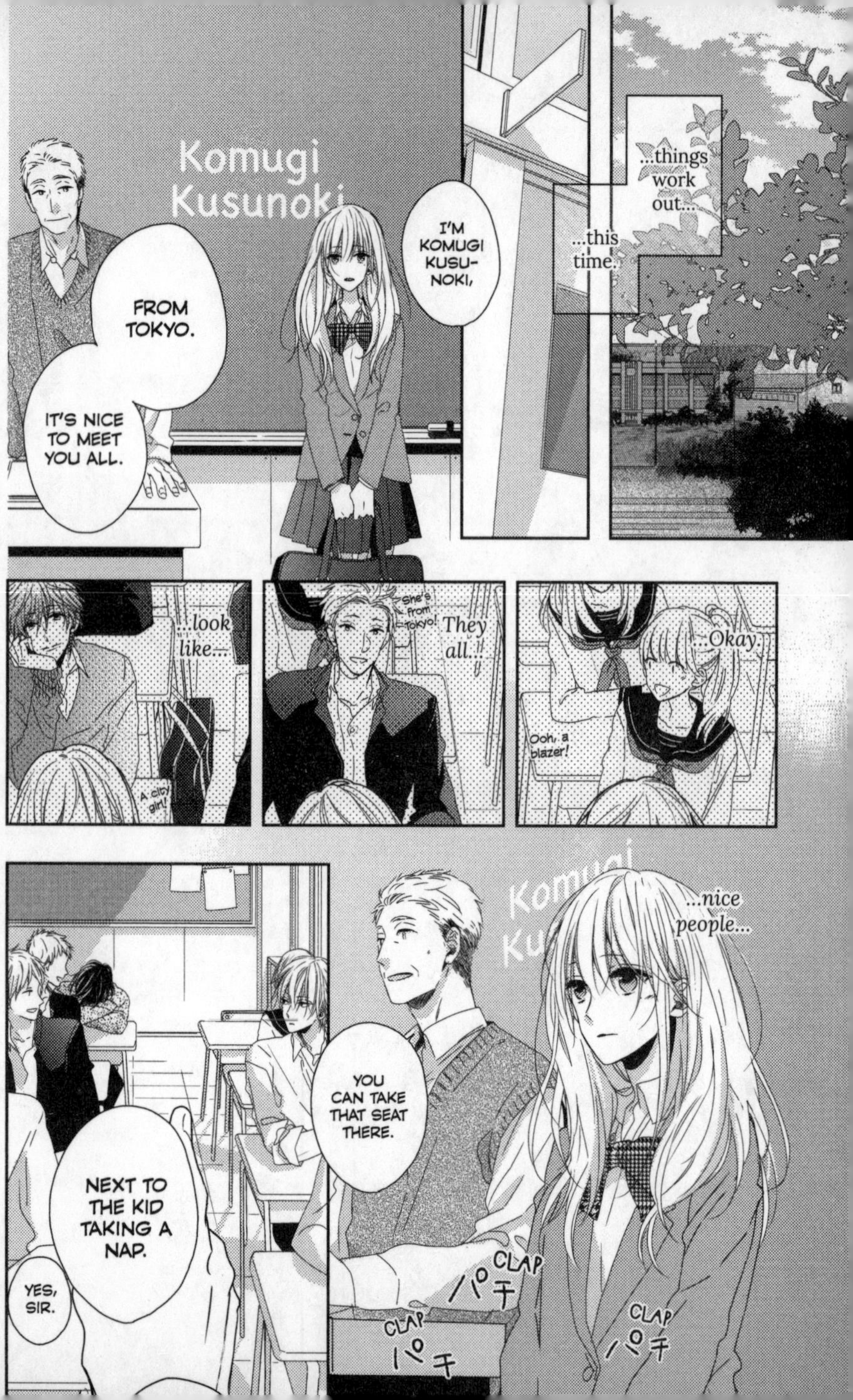

...things work out...
...this time.
Komugi Kusunoki
I'M KOMUGI KUSUNOKI,
FROM TOKYO.
IT'S NICE TO MEET YOU ALL.
...Okay.
Ooh, a blazer!
She's from Tokyo!
They all...
...look like...
A city girl!
...nice people...
YOU CAN TAKE THAT SEAT THERE.
CLAP パチ
CLAP パチ
CLAP パチ
NEXT TO THE KID TAKING A NAP.
YES, SIR.

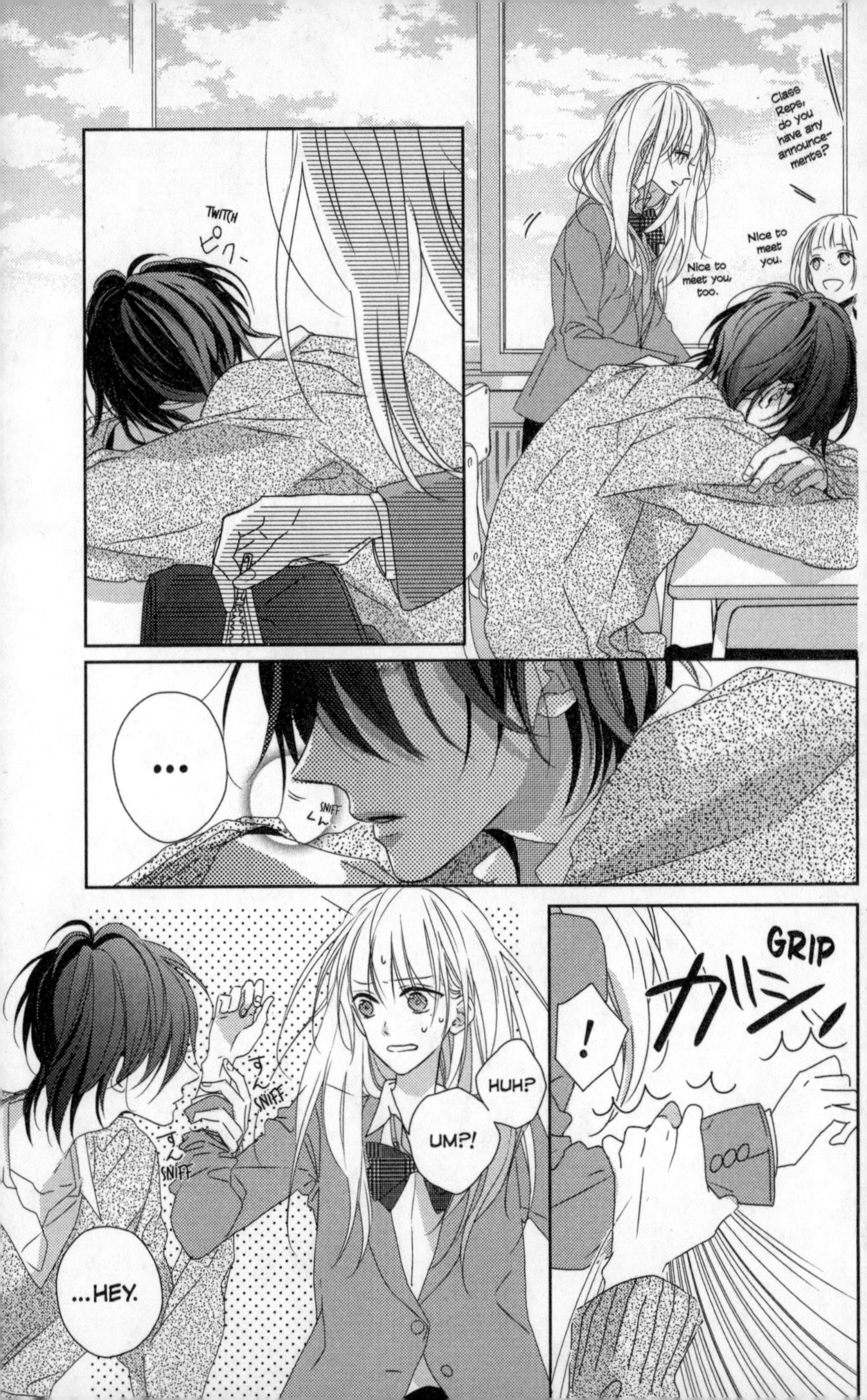
Class Reps, do you have any announcements?
Nice to meet you.
Nice to meet you, too.
TWITCH
...
SNIFF
GRIP
!
HUH?
UM?!
SNIFF
SNIFF
...HEY.

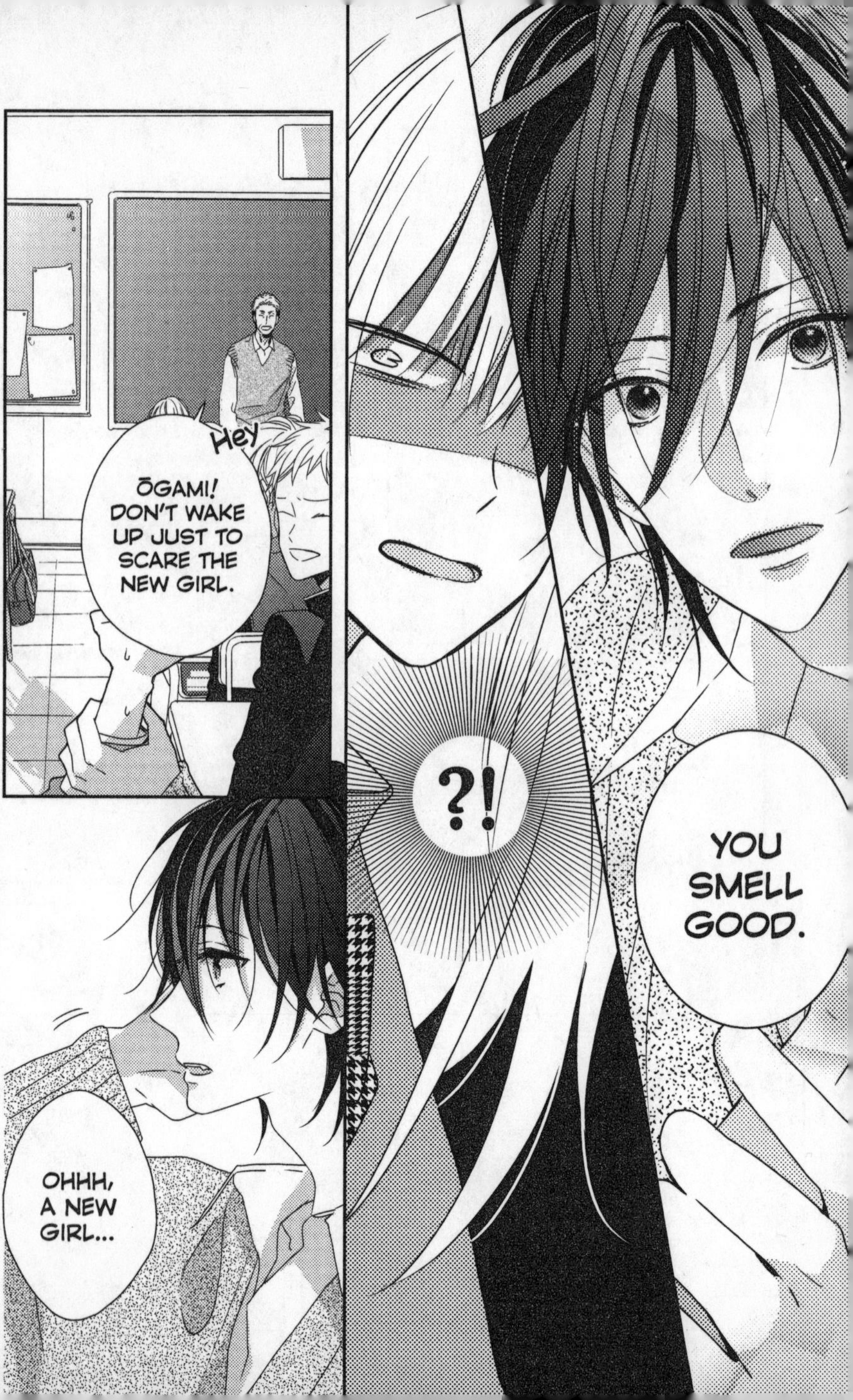
?!
YOU SMELL GOOD.
Hey
ŌGAMI! DON'T WAKE UP JUST TO SCARE THE NEW GIRL.
OHHH, A NEW GIRL...

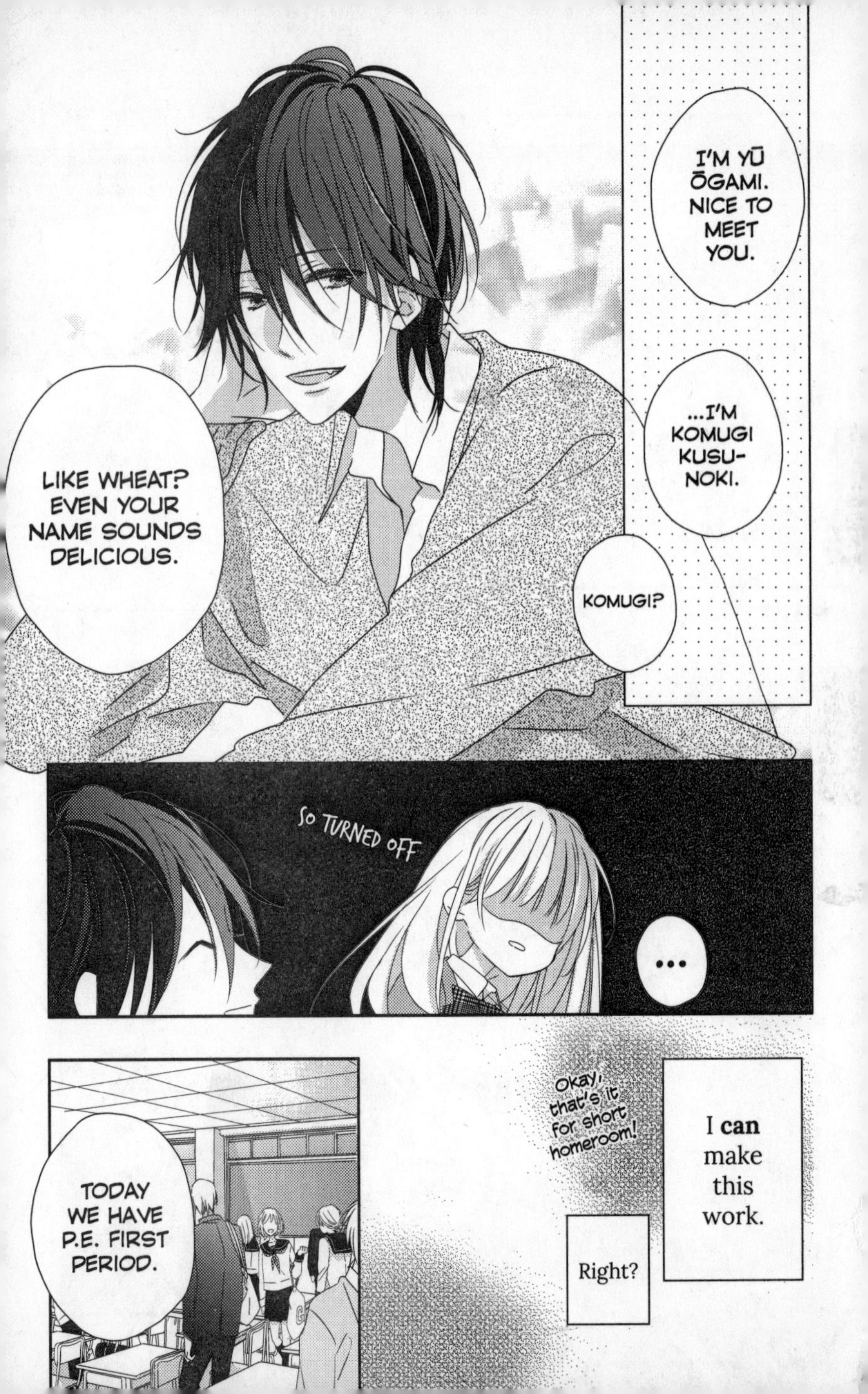
I'M YŪ ŌGAMI. NICE TO MEET YOU.
...I'M KOMUGI KUSUNOKI.
KOMUGI?
LIKE WHEAT? EVEN YOUR NAME SOUNDS DELICIOUS.
...
SO TURNED OFF
I **can** make this work.
Right?
Okay, that's it for short homeroom!
TODAY WE HAVE P.E. FIRST PERIOD.

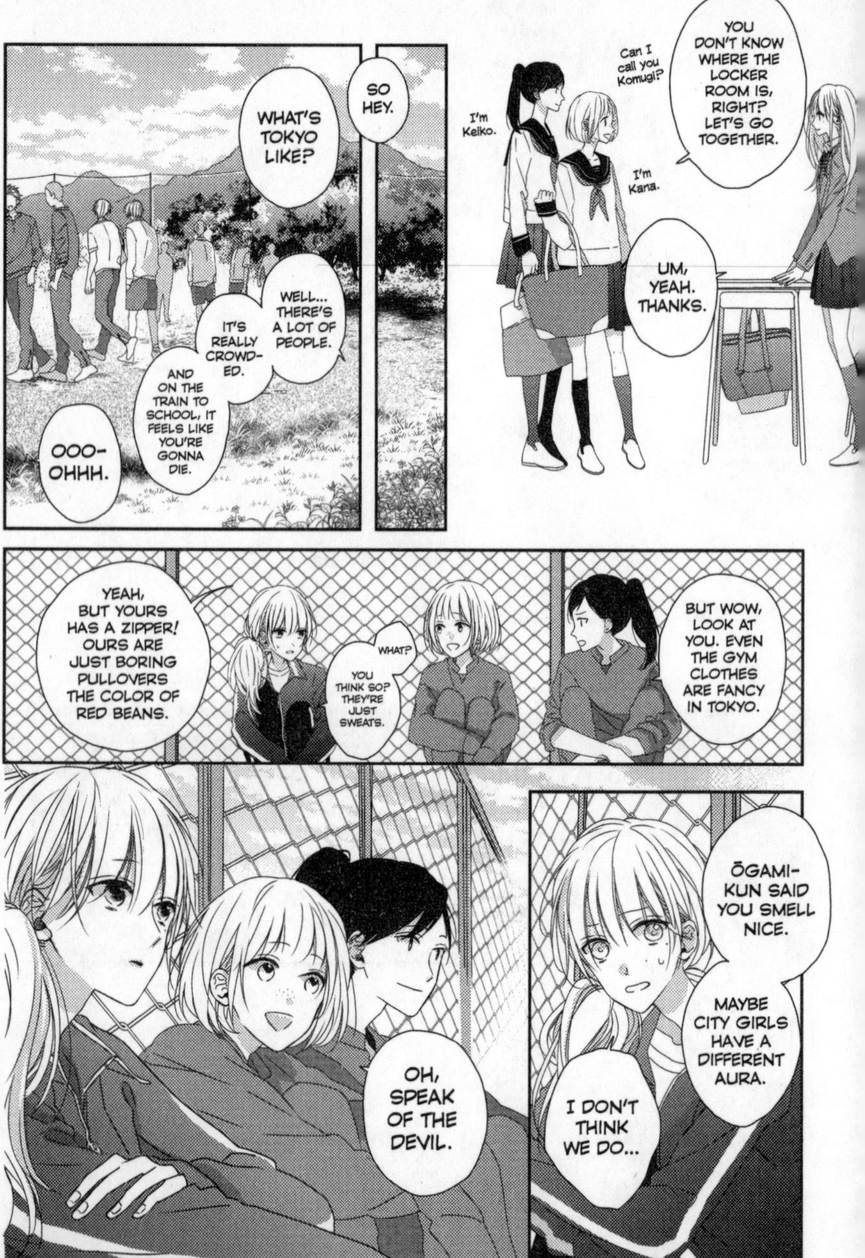
YOU DON'T KNOW WHERE THE LOCKER ROOM IS, RIGHT? LET'S GO TOGETHER.
Can I call you Komugi?
I'm Keiko.
I'm Kana.
UM, YEAH. THANKS.
SO HEY.
WHAT'S TOKYO LIKE?
WELL... THERE'S A LOT OF PEOPLE.
IT'S REALLY CROWD-ED.
AND ON THE TRAIN TO SCHOOL, IT FEELS LIKE YOU'RE GONNA DIE.
OOO-OHHH.
BUT WOW, LOOK AT YOU. EVEN THE GYM CLOTHES ARE FANCY IN TOKYO.
WHAT?
YOU THINK SO? THEY'RE JUST SWEATS.
YEAH, BUT YOURS HAS A ZIPPER! OURS ARE JUST BORING PULLOVERS THE COLOR OF RED BEANS.
ŌGAMI-KUN SAID YOU SMELL NICE.
MAYBE CITY GIRLS HAVE A DIFFERENT AURA.
I DON'T THINK WE DO...
OH, SPEAK OF THE DEVIL.

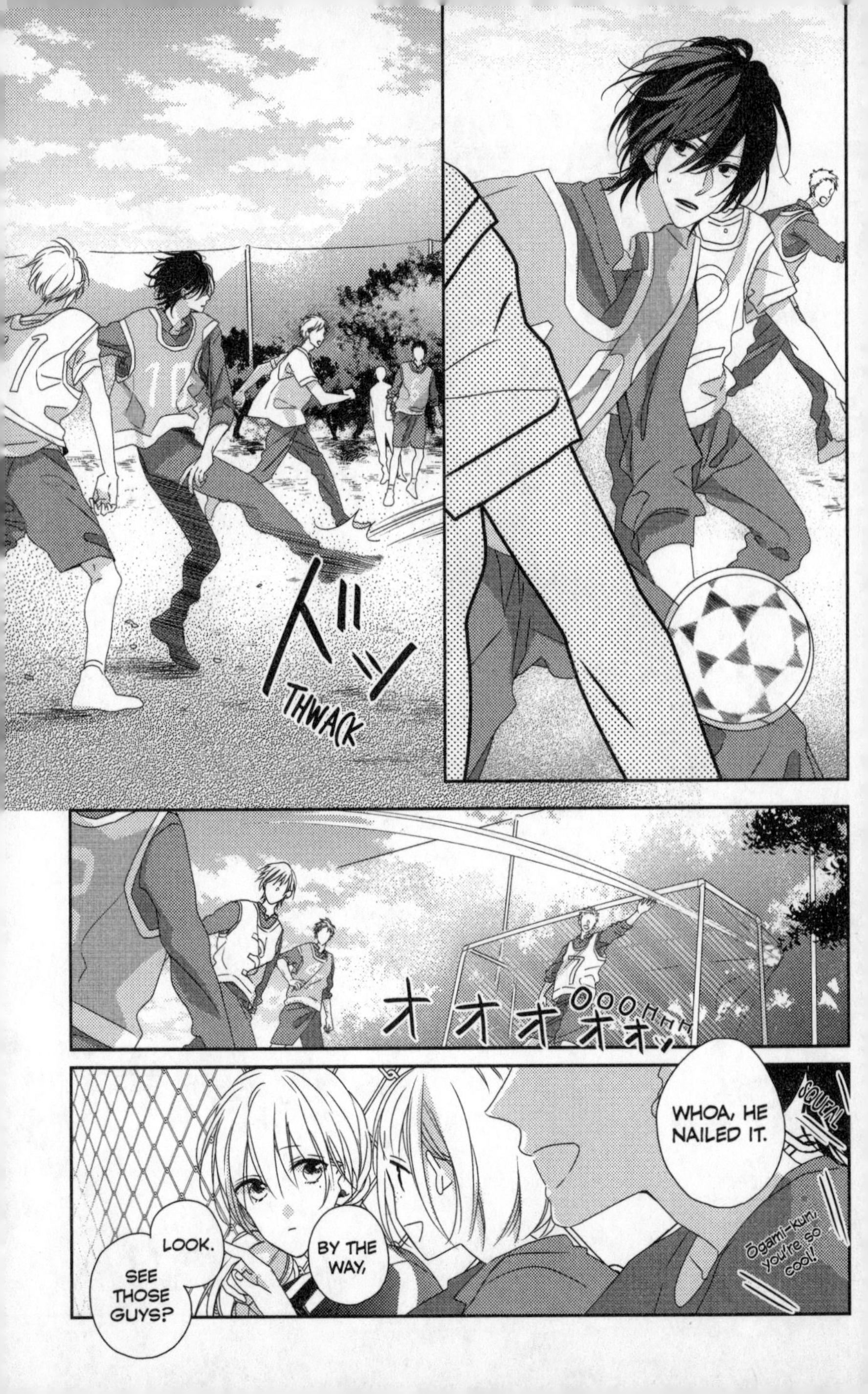
ドッ
THWACK
オオオオオッ
OOOHHH
SQUEAL
Ōgami-kun, you're so cool!
WHOA, HE NAILED IT.
BY THE WAY,
LOOK.
SEE THOSE GUYS?

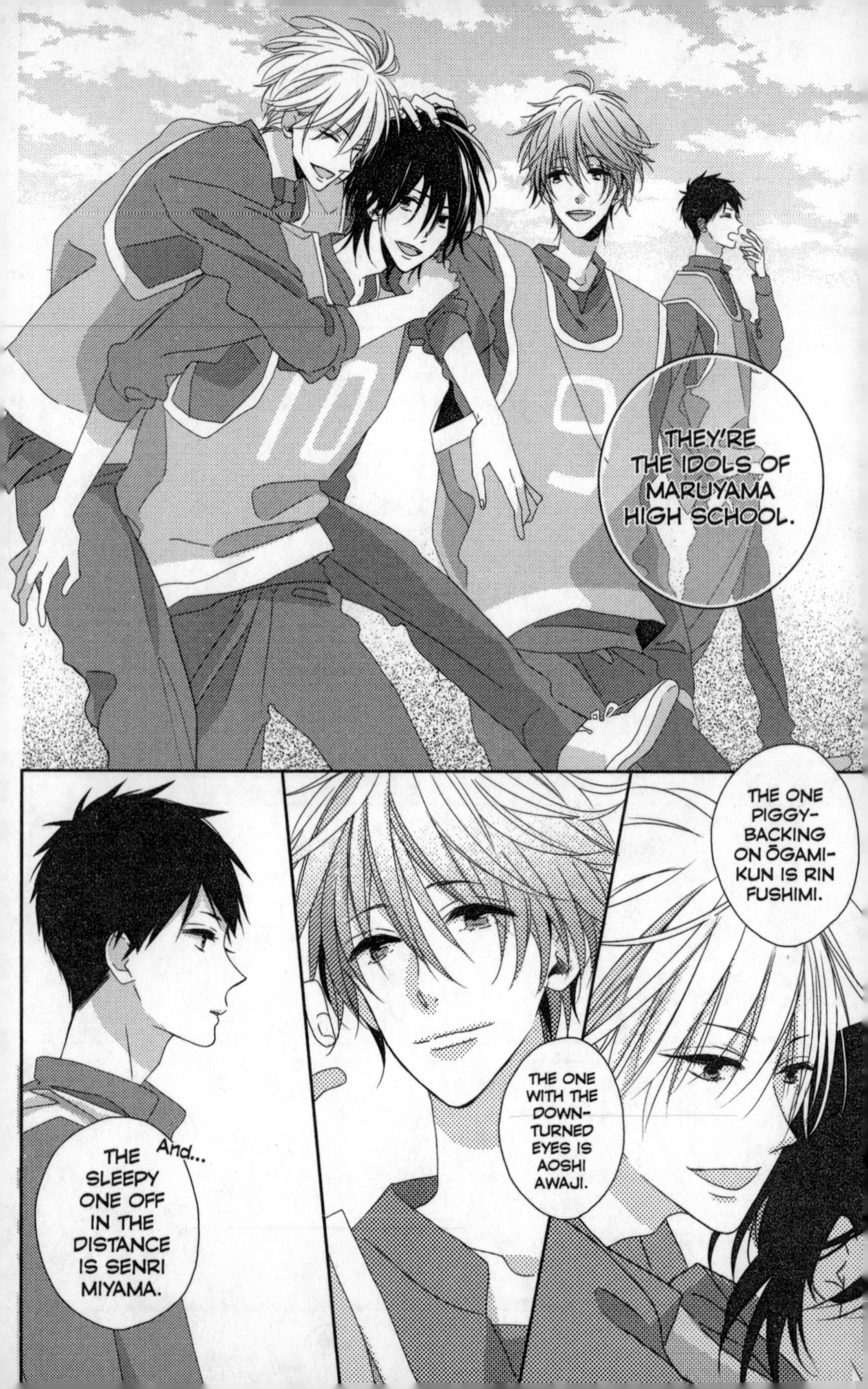
THEY'RE THE IDOLS OF MARUYAMA HIGH SCHOOL.
THE ONE PIGGY-BACKING ON ŌGAMI-KUN IS RIN FUSHIMI.
THE ONE WITH THE DOWN-TURNED EYES IS AOSHI AWAJI.
And...
THE SLEEPY ONE OFF IN THE DISTANCE IS SENRI MIYAMA.

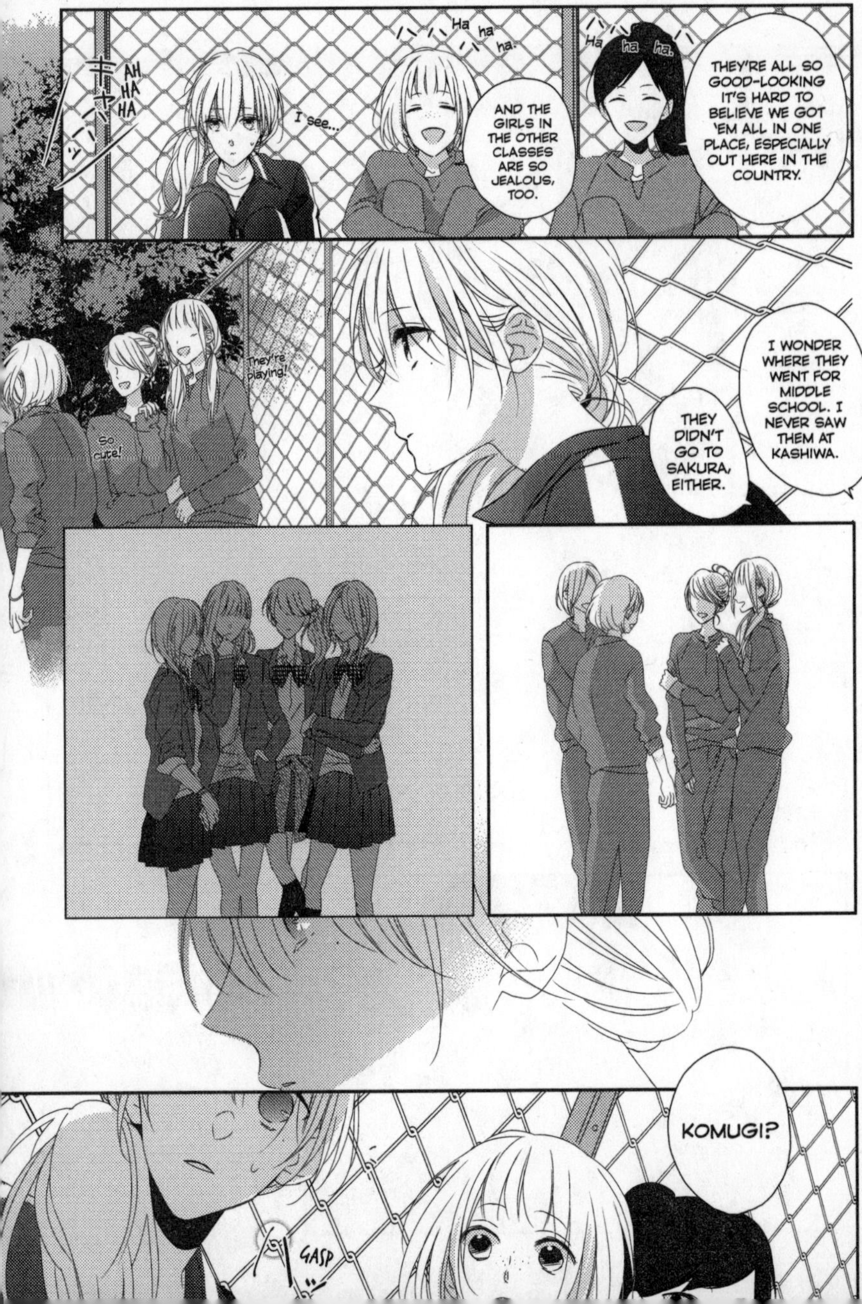

Ha ha ha.
THEY'RE ALL SO GOOD-LOOKING IT'S HARD TO BELIEVE WE GOT 'EM ALL IN ONE PLACE, ESPECIALLY OUT HERE IN THE COUNTRY.
Ha ha ha.
AND THE GIRLS IN THE OTHER CLASSES ARE SO JEALOUS, TOO.
I see...
AH HA HA
I WONDER WHERE THEY WENT FOR MIDDLE SCHOOL. I NEVER SAW THEM AT KASHIWA.
THEY DIDN'T GO TO SAKURA, EITHER.
They're playing!
So cute!
KOMUGI?
GASP

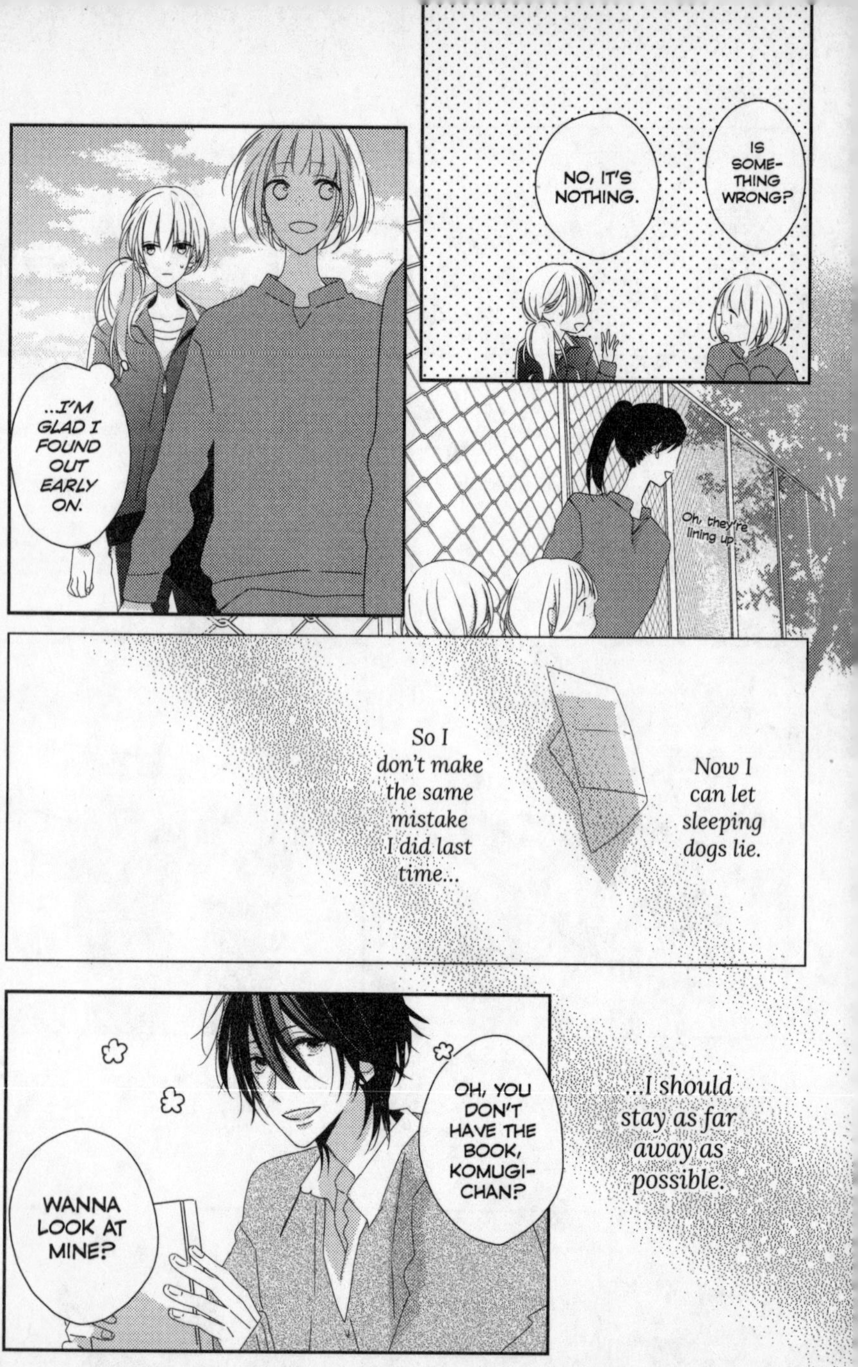
IS SOMETHING WRONG?
NO, IT'S NOTHING.
Oh, they're lining up.
...I'M GLAD I FOUND OUT EARLY ON.
Now I can let sleeping dogs lie.
So I don't make the same mistake I did last time...
...I should stay as far away as possible.
OH, YOU DON'T HAVE THE BOOK, KOMUGI-CHAN?
WANNA LOOK AT MINE?

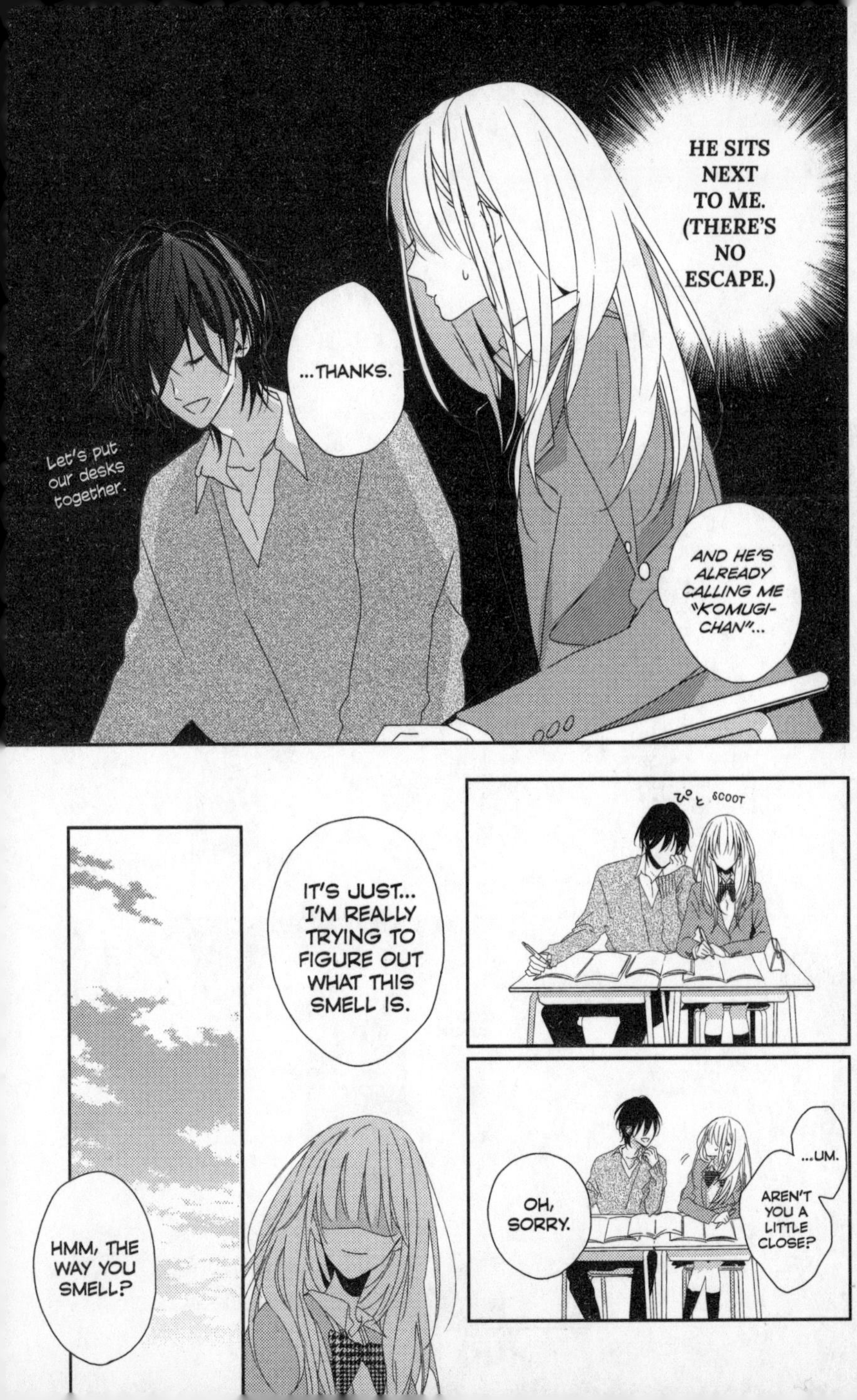
HE SITS NEXT TO ME. (THERE'S NO ESCAPE.)
...THANKS.
AND HE'S ALREADY CALLING ME "KOMUGI-CHAN"...
Let's put our desks together.
ぴと SCOOT
...UM.
AREN'T YOU A LITTLE CLOSE?
OH, SORRY.
IT'S JUST... I'M REALLY TRYING TO FIGURE OUT WHAT THIS SMELL IS.
HMM, THE WAY YOU SMELL?

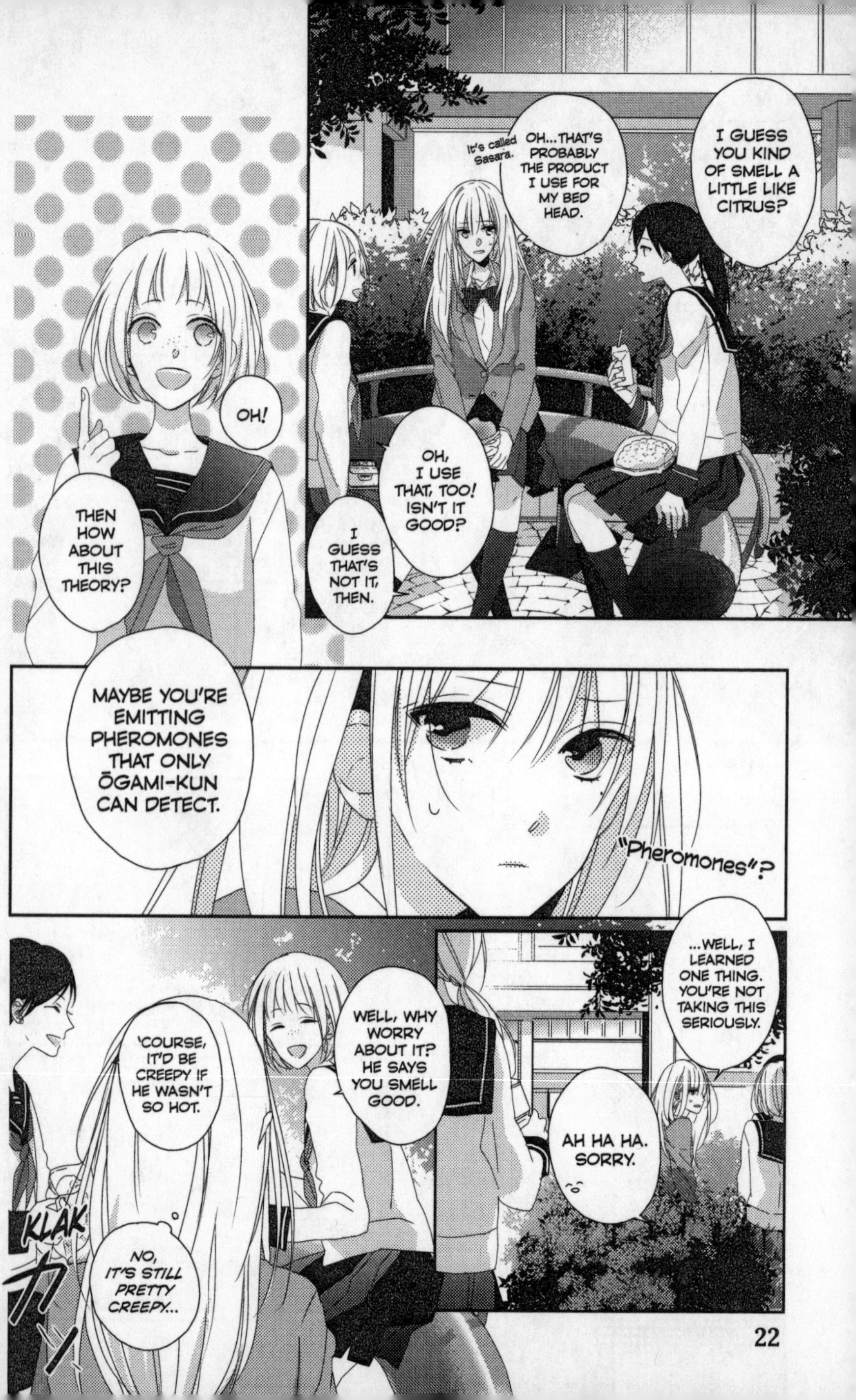

I GUESS YOU KIND OF SMELL A LITTLE LIKE CITRUS?
OH...THAT'S PROBABLY THE PRODUCT I USE FOR MY BED HEAD.
It's called Sasara.
OH, I USE THAT, TOO! ISN'T IT GOOD?
I GUESS THAT'S NOT IT, THEN.
OH!
THEN HOW ABOUT THIS THEORY?
MAYBE YOU'RE EMITTING PHEROMONES THAT ONLY ŌGAMI-KUN CAN DETECT.
"Pheromones"?
...WELL, I LEARNED ONE THING. YOU'RE NOT TAKING THIS SERIOUSLY.
AH HA HA. SORRY.
WELL, WHY WORRY ABOUT IT? HE SAYS YOU SMELL GOOD.
'COURSE, IT'D BE CREEPY IF HE WASN'T SO HOT.
NO, IT'S STILL PRETTY CREEPY...
KLAK

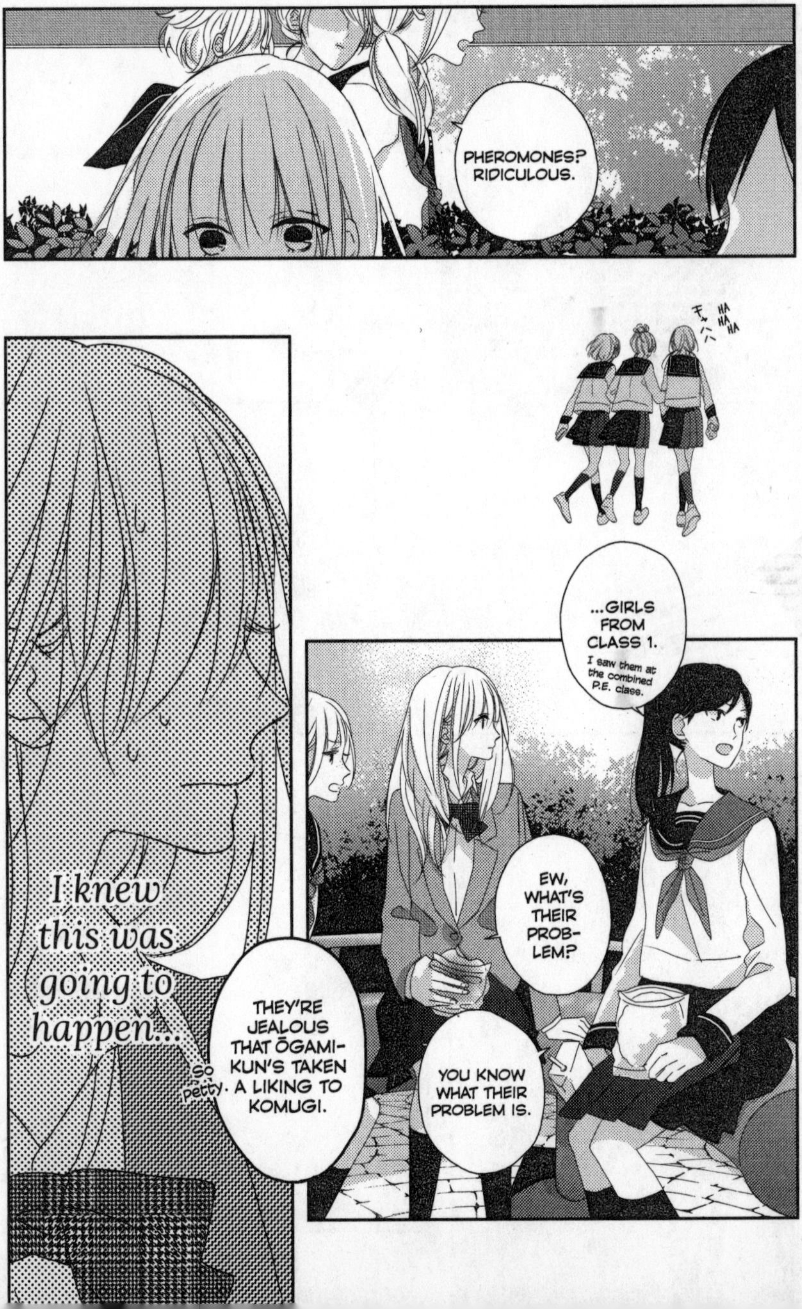
PHEROMONES? RIDICULOUS.
HA HA HA
...GIRLS FROM CLASS 1.
I saw them at the combined P.E. class.
EW, WHAT'S THEIR PROB-LEM?
YOU KNOW WHAT THEIR PROBLEM IS.
THEY'RE JEALOUS THAT ŌGAMI-KUN'S TAKEN A LIKING TO KOMUGI.
So petty.
I knew this was going to happen...

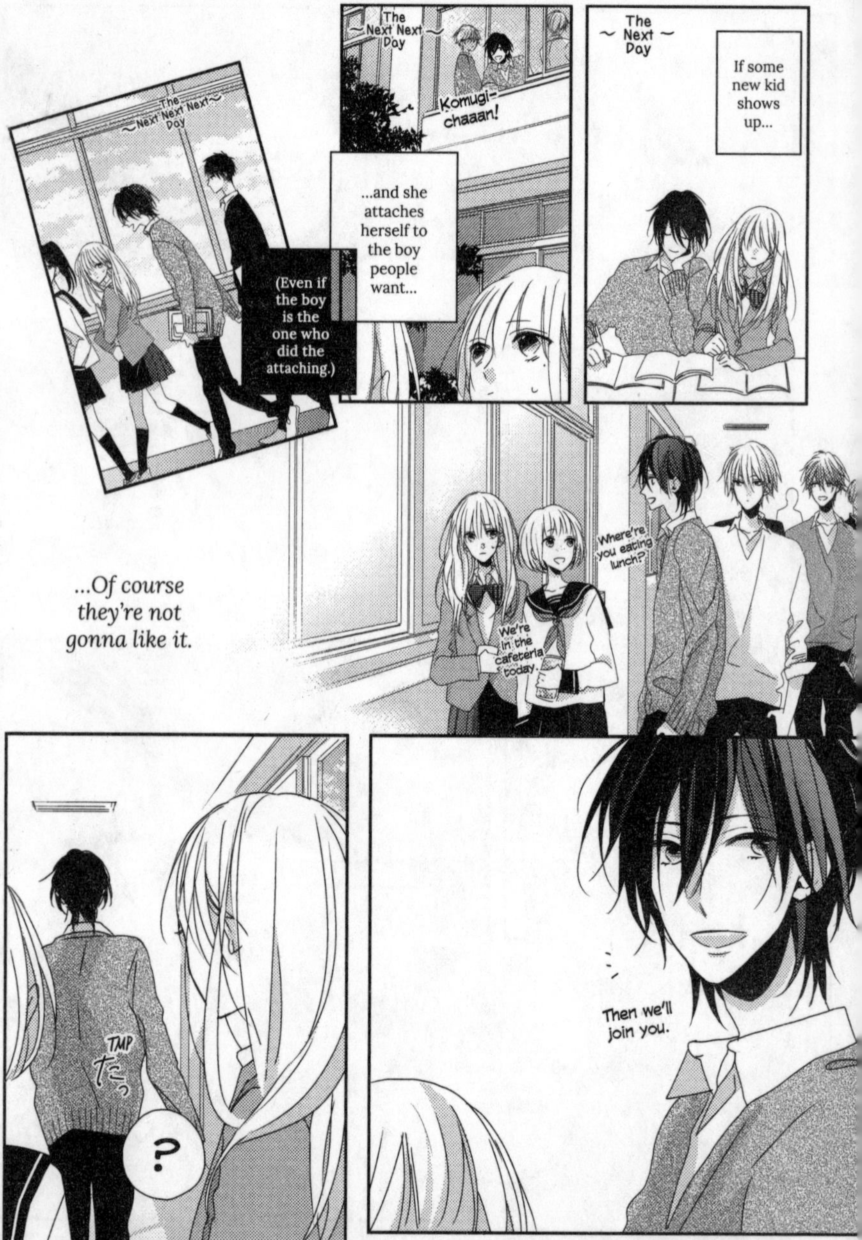
~ The Next Day ~
If some new kid shows up...
~ The Next Next Day ~
Komugi-chaaan!
...and she attaches herself to the boy people want...
~ The Next Next Next Day ~
(Even if the boy is the one who did the attaching.)
Where're you eating lunch?
We're in the cafeteria today.
...Of course they're not gonna like it.
Then we'll join you.
TMP
?

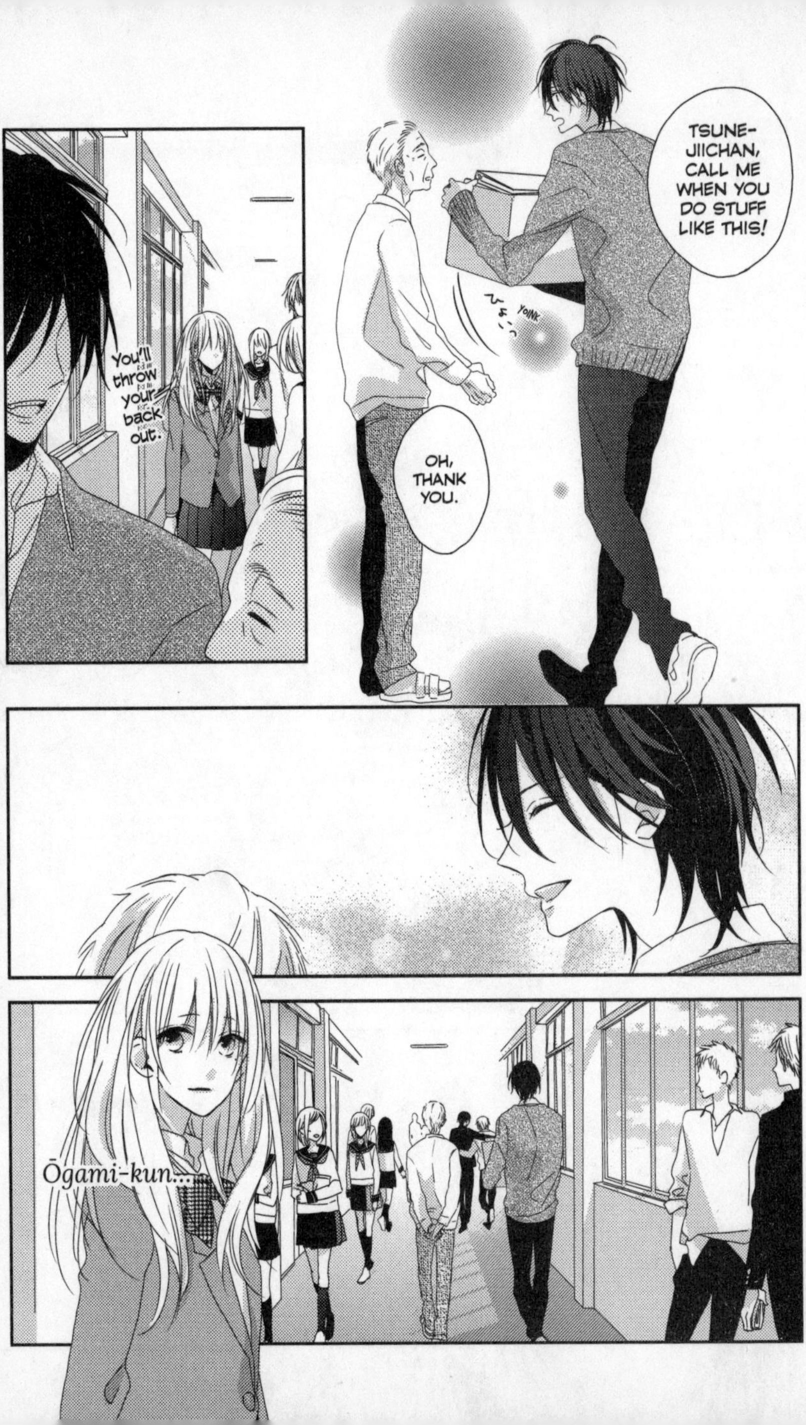
TSUNE-JIICHAN, CALL ME WHEN YOU DO STUFF LIKE THIS!
YOINK
OH, THANK YOU.
You'll throw your back out.
Ōgami-kun...

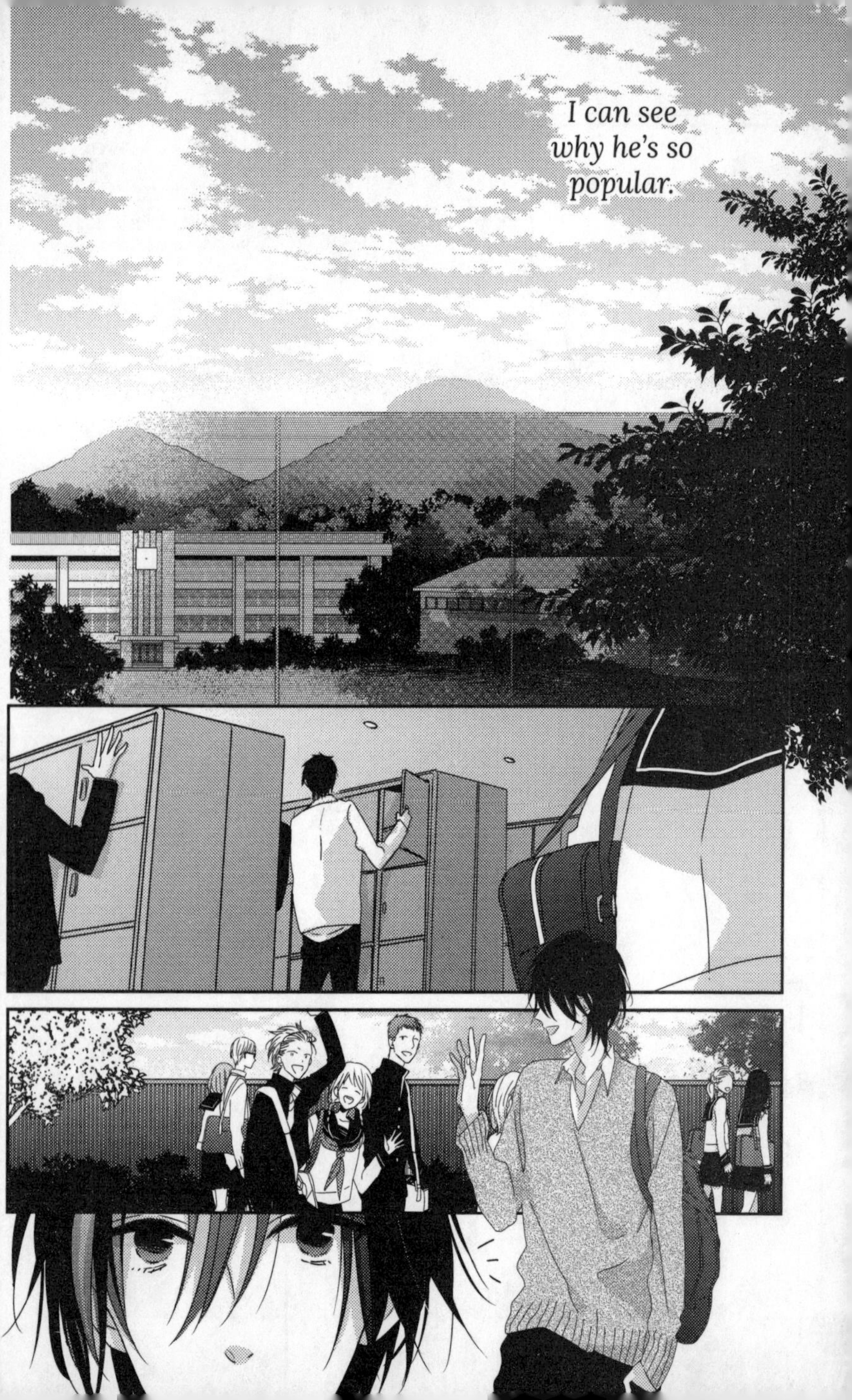
I can see why he's so popular.

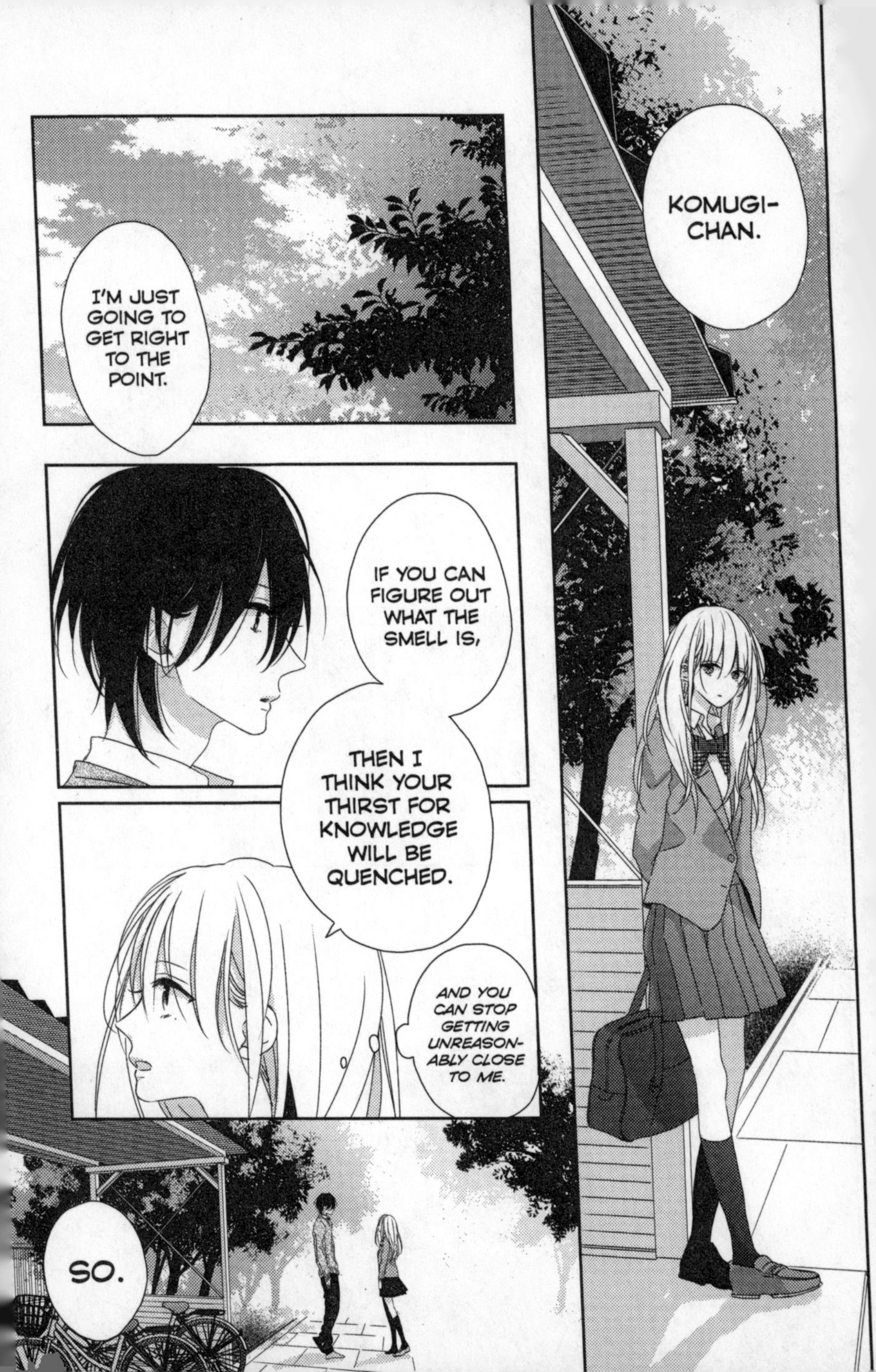
KOMUGI-CHAN.
I'M JUST GOING TO GET RIGHT TO THE POINT.
IF YOU CAN FIGURE OUT WHAT THE SMELL IS,
THEN I THINK YOUR THIRST FOR KNOWLEDGE WILL BE QUENCHED.
AND YOU CAN STOP GETTING UNREASONABLY CLOSE TO ME.
SO.

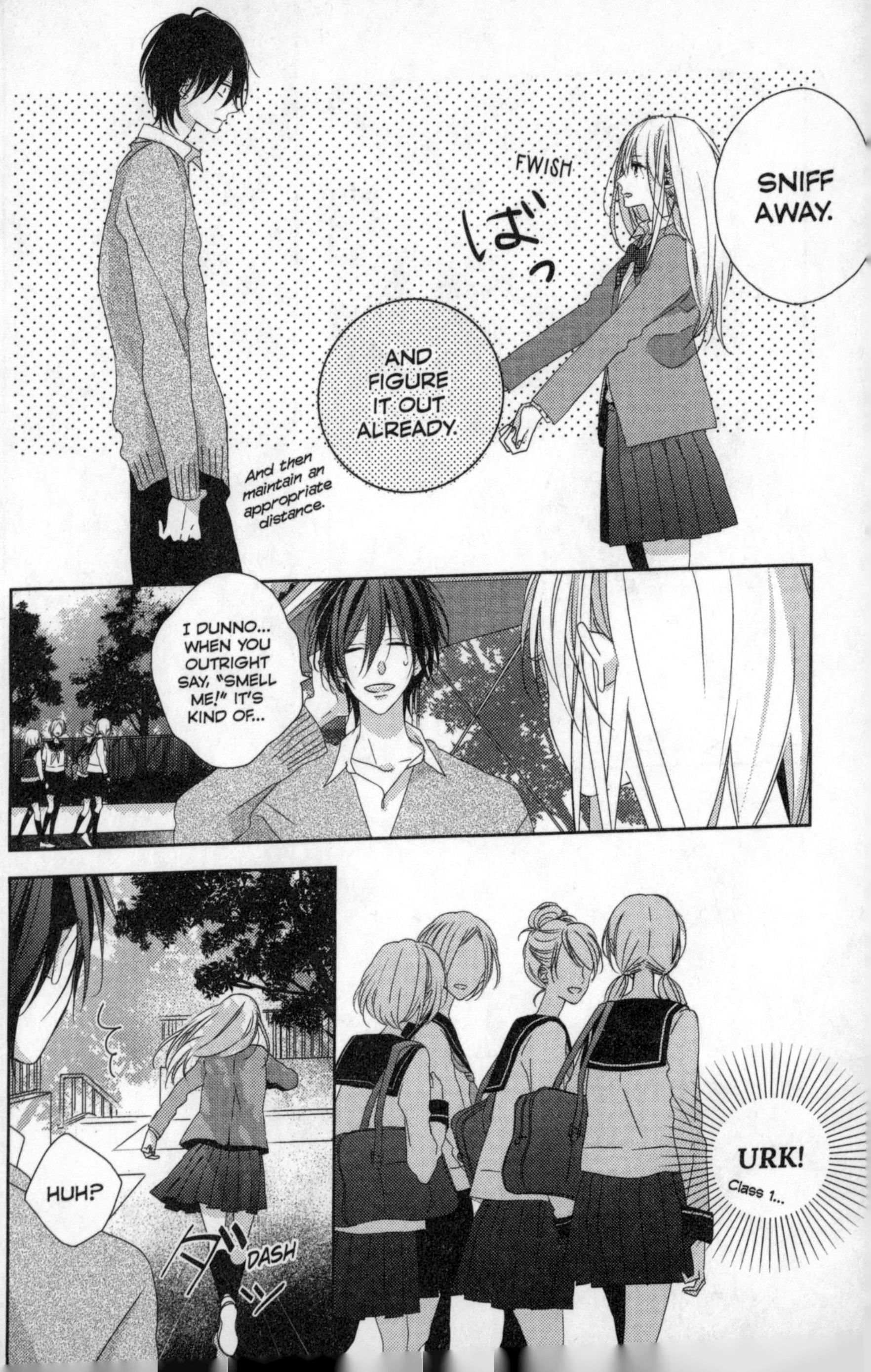
SNIFF AWAY.
FWISH
ばっ
AND FIGURE IT OUT ALREADY.
And then maintain an appropriate distance.
I DUNNO... WHEN YOU OUTRIGHT SAY, "SMELL ME!" IT'S KIND OF...
URK!
Class 1...
HUH?
ダッ
DASH

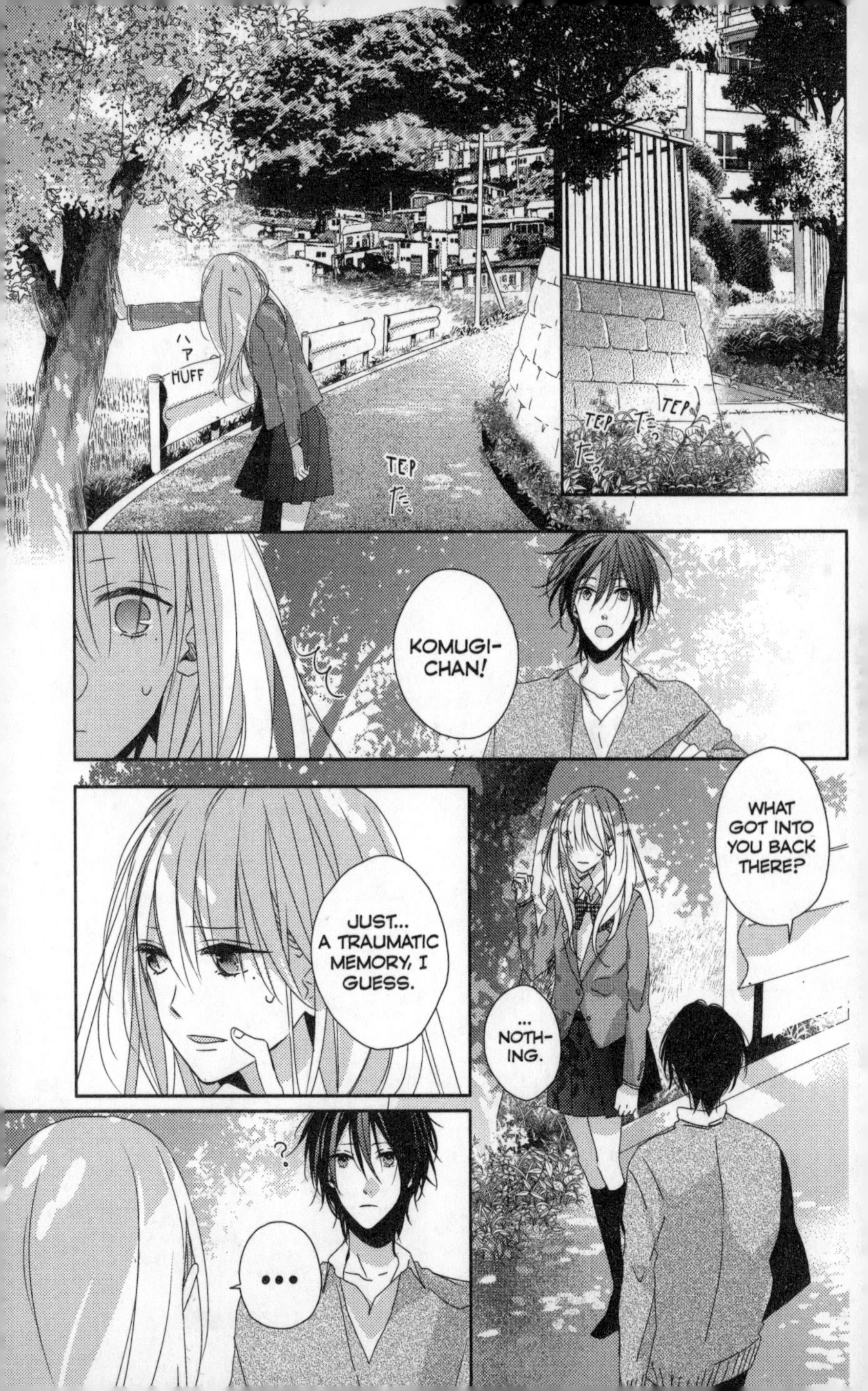

TEP
TEP
ハァ
HUFF
TEP
KOMUGI-CHAN!
WHAT GOT INTO YOU BACK THERE?
... NOTHING.
JUST... A TRAUMATIC MEMORY, I GUESS.
...

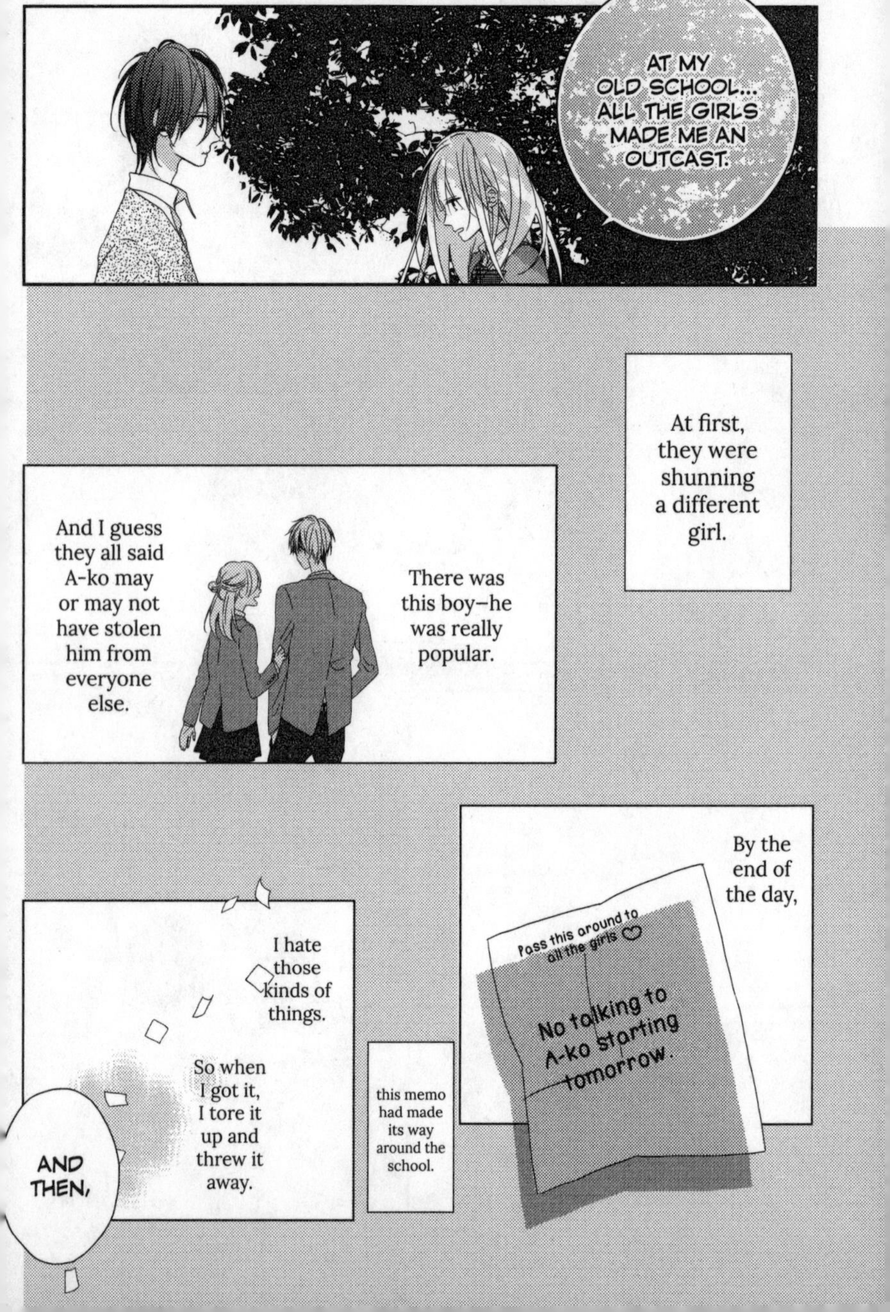
AT MY OLD SCHOOL... ALL THE GIRLS MADE ME AN OUTCAST.
At first, they were shunning a different girl.
There was this boy—he was really popular.
And I guess they all said A-ko may or may not have stolen him from everyone else.
By the end of the day,
Pass this around to all the girls
No talking to A-ko starting tomorrow.
this memo had made its way around the school.
I hate those kinds of things.
So when I got it, I tore it up and threw it away.
AND THEN,

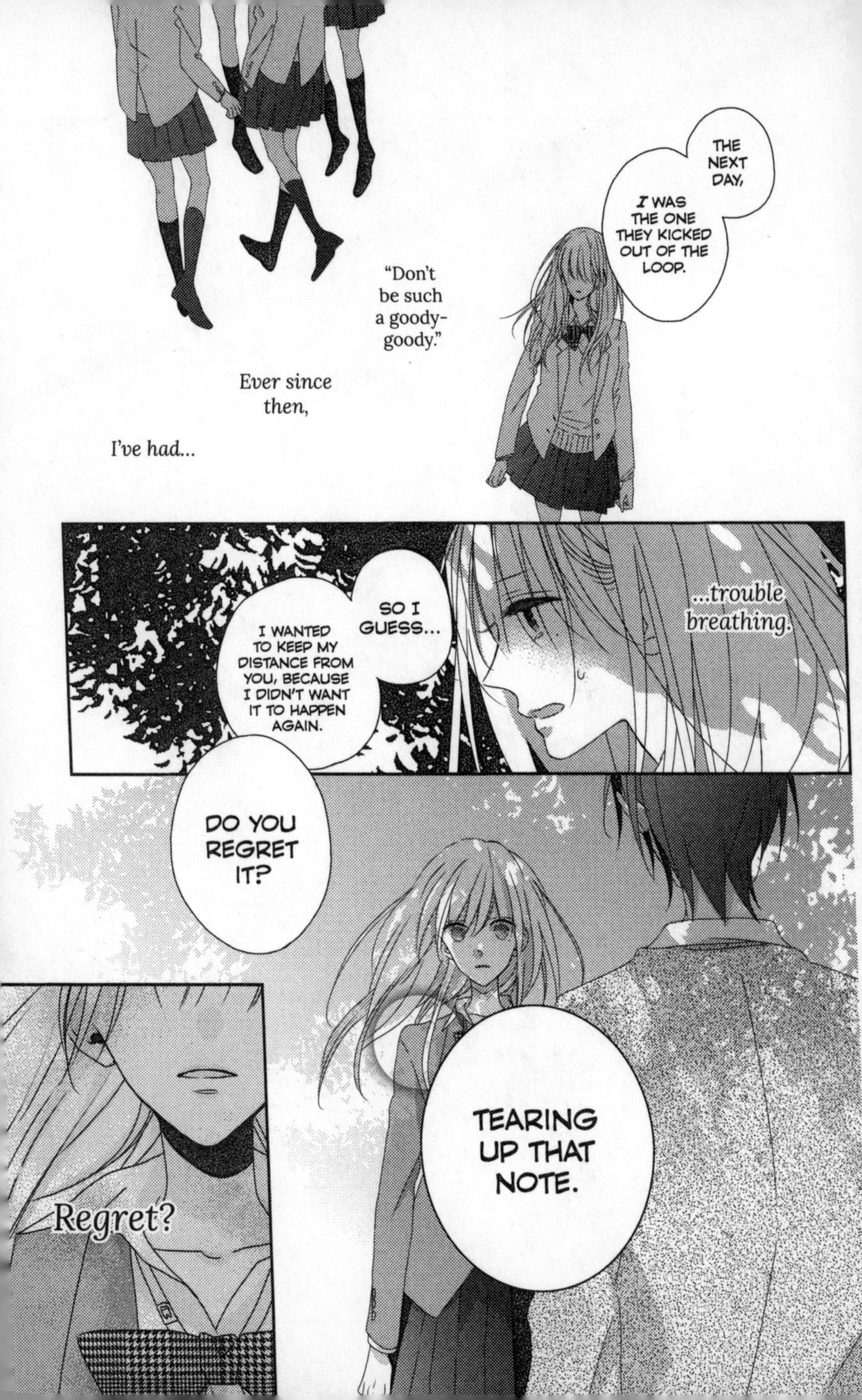
THE NEXT DAY, *I* WAS THE ONE THEY KICKED OUT OF THE LOOP.
"Don't be such a goody-goody."
Ever since then,
I've had...
...trouble breathing.
SO I GUESS... I WANTED TO KEEP MY DISTANCE FROM YOU, BECAUSE I DIDN'T WANT IT TO HAPPEN AGAIN.
DO YOU REGRET IT?
TEARING UP THAT NOTE.
Regret?

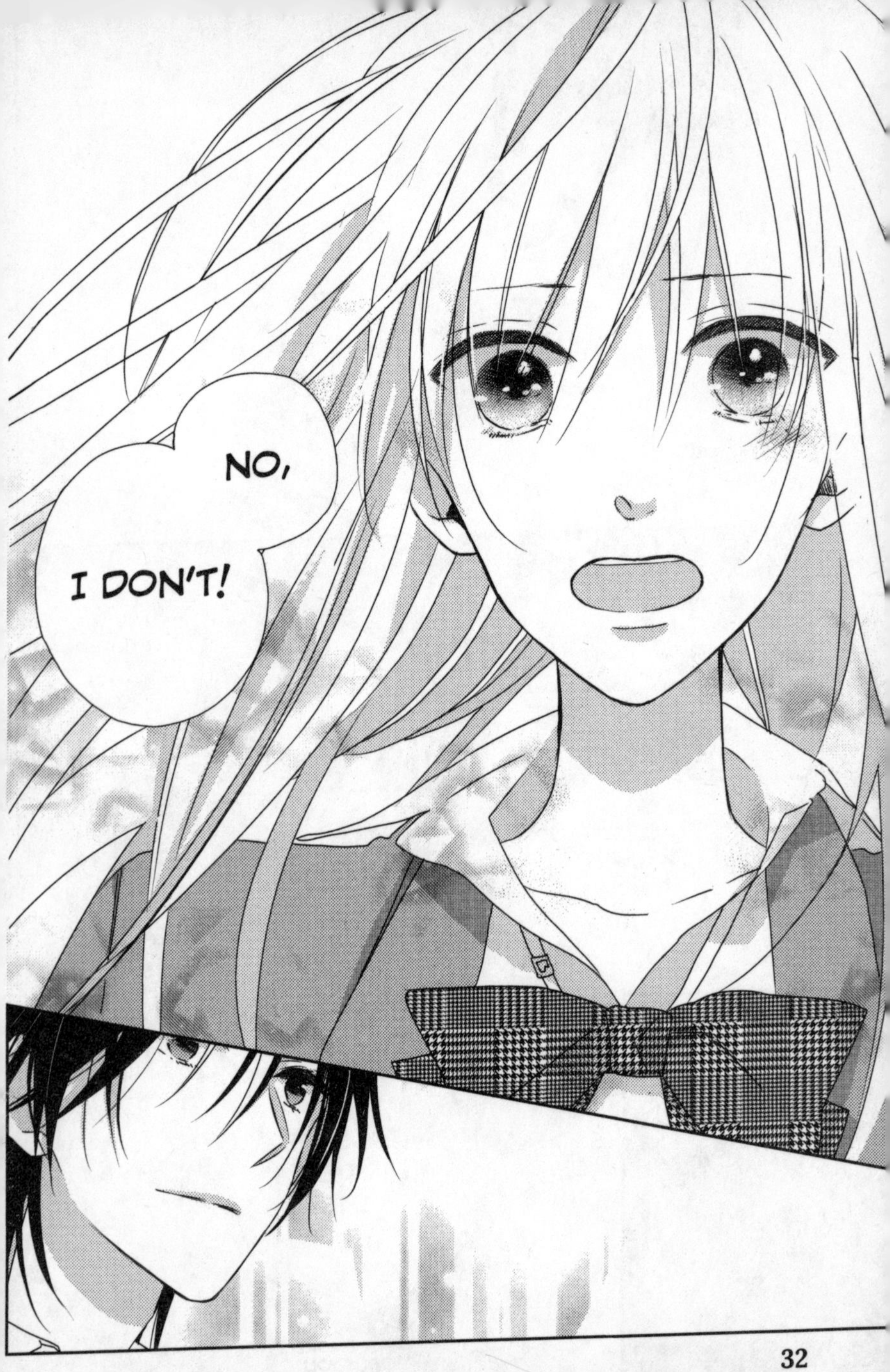
NO, I DON'T!

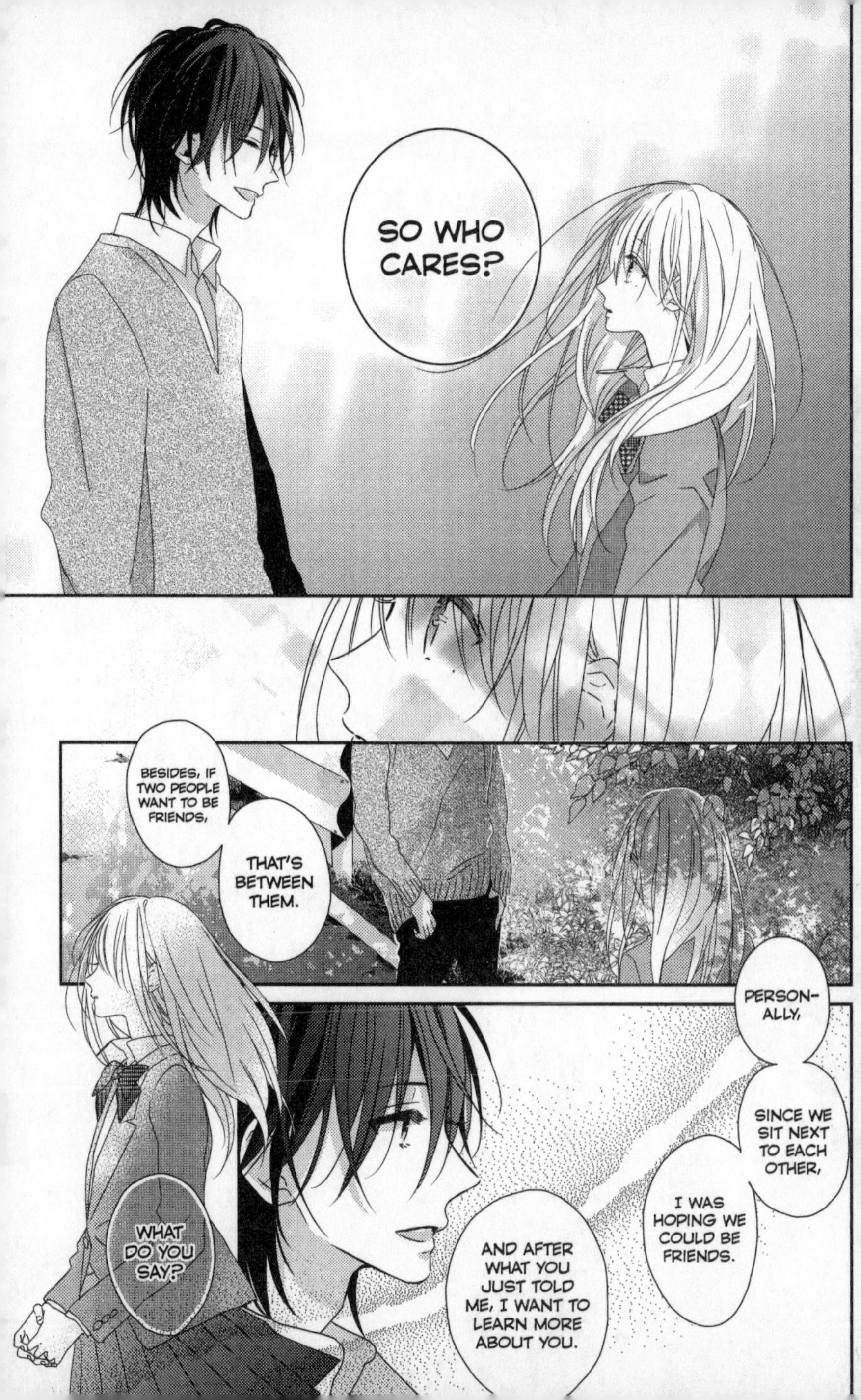
SO WHO CARES?
BESIDES, IF TWO PEOPLE WANT TO BE FRIENDS,
THAT'S BETWEEN THEM.
PERSONALLY,
SINCE WE SIT NEXT TO EACH OTHER,
I WAS HOPING WE COULD BE FRIENDS.
AND AFTER WHAT YOU JUST TOLD ME, I WANT TO LEARN MORE ABOUT YOU.
WHAT DO YOU SAY?

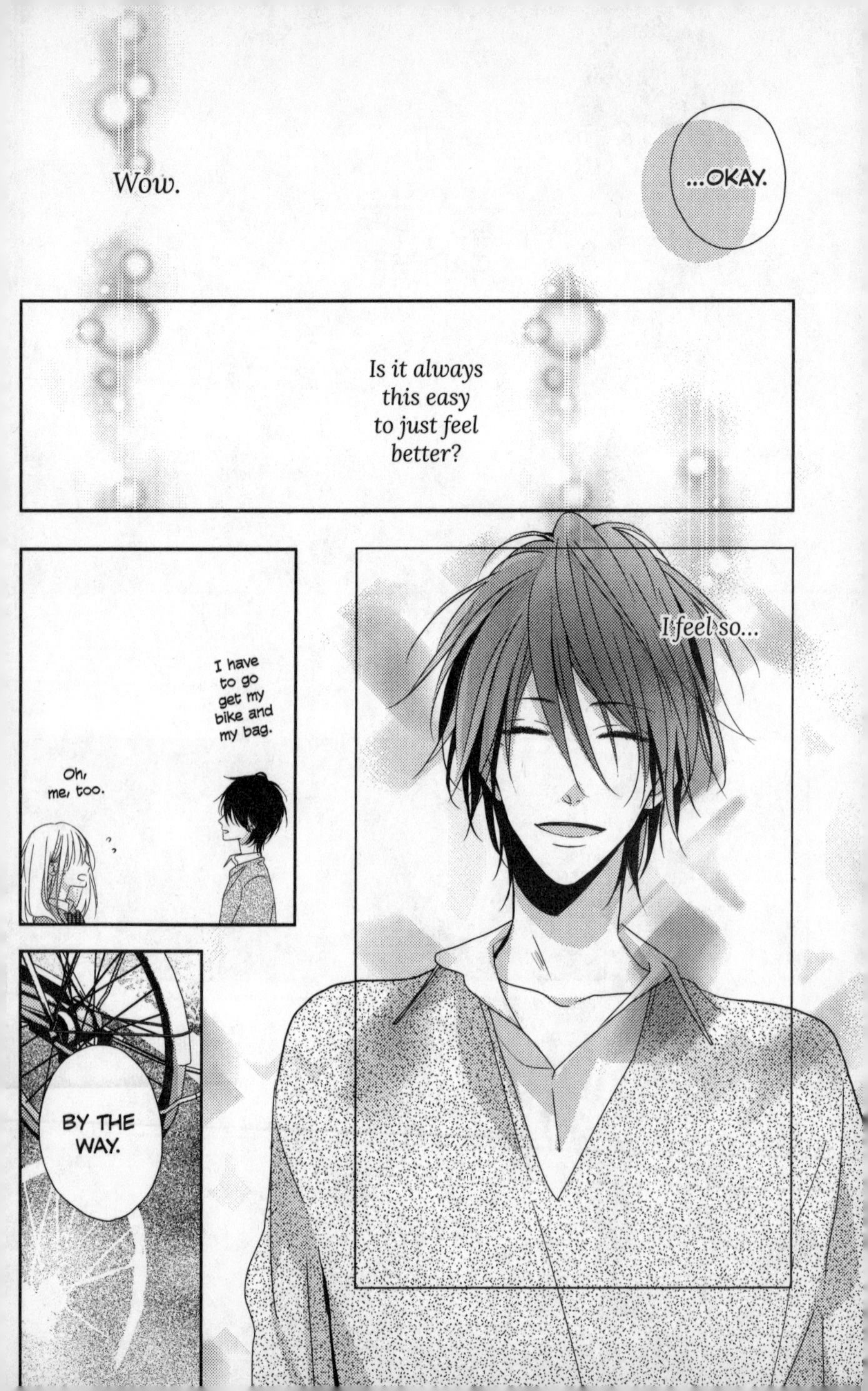
...OKAY.
Wow.
Is it always this easy to just feel better?
I feel so...
I have to go get my bike and my bag.
Oh, me, too.
BY THE WAY.

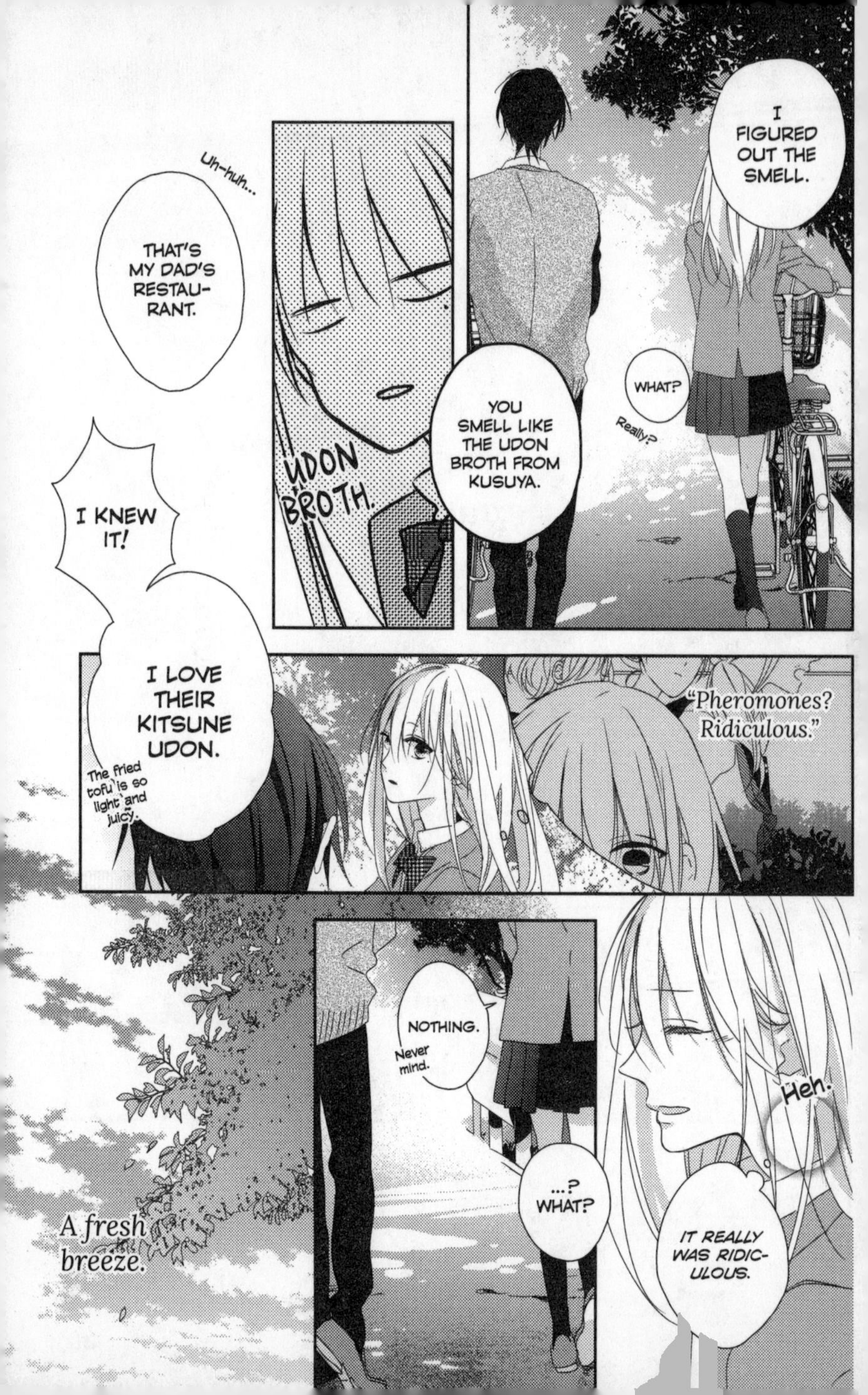
I FIGURED OUT THE SMELL.
WHAT?
Really?
YOU SMELL LIKE THE UDON BROTH FROM KUSUYA.
UDON BROTH.
Uh-huh...
THAT'S MY DAD'S RESTAU-RANT.
I KNEW IT!
I LOVE THEIR KITSUNE UDON.
The fried tofu is so light and juicy.
“Pheromones? Ridiculous.”
Heh.
IT REALLY WAS RIDIC-ULOUS.
...? WHAT?
NOTHING.
Never mind.
A fresh breeze.

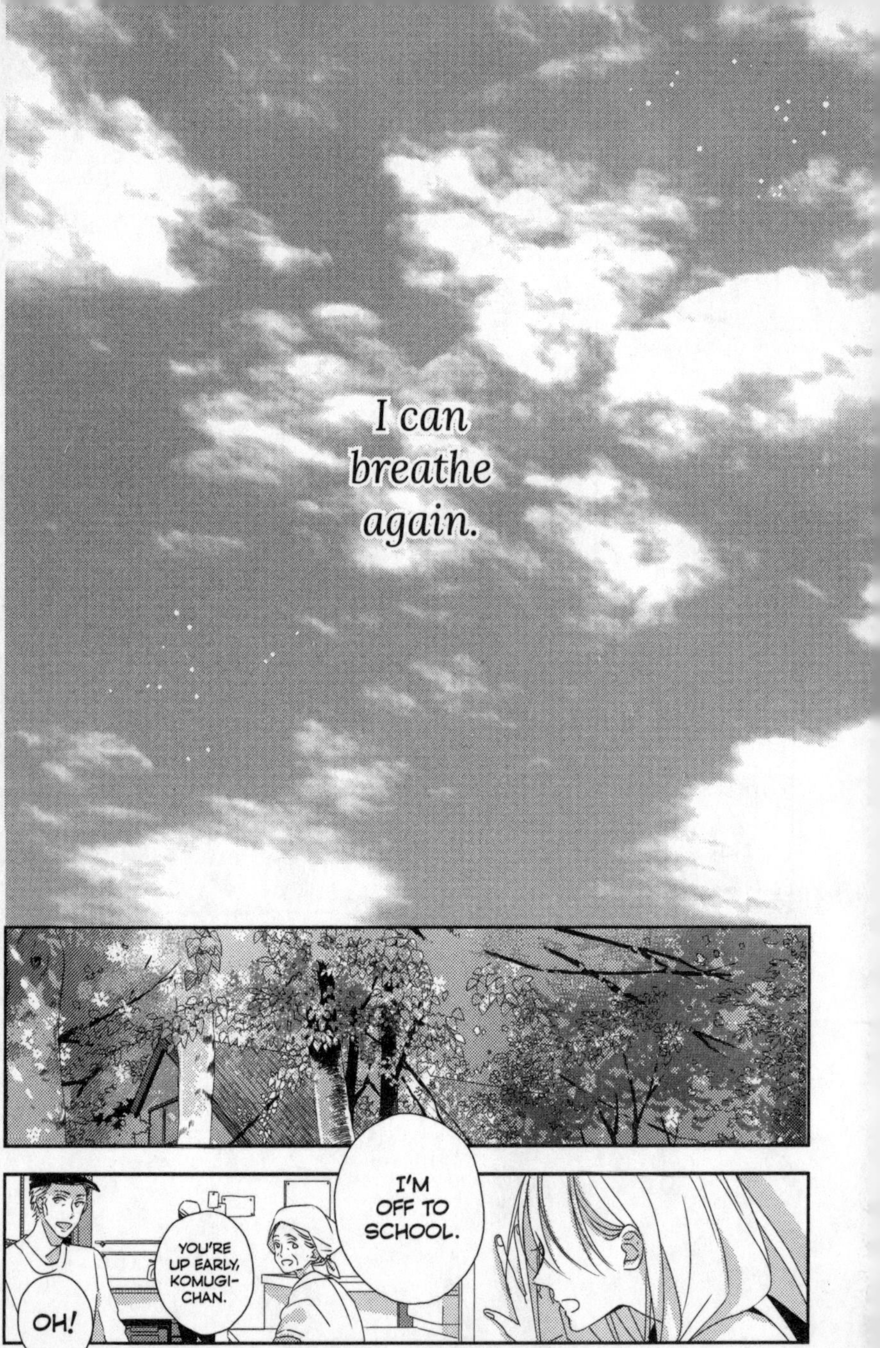
I can breathe again.
I'M OFF TO SCHOOL.
YOU'RE UP EARLY, KOMUGI-CHAN.
OH!

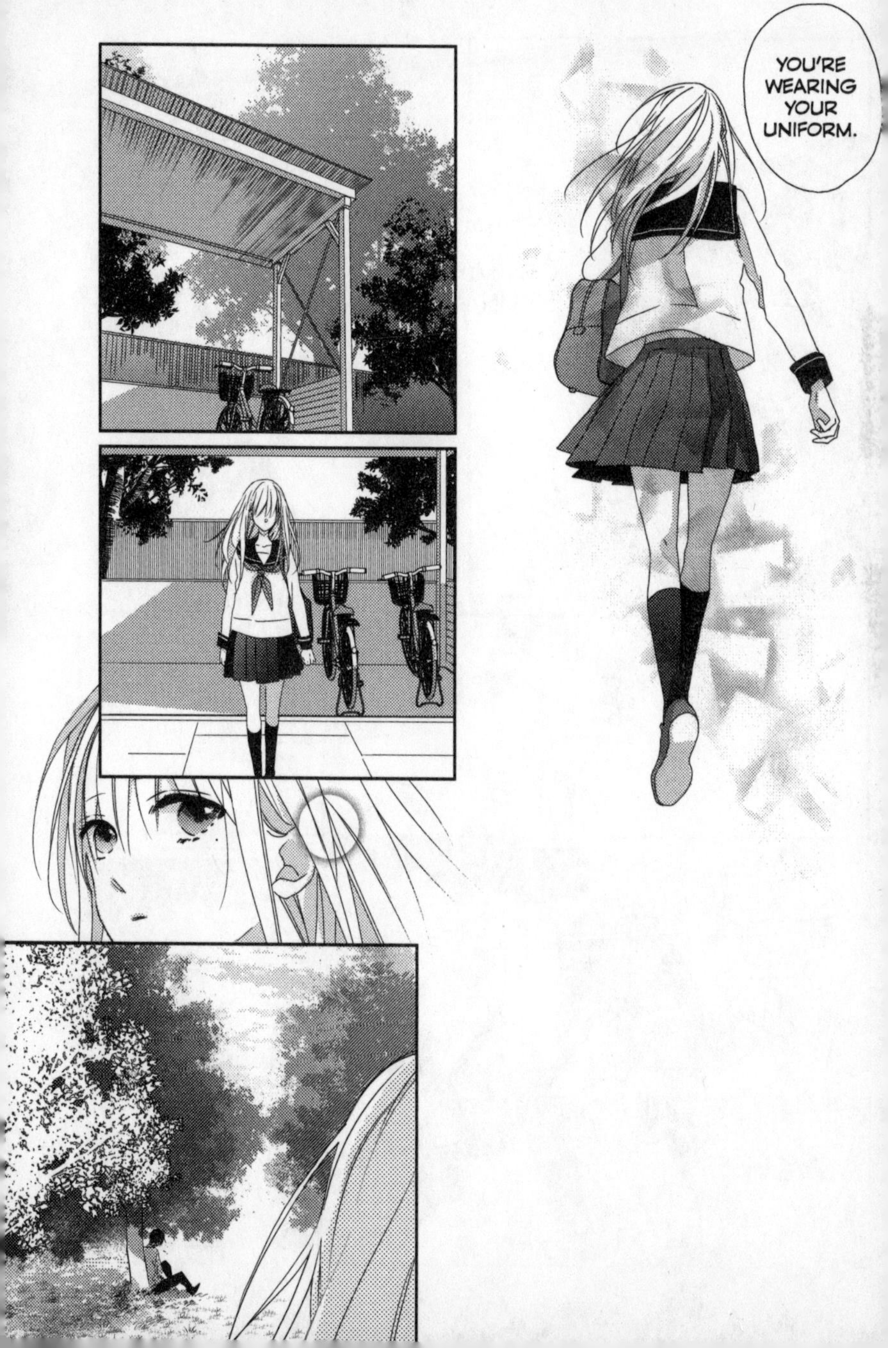
YOU'RE WEARING YOUR UNIFORM.

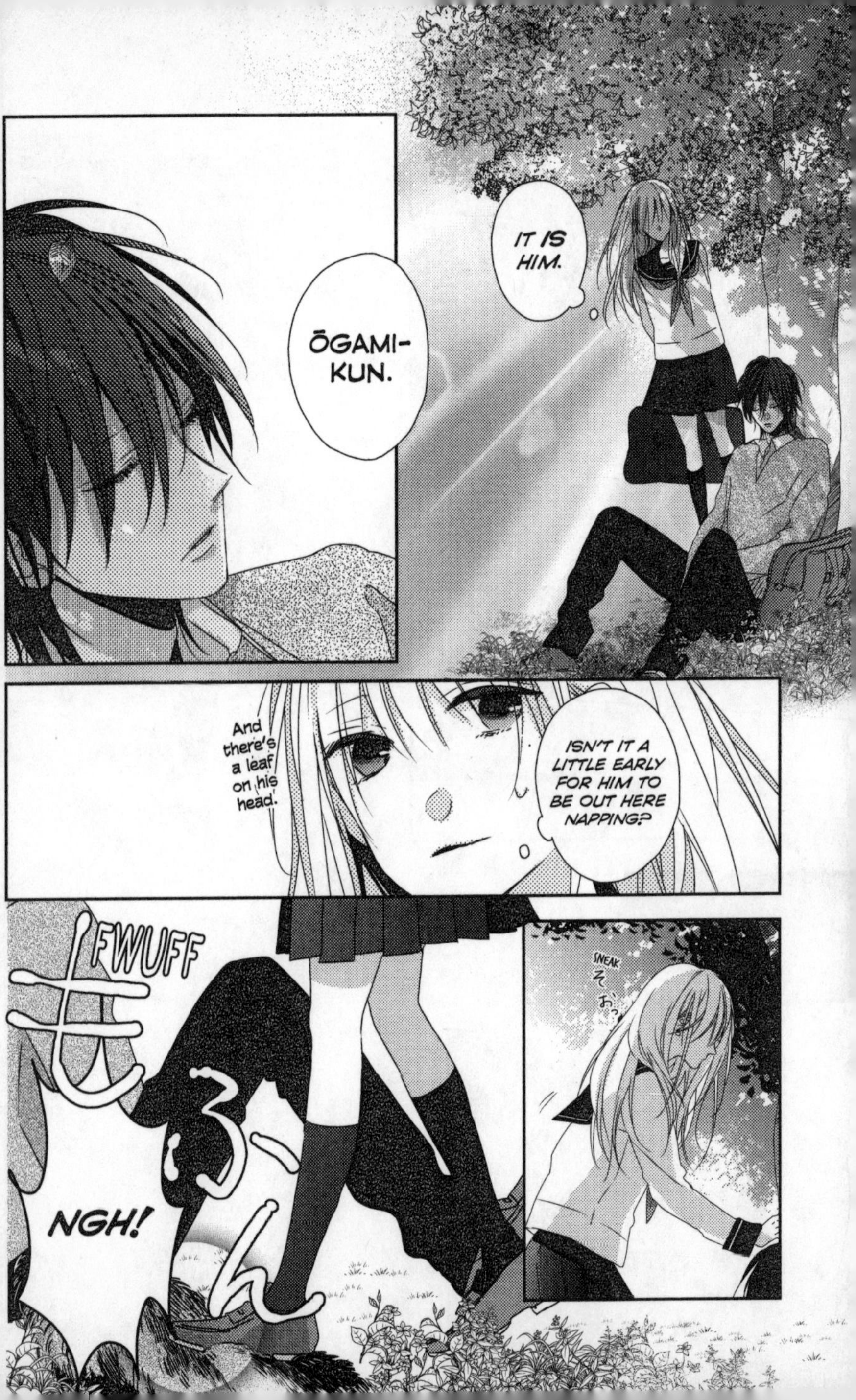
IT IS HIM.
ŌGAMI-KUN.
ISN'T IT A LITTLE EARLY FOR HIM TO BE OUT HERE NAPPING?
And there's a leaf on his head.
SNEAK
そぉ
FWUFF
もふーん
NGH!

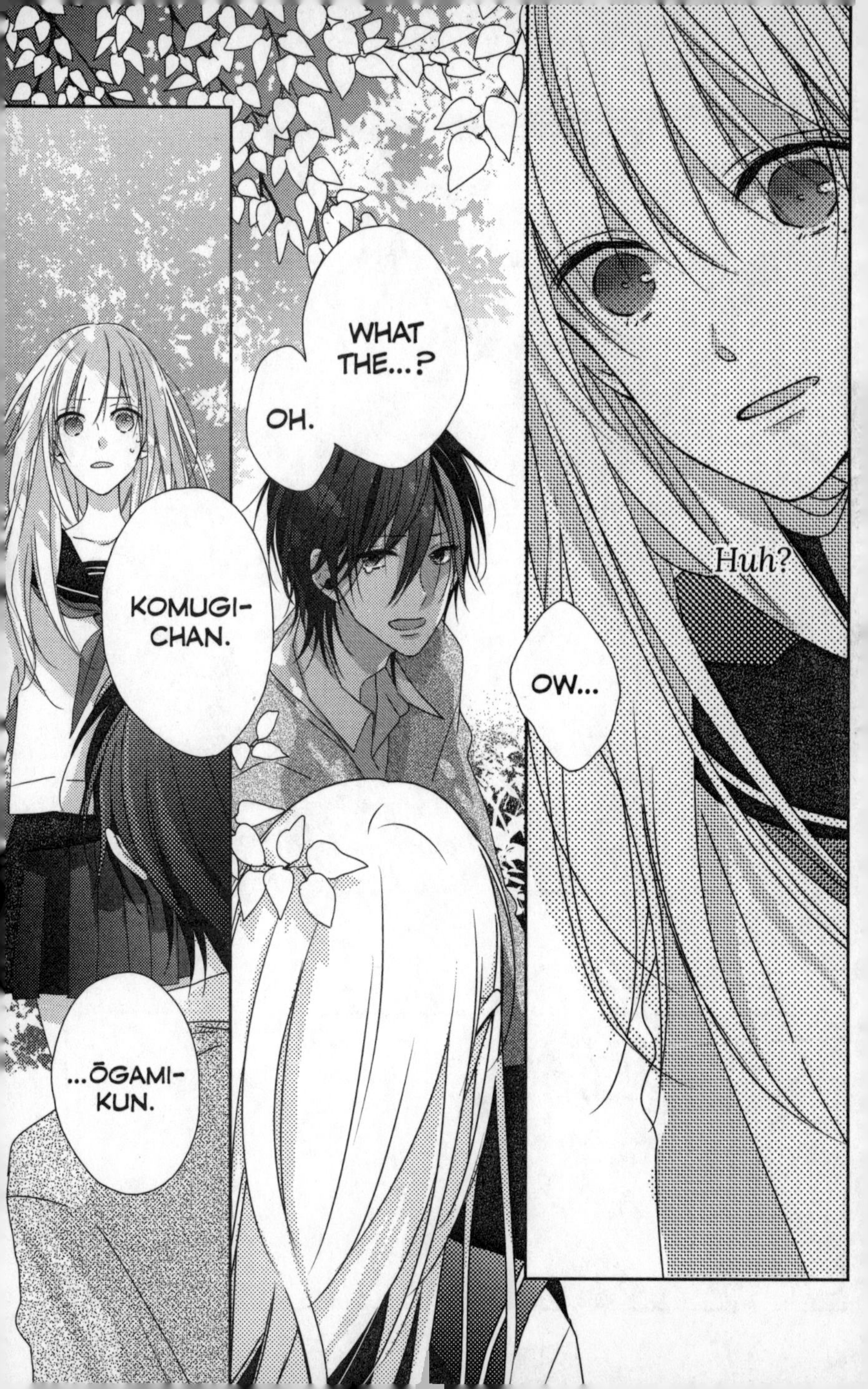
Huh?
OW...
WHAT THE...?
OH.
KOMUGI-CHAN.
...ŌGAMI-KUN.

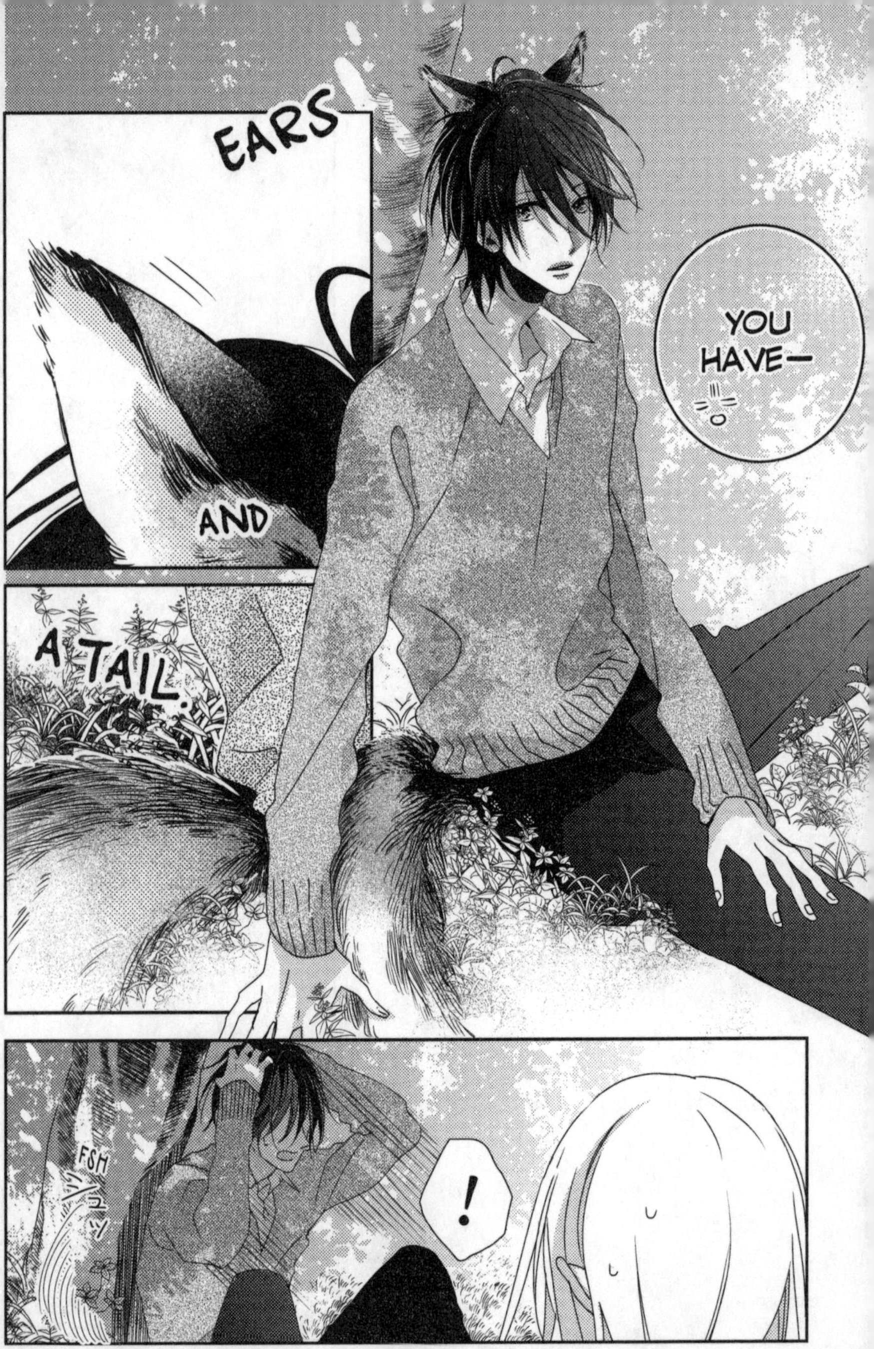
YOU HAVE—
EARS
AND
A TAIL.
!
FSH

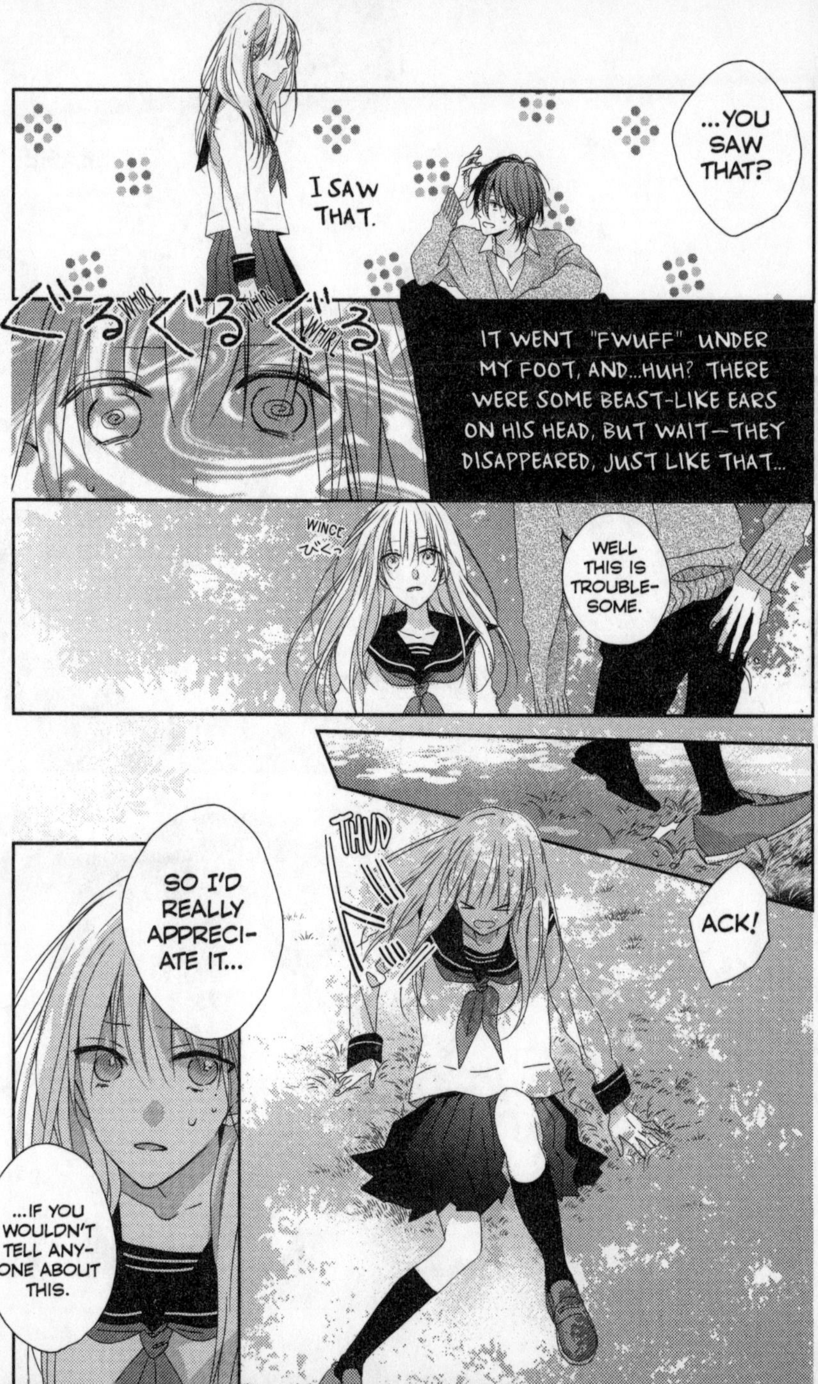
...YOU SAW THAT?
I SAW THAT.
IT WENT "FWUFF" UNDER MY FOOT, AND...HUH? THERE WERE SOME BEAST-LIKE EARS ON HIS HEAD, BUT WAIT—THEY DISAPPEARED, JUST LIKE THAT...
WHIRL WHIRL WHIRL
WELL THIS IS TROUBLE-SOME.
WINCE
ACK!
THUD
SO I'D REALLY APPRECI-ATE IT...
...IF YOU WOULDN'T TELL ANY-ONE ABOUT THIS.

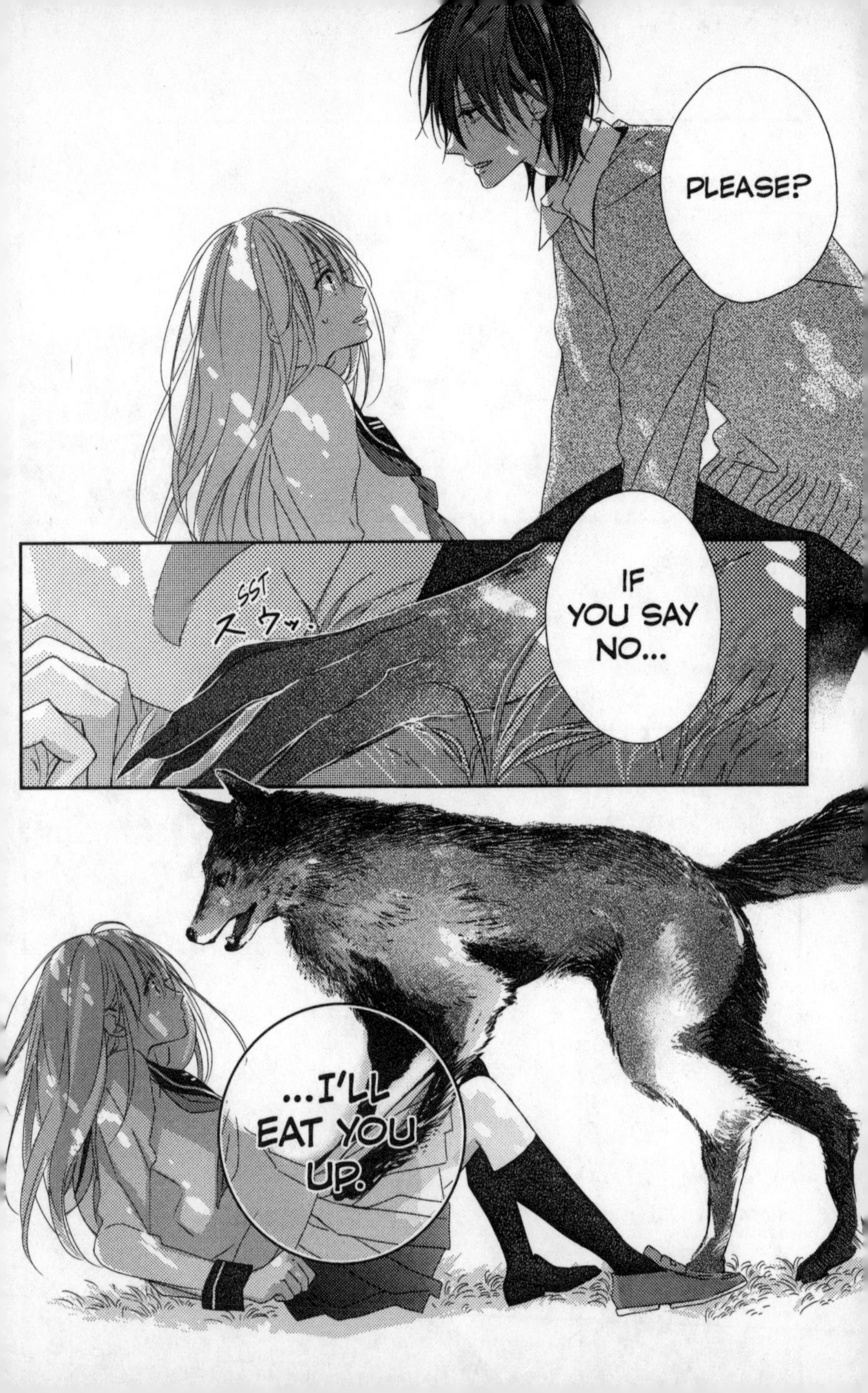
PLEASE?
IF YOU SAY NO...
SST
スゥッ
...I'LL EAT YOU UP.

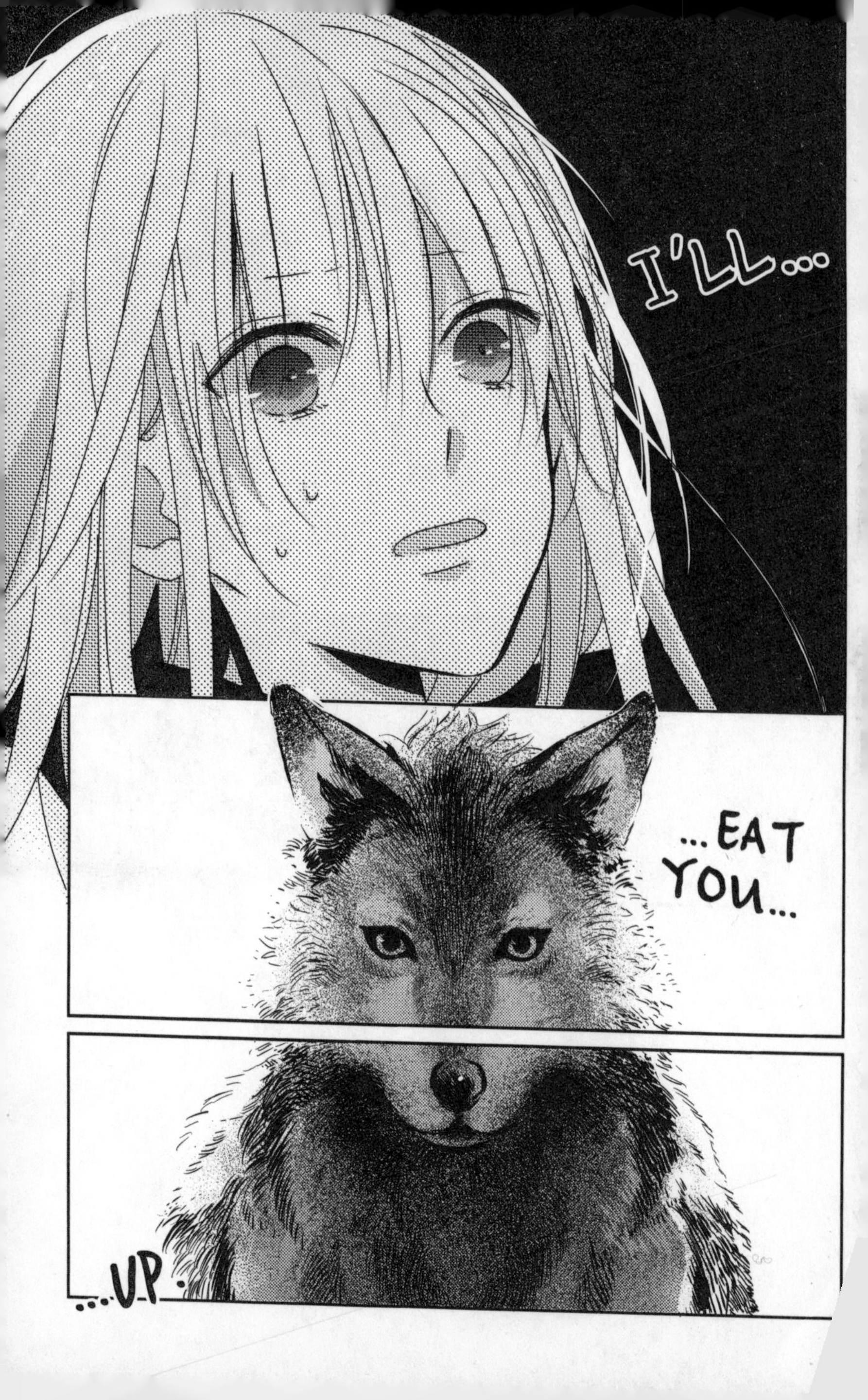
I'LL...
...EAT YOU...
...UP.

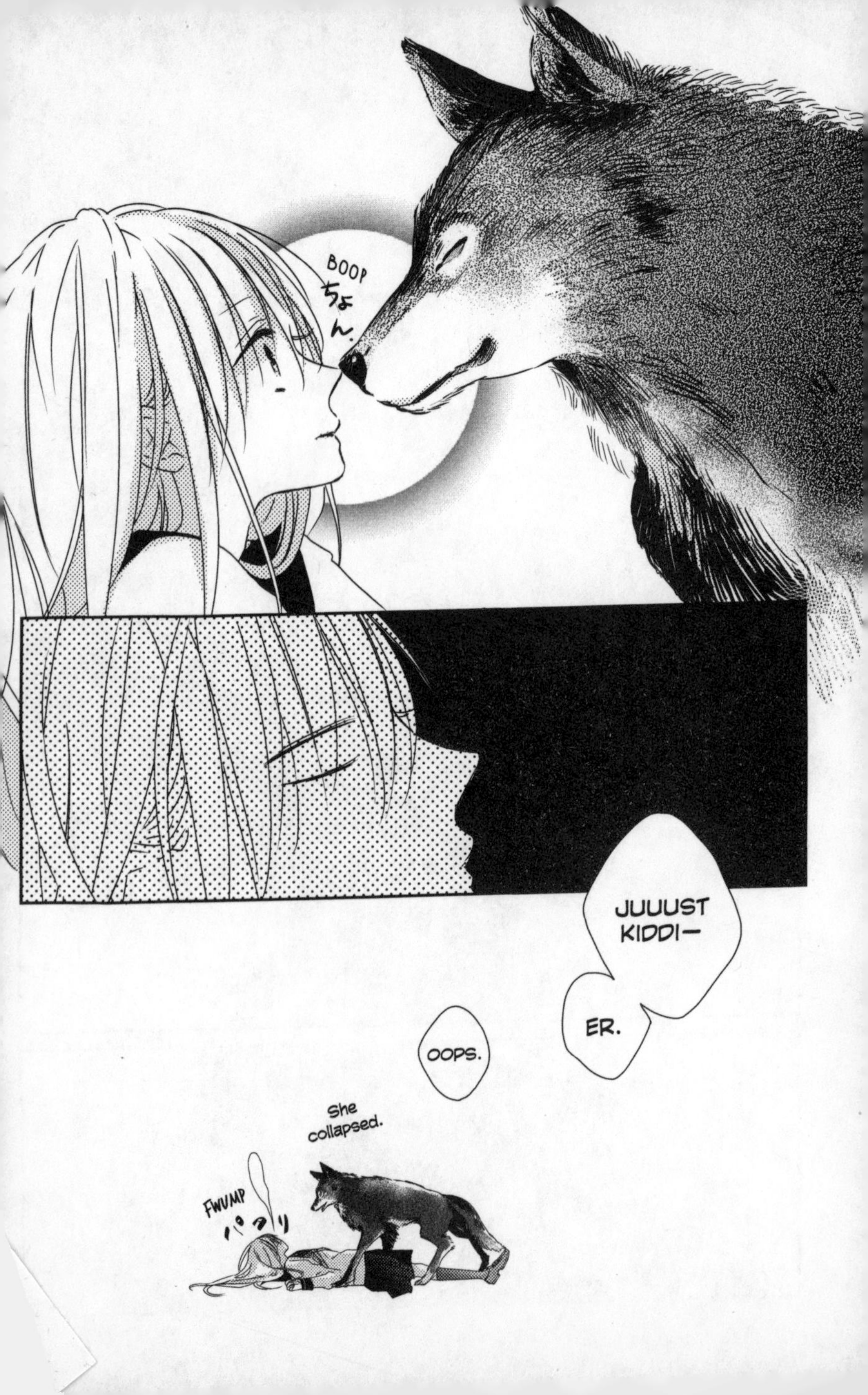
BOOP
ちょん.
JUUUST KIDDI—
ER.
OOPS.
She collapsed.
FWUMP
パタリ

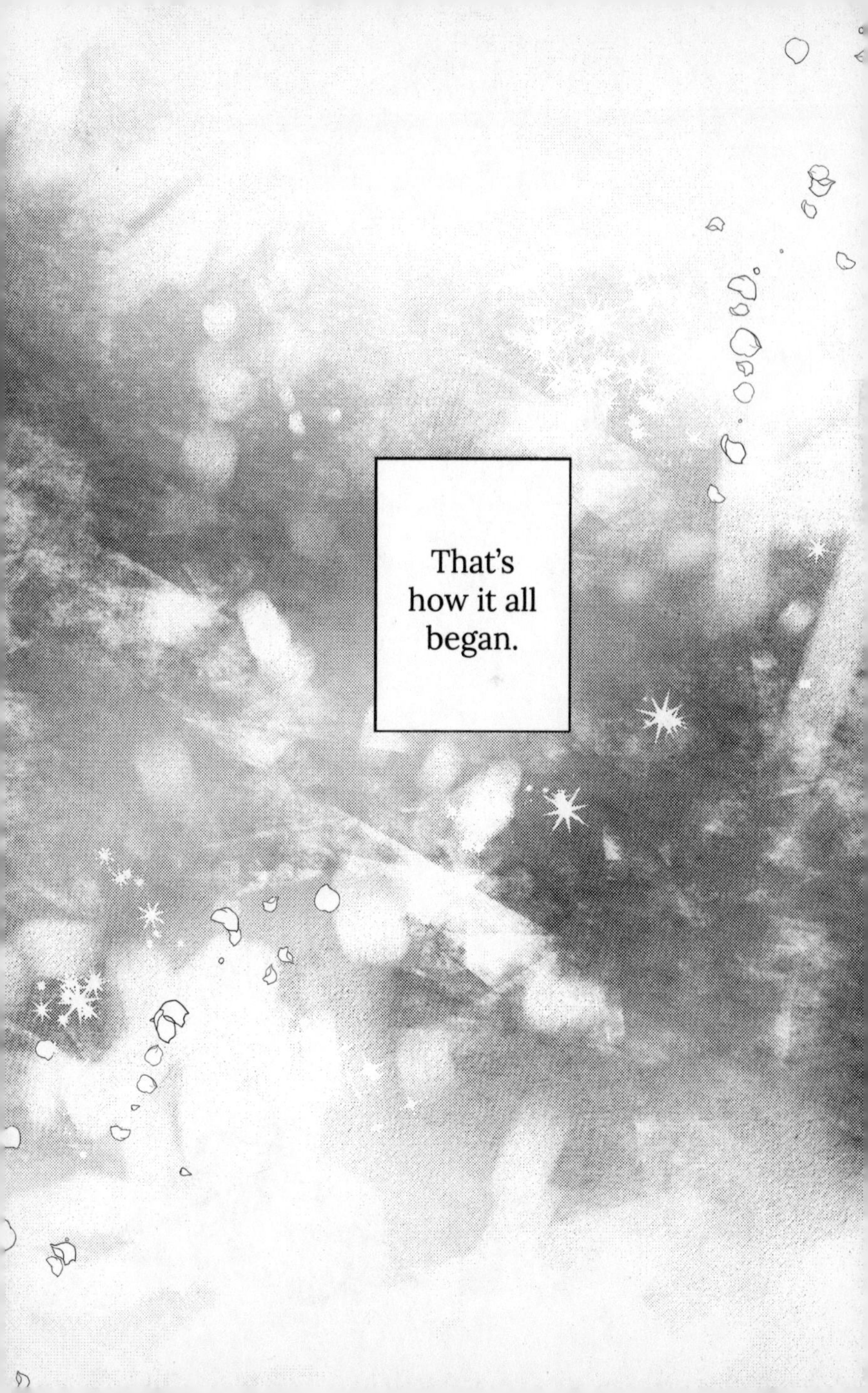
That's how it all began.

That Wolf-Boy is Mine!

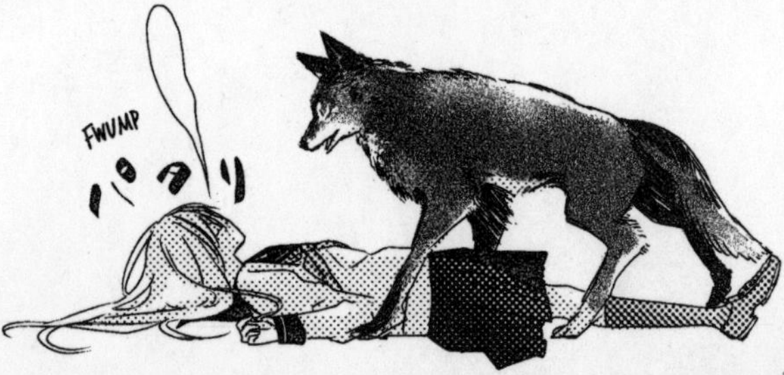
FWUMP
パタリ

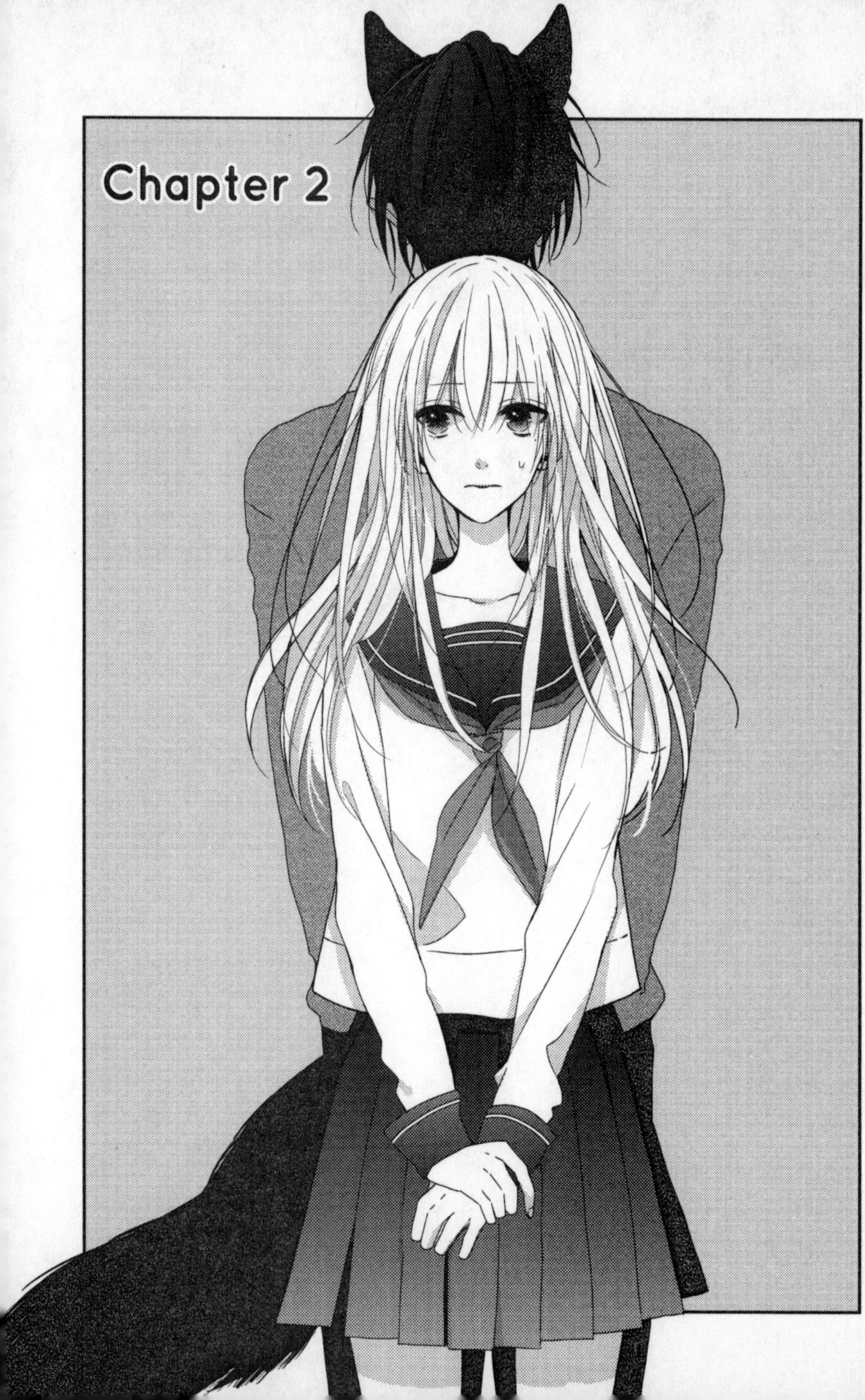
Chapter 2

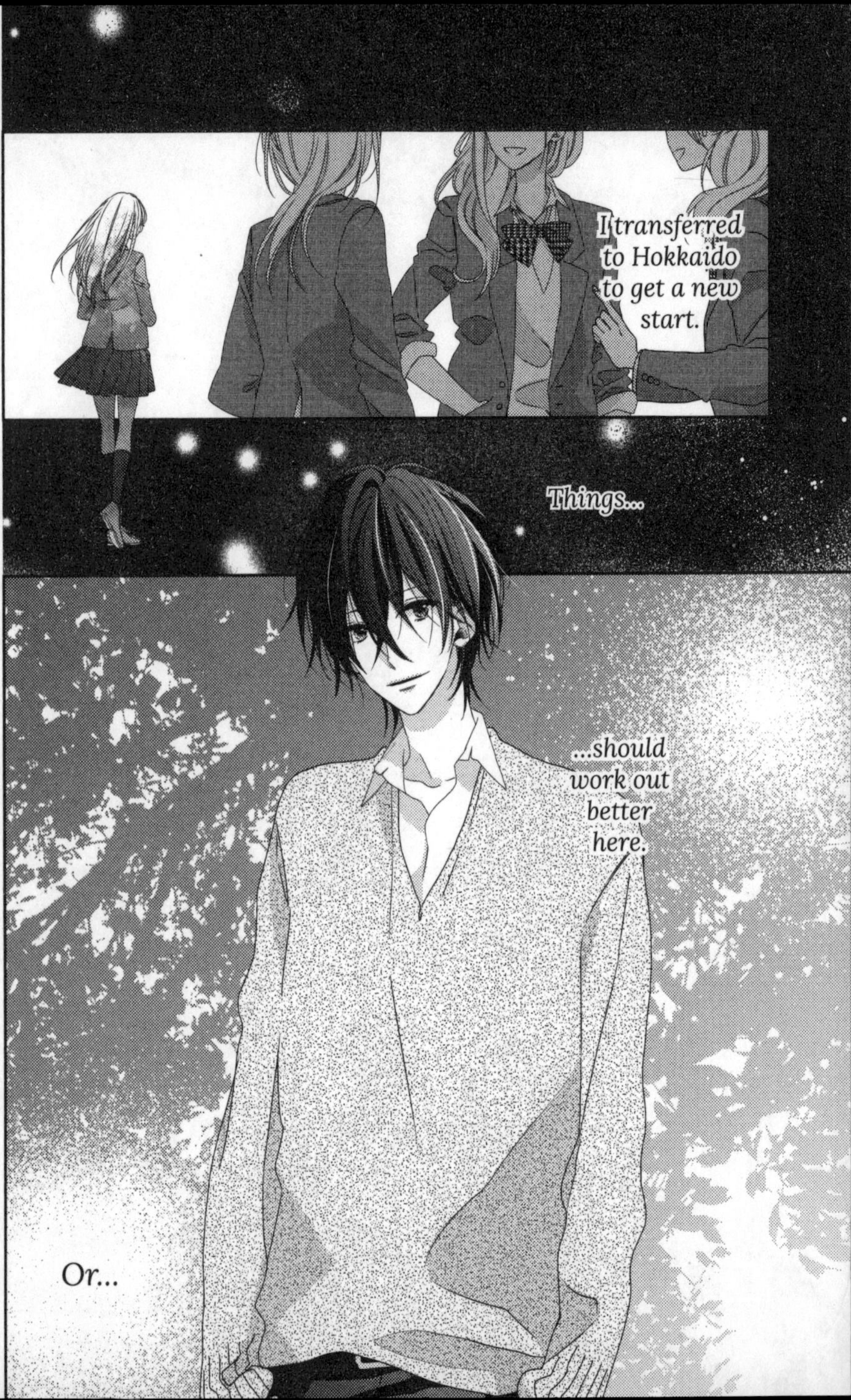
I transferred to Hokkaido to get a new start.
Things...
...should work out better here.
Or...

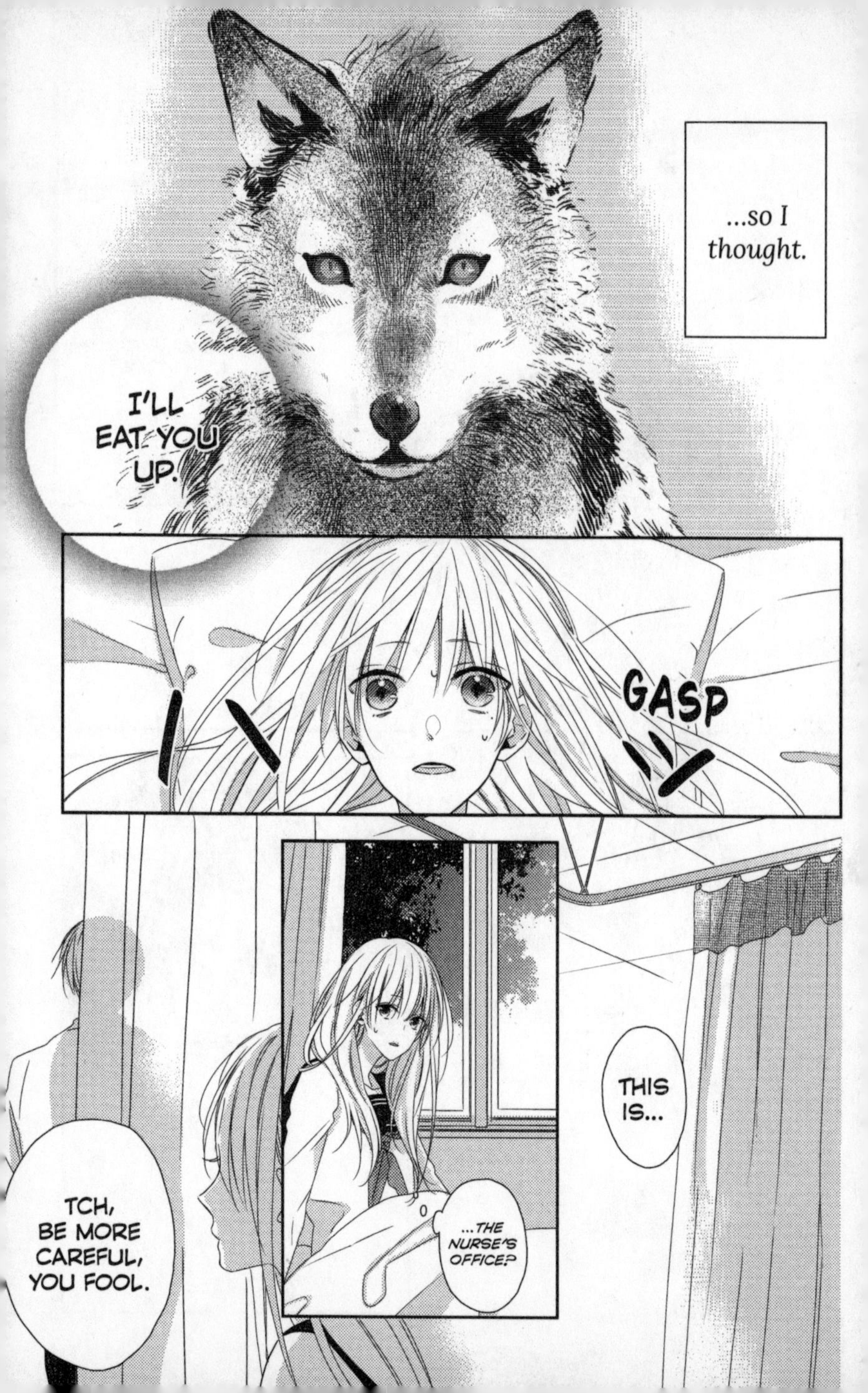
...so I thought.
I'LL EAT YOU UP.
GASP
THIS IS...
...THE NURSE'S OFFICE?
TCH, BE MORE CAREFUL, YOU FOOL.

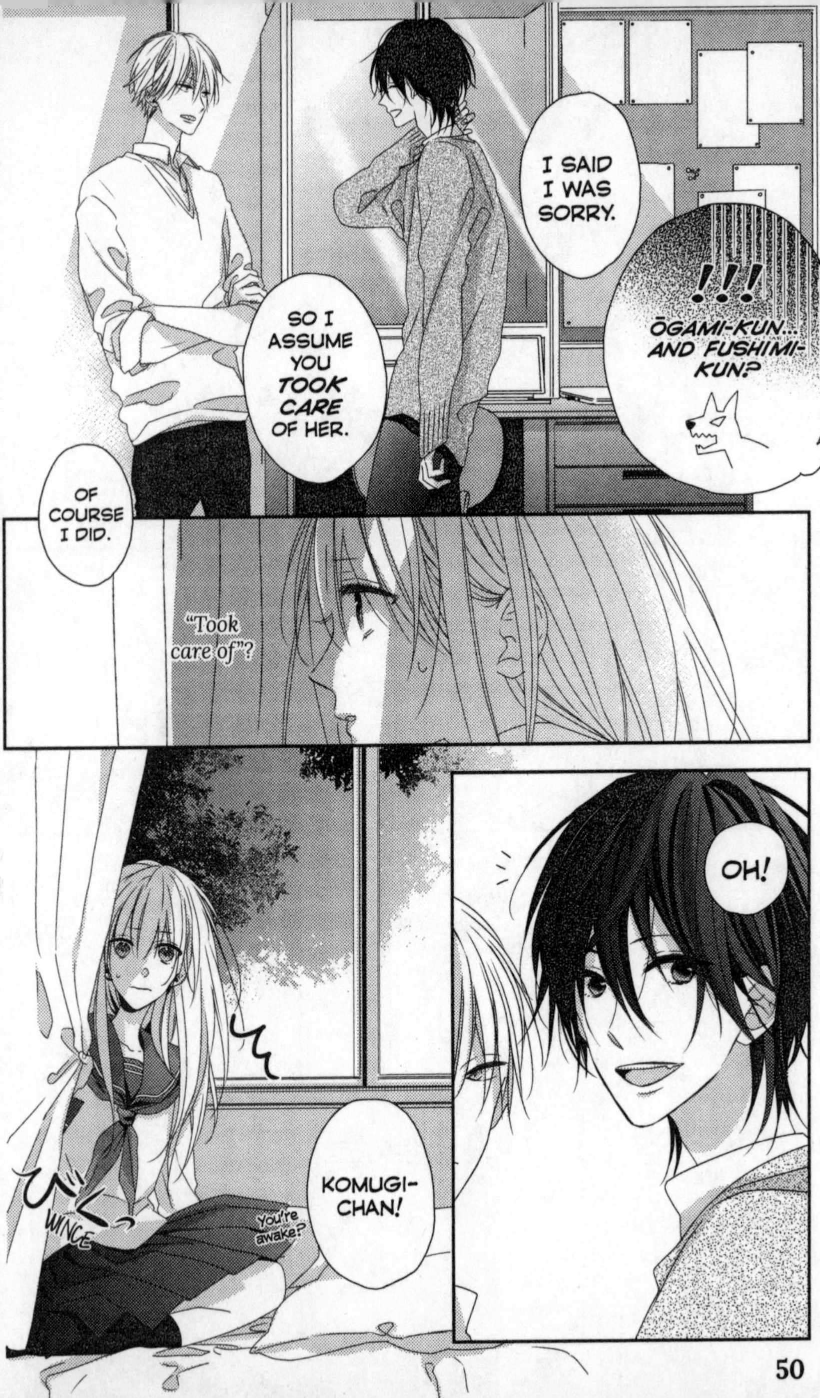
I SAID I WAS SORRY.
!!!
ŌGAMI-KUN... AND FUSHIMI-KUN?
SO I ASSUME YOU *TOOK CARE* OF HER.
OF COURSE I DID.
"Took care of"?
OH!
KOMUGI-CHAN!
You're awake?
びくっ
WINCE

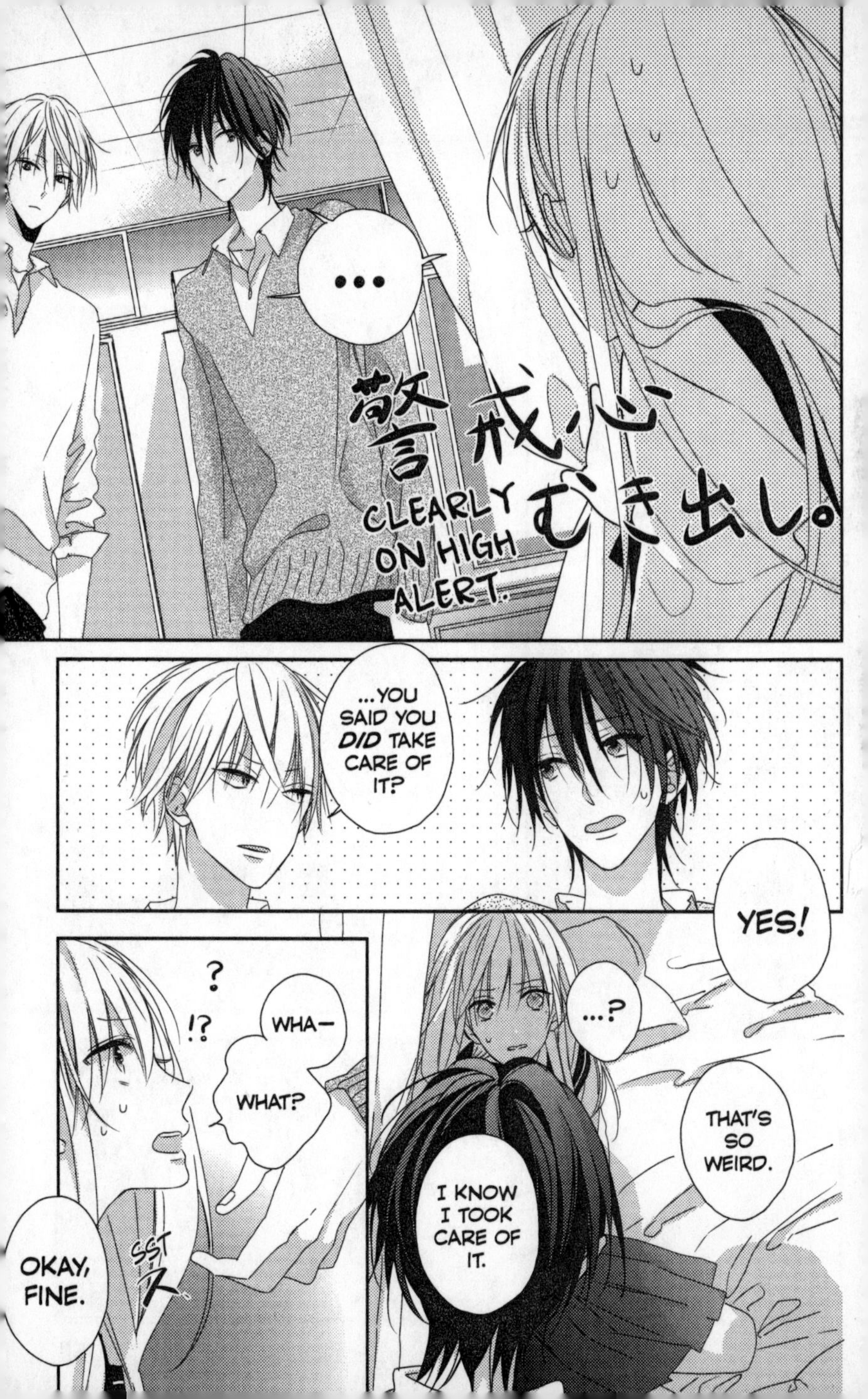
...
警戒心むき出し。
CLEARLY ON HIGH ALERT.
...YOU SAID YOU *DID* TAKE CARE OF IT?
YES!
...?
THAT'S SO WEIRD.
I KNOW I TOOK CARE OF IT.
?
!?
WHA—
WHAT?
SST
ス
OKAY, FINE.

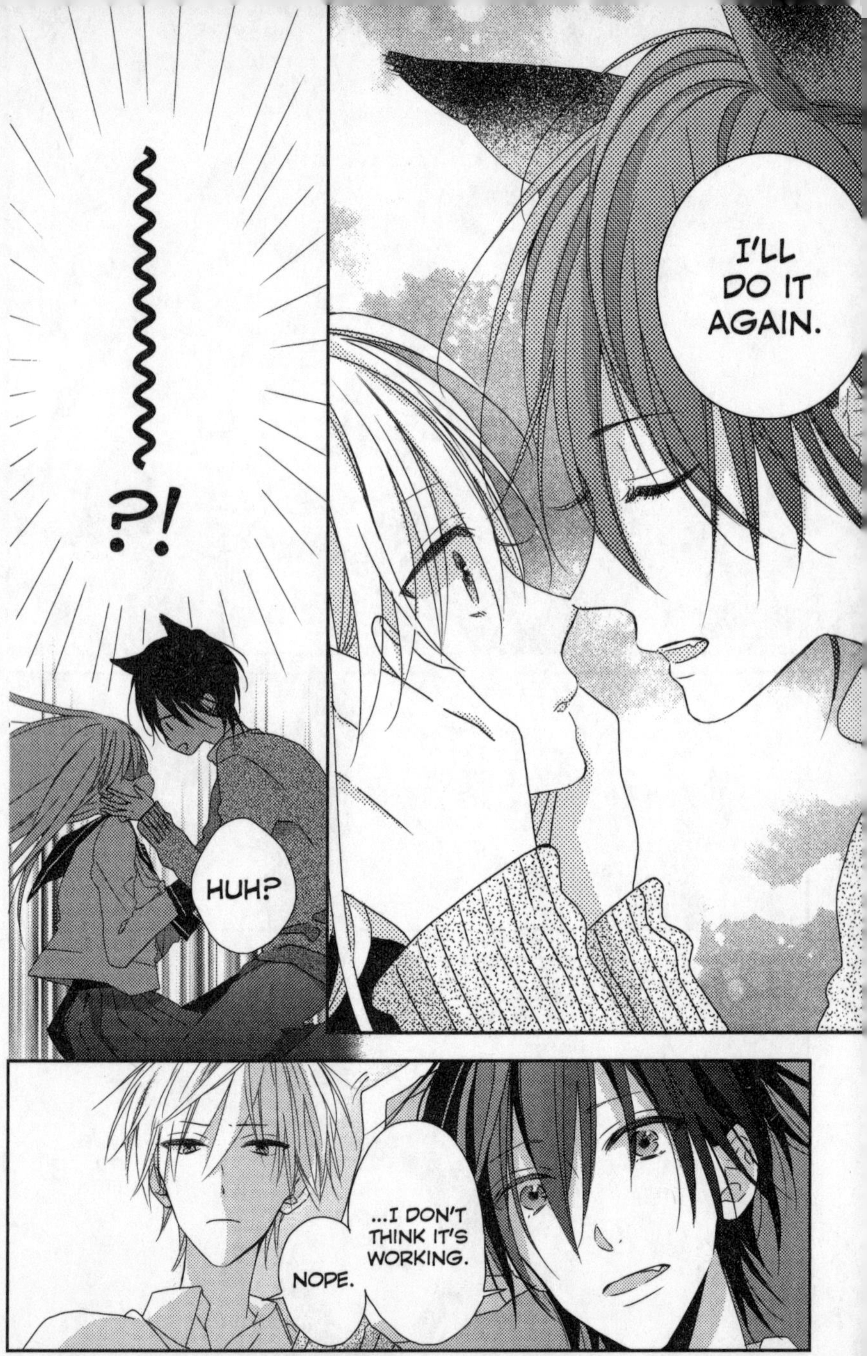
I'LL DO IT AGAIN.
~?!
HUH?
...I DON'T THINK IT'S WORKING.
NOPE.

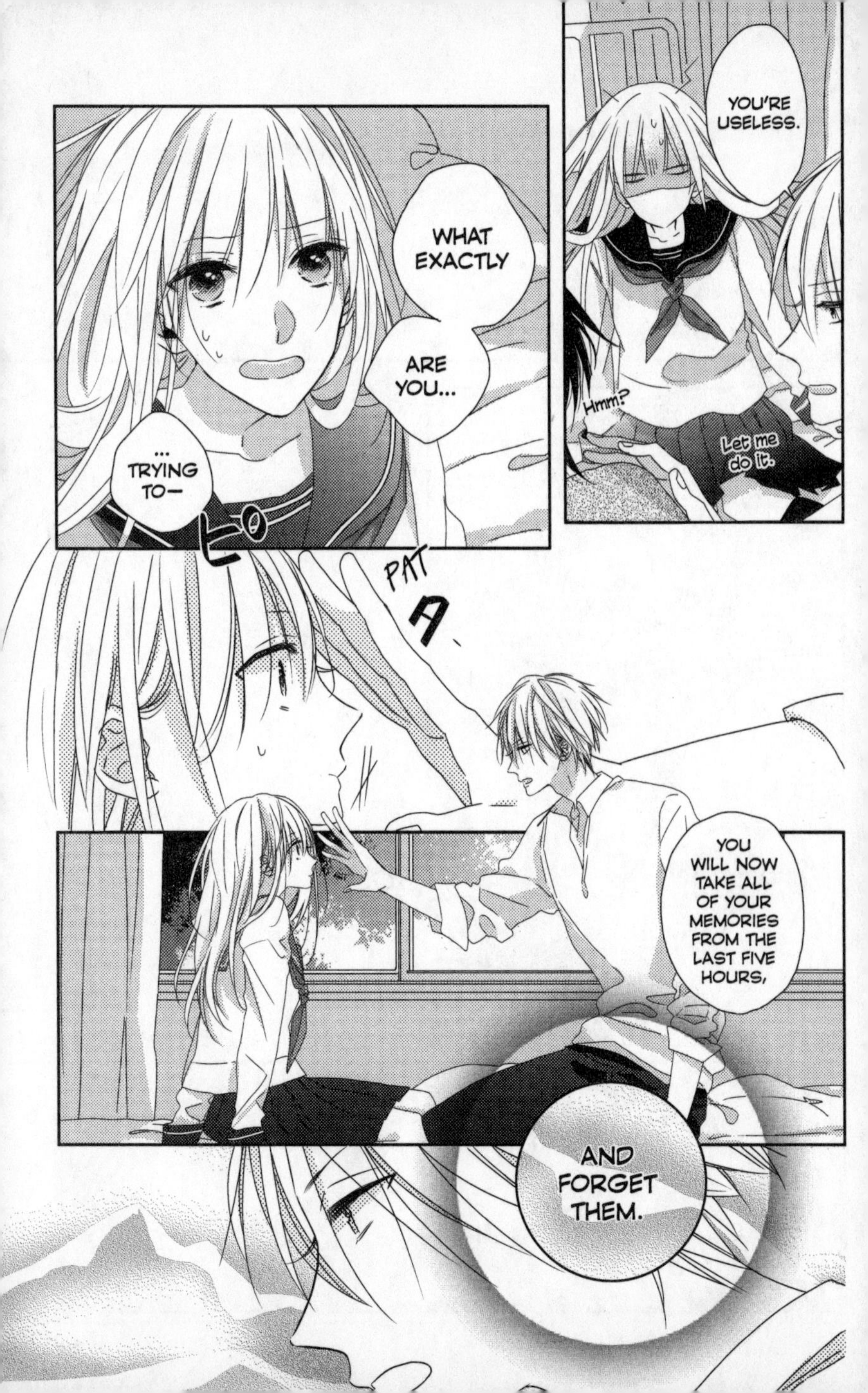
YOU'RE USELESS.
Hmm?
Let me do it.
WHAT EXACTLY
ARE YOU...
... TRYING TO—
ピ
PAT
タ
YOU WILL NOW TAKE ALL OF YOUR MEMORIES FROM THE LAST FIVE HOURS,
AND FORGET THEM.

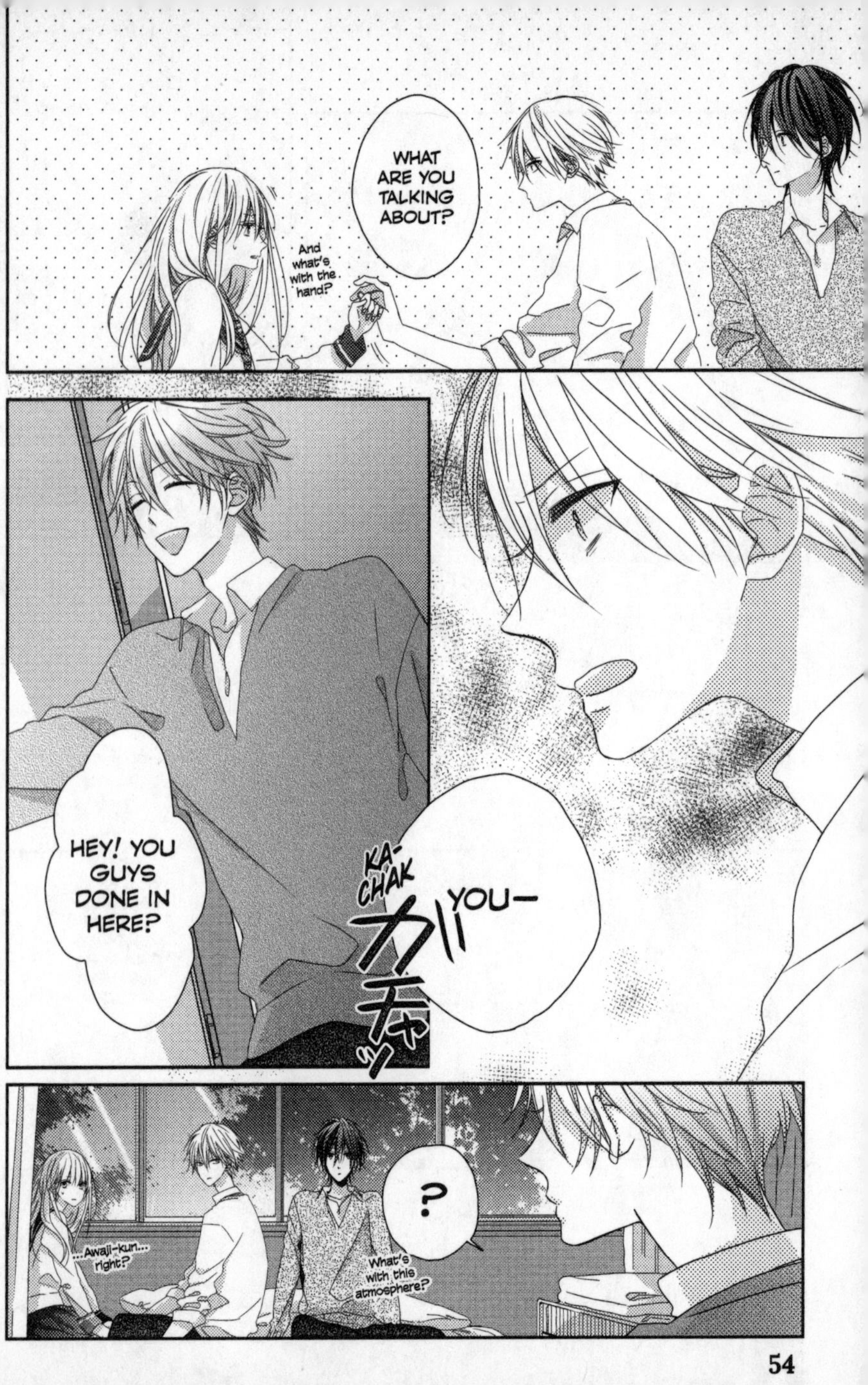
WHAT ARE YOU TALKING ABOUT?
And what's with the hand?
YOU—
KA-CHAK
HEY! YOU GUYS DONE IN HERE?
?
What's with this atmosphere?
...Awaji-kun... right?

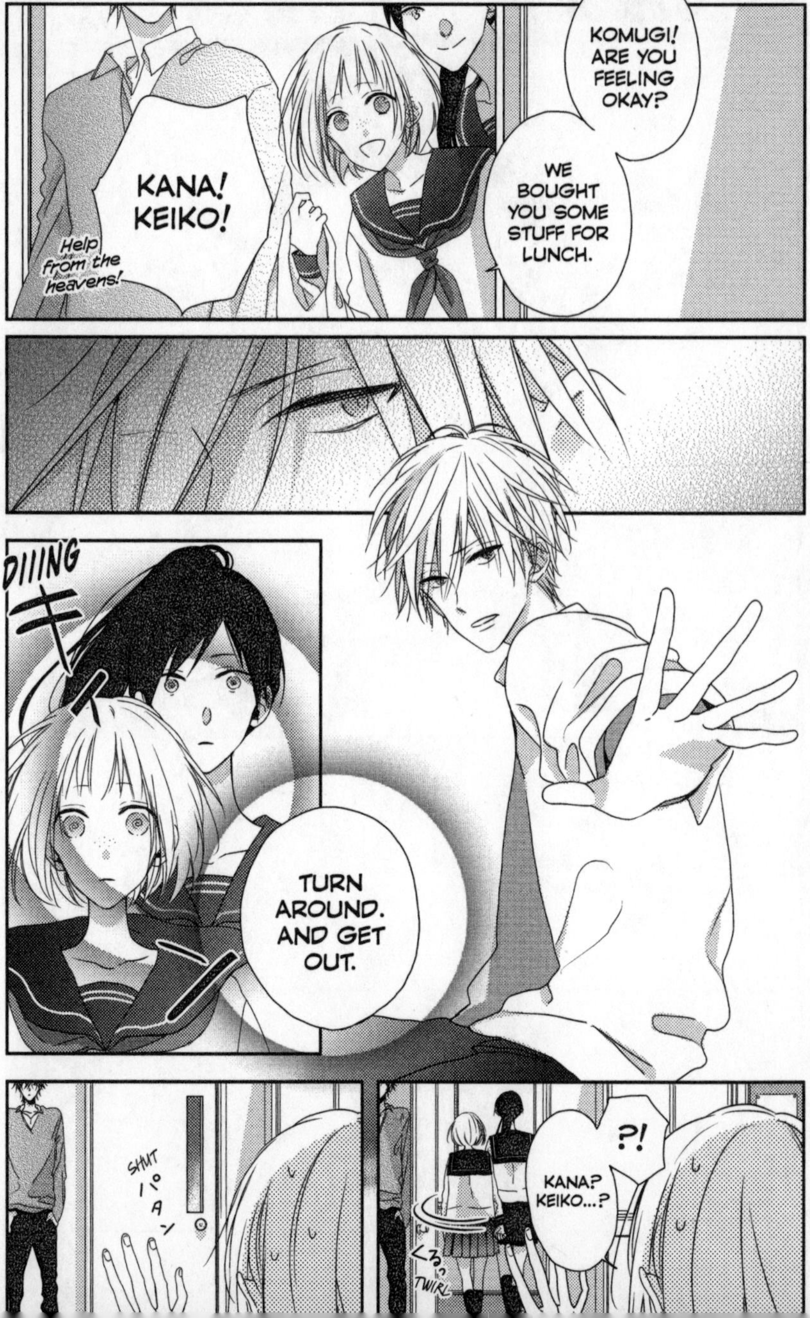
KOMUGI! ARE YOU FEELING OKAY?
WE BOUGHT YOU SOME STUFF FOR LUNCH.
KANA! KEIKO!
Help from the heavens!
DIIING
TURN AROUND. AND GET OUT.
?!
KANA? KEIKO...?
くるっ
TWIRL
SHUT
パタン

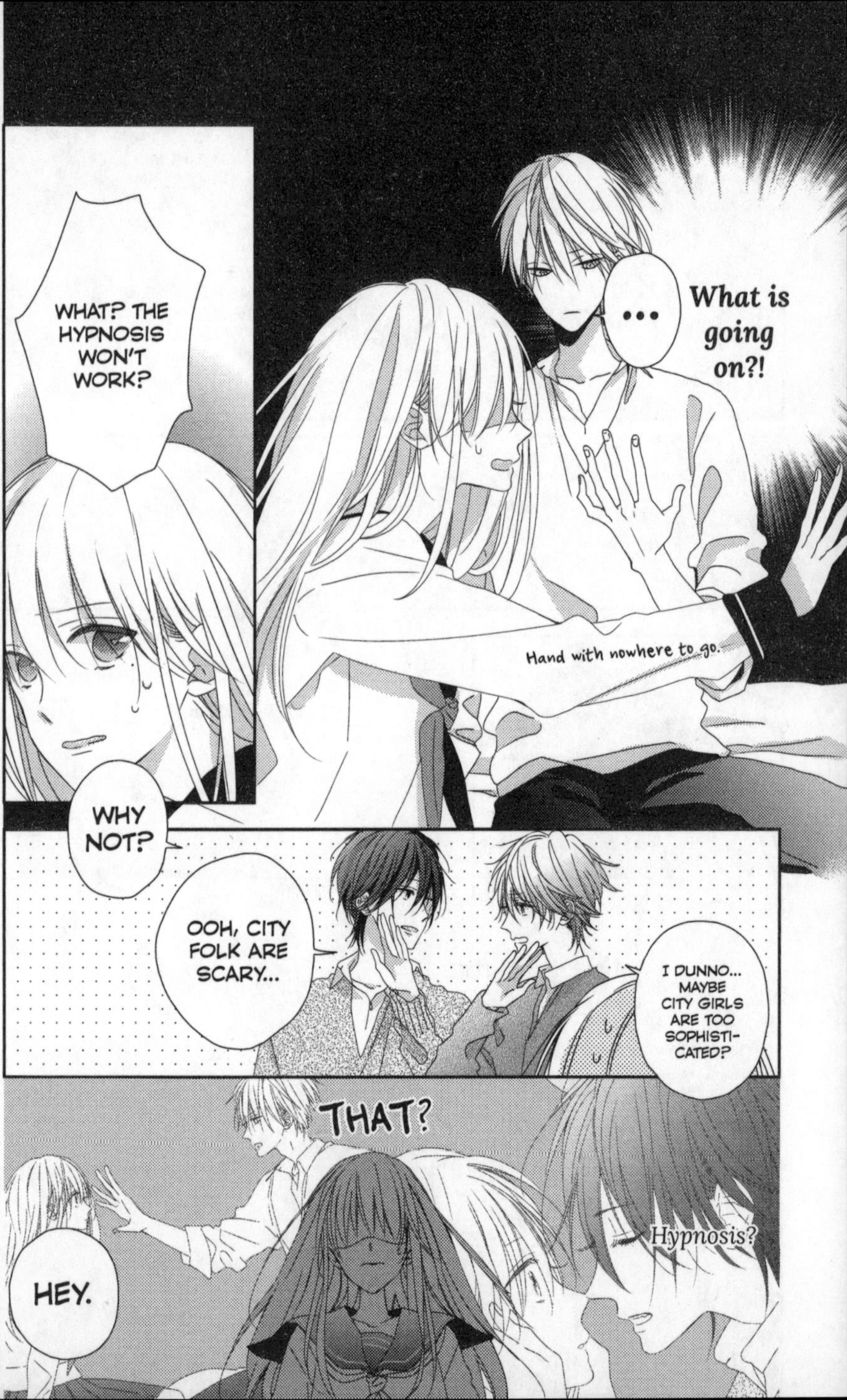
...
What is going on?!
Hand with nowhere to go.
WHAT? THE HYPNOSIS WON'T WORK?
WHY NOT?
I DUNNO... MAYBE CITY GIRLS ARE TOO SOPHISTI-CATED?
OOH, CITY FOLK ARE SCARY...
Hypnosis?
THAT?
HEY.

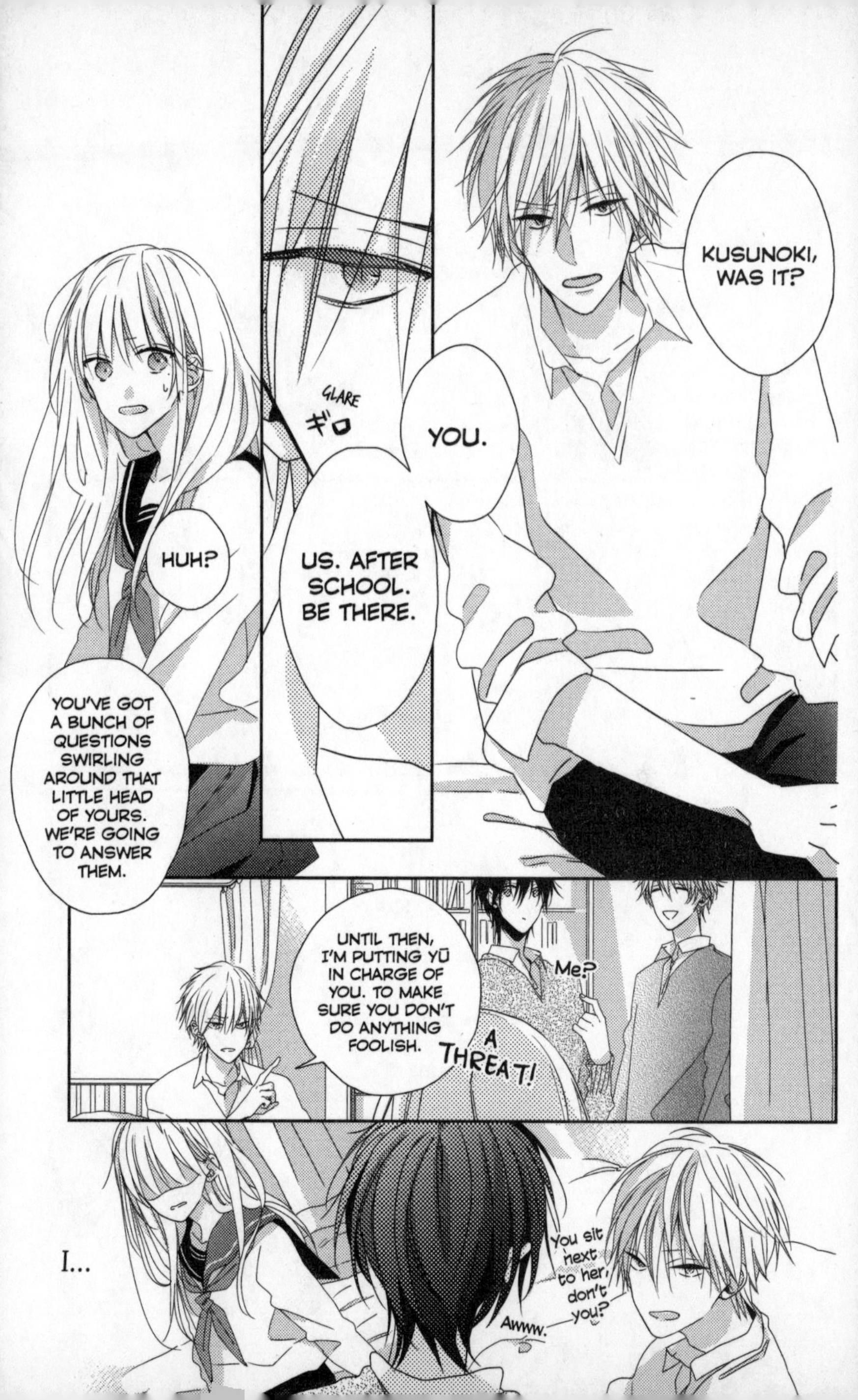
KUSUNOKI, WAS IT?
YOU.
GLARE
ギロ
US. AFTER SCHOOL. BE THERE.
HUH?
YOU'VE GOT A BUNCH OF QUESTIONS SWIRLING AROUND THAT LITTLE HEAD OF YOURS. WE'RE GOING TO ANSWER THEM.
UNTIL THEN, I'M PUTTING YŪ IN CHARGE OF YOU. TO MAKE SURE YOU DON'T DO ANYTHING FOOLISH.
Me?
A THREAT!
You sit next to her, don't you?
Awww.
I...

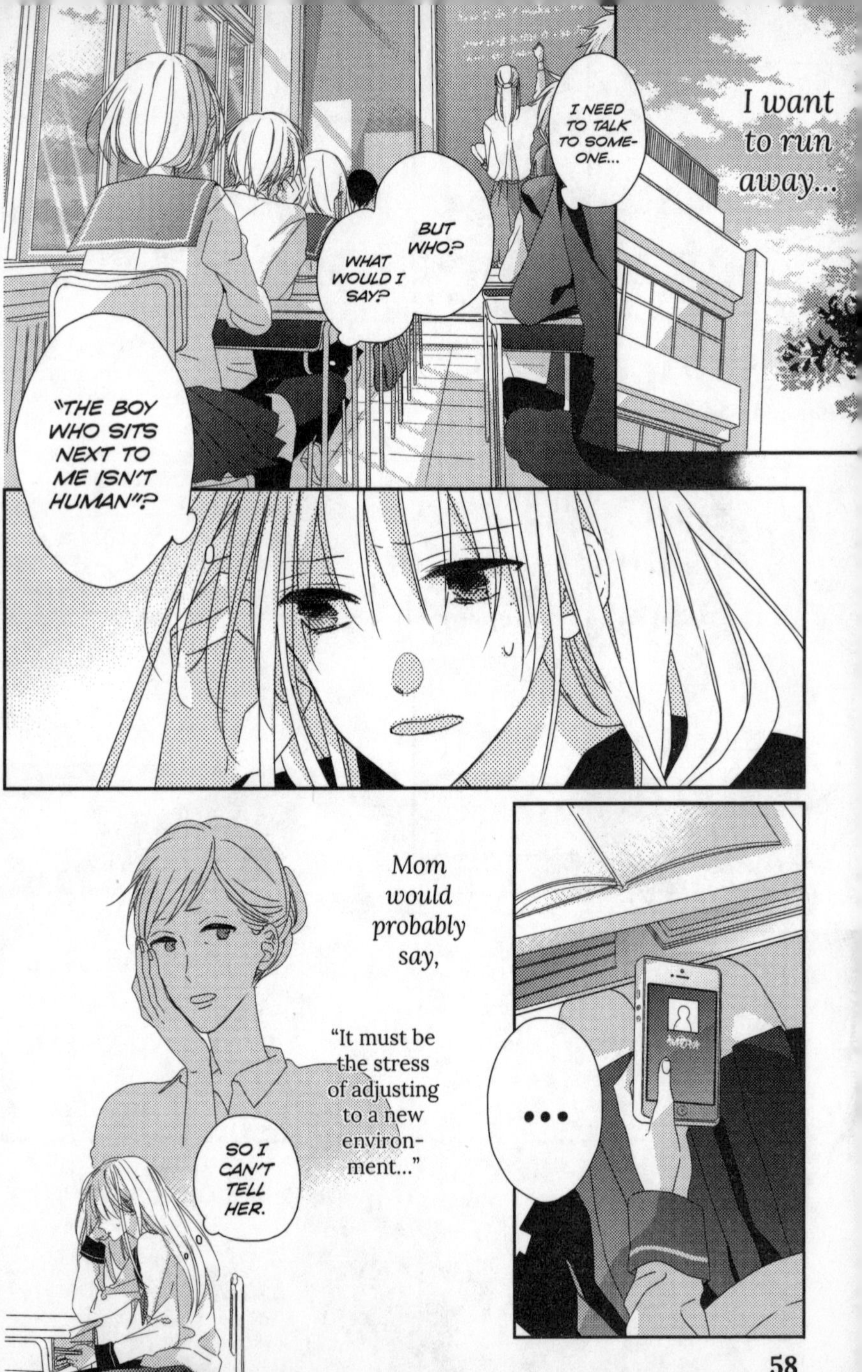
I want to run away...
I NEED TO TALK TO SOME-ONE...
BUT WHO?
WHAT WOULD I SAY?
"THE BOY WHO SITS NEXT TO ME ISN'T HUMAN"?
...
Mom would probably say,
"It must be the stress of adjusting to a new environ-ment..."
SO I CAN'T TELL HER.

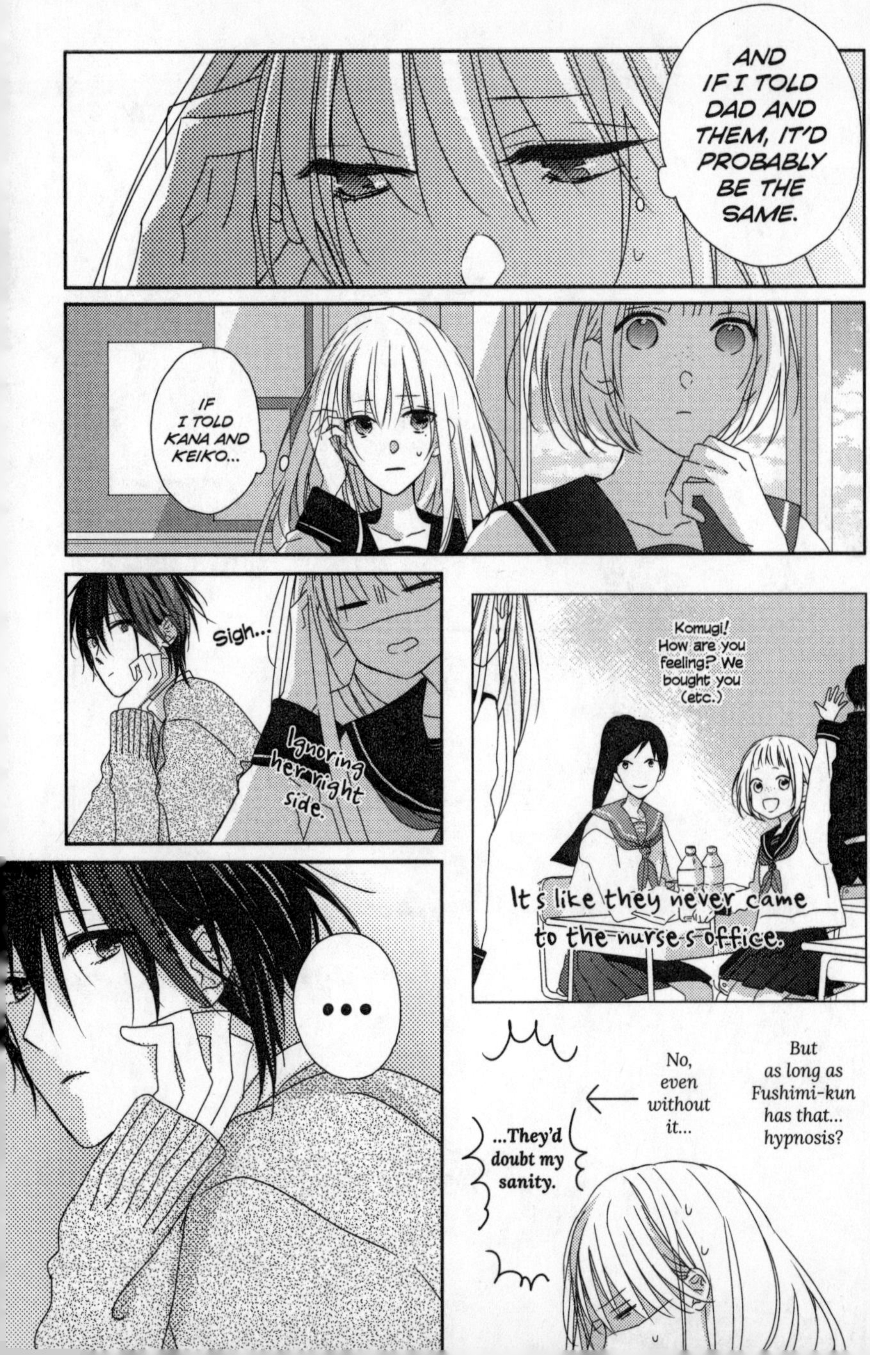
AND IF I TOLD DAD AND THEM, IT'D PROBABLY BE THE SAME.
IF I TOLD KANA AND KEIKO...
Komugi! How are you feeling? We bought you (etc.)
It's like they never came to the nurse's office.
Sigh...
Ignoring her right side.
But as long as Fushimi-kun has that... hypnosis?
No, even without it...
...They'd doubt my sanity.
...

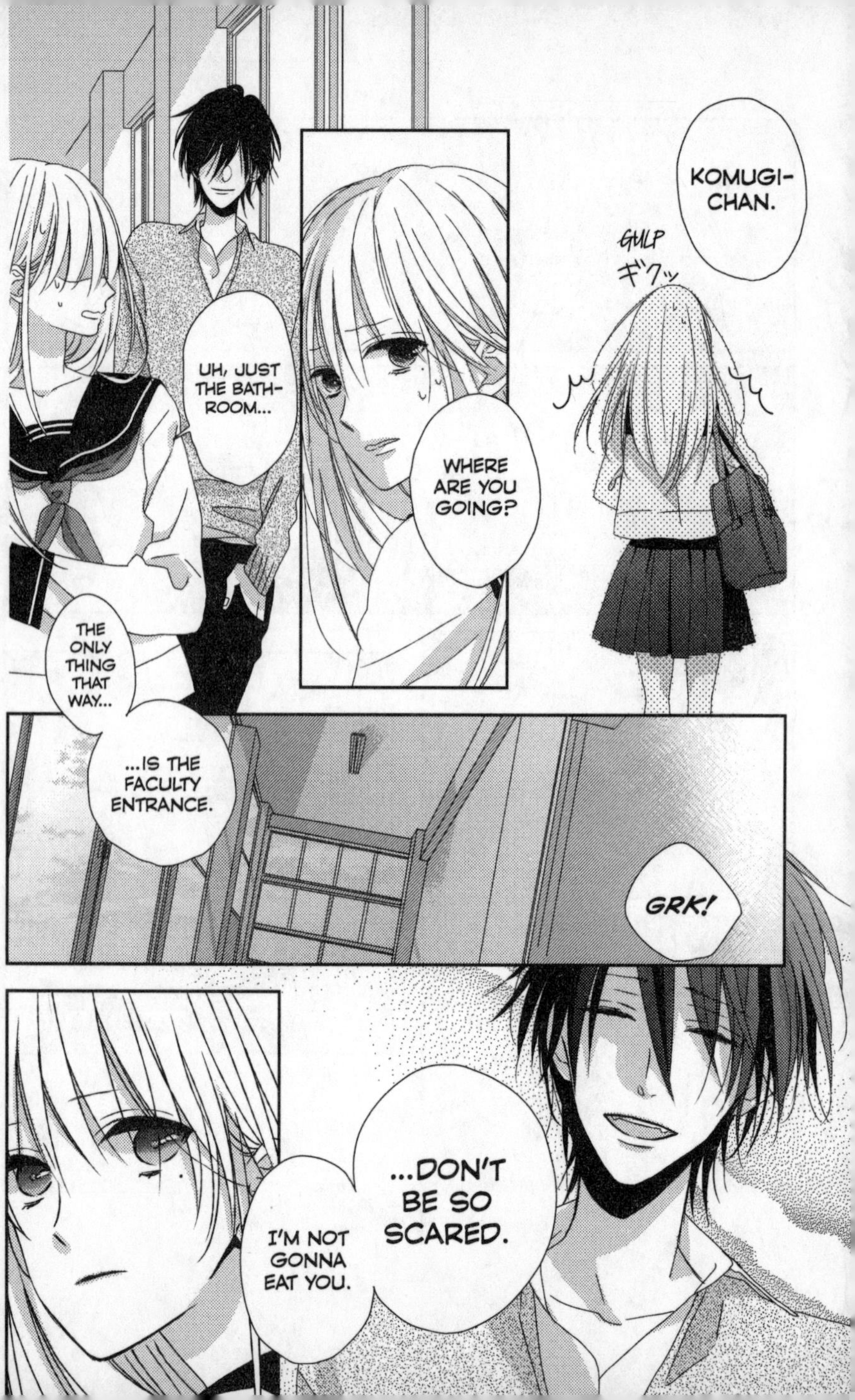
KOMUGI-CHAN.
GULP
ギクッ
WHERE ARE YOU GOING?
UH, JUST THE BATH-ROOM...
THE ONLY THING THAT WAY...
...IS THE FACULTY ENTRANCE.
GRK!
...DON'T BE SO SCARED.
I'M NOT GONNA EAT YOU.

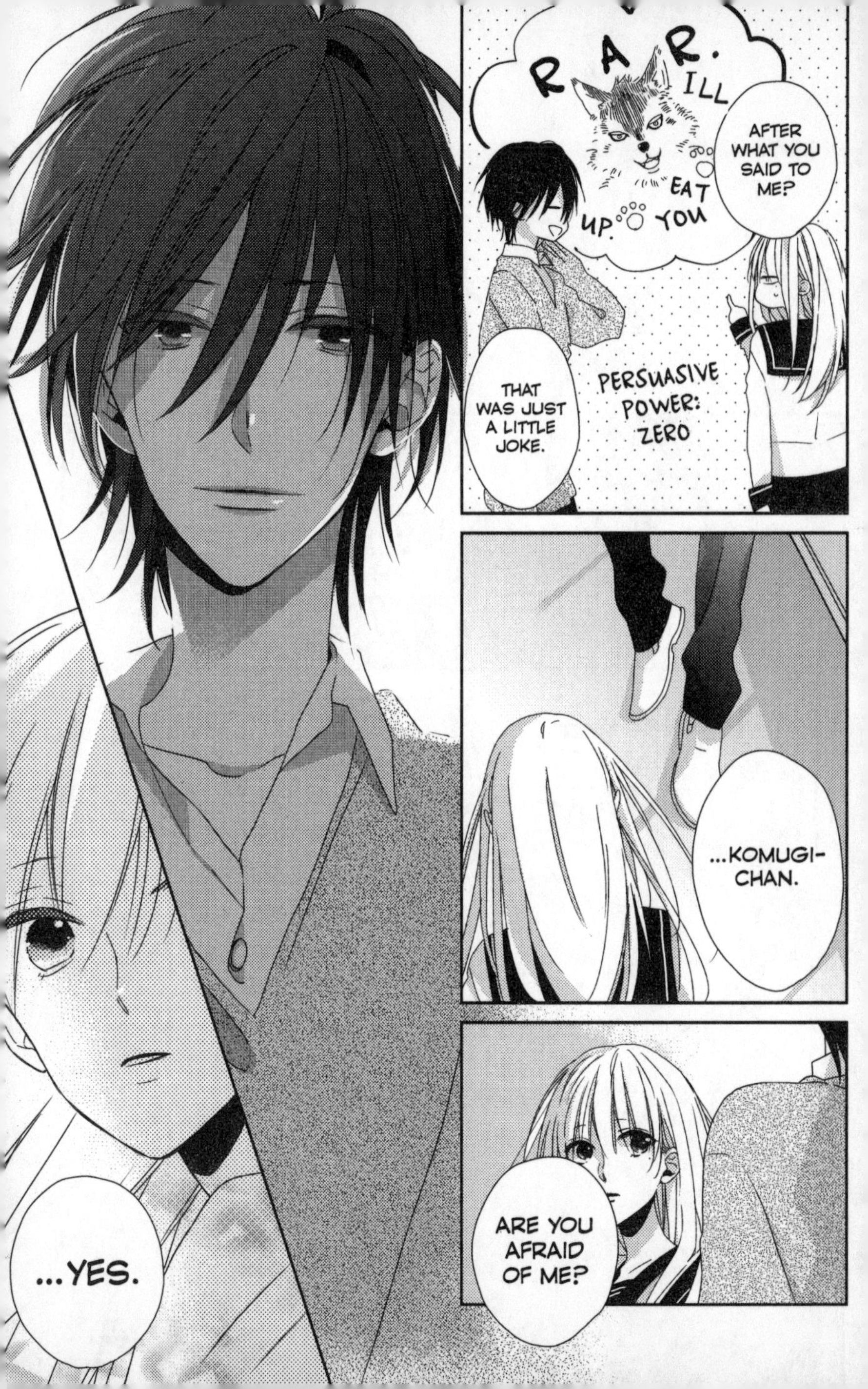
RAR. ILL EAT YOU UP.
AFTER WHAT YOU SAID TO ME?
PERSUASIVE POWER: ZERO
THAT WAS JUST A LITTLE JOKE.
...KOMUGI-CHAN.
ARE YOU AFRAID OF ME?
...YES.

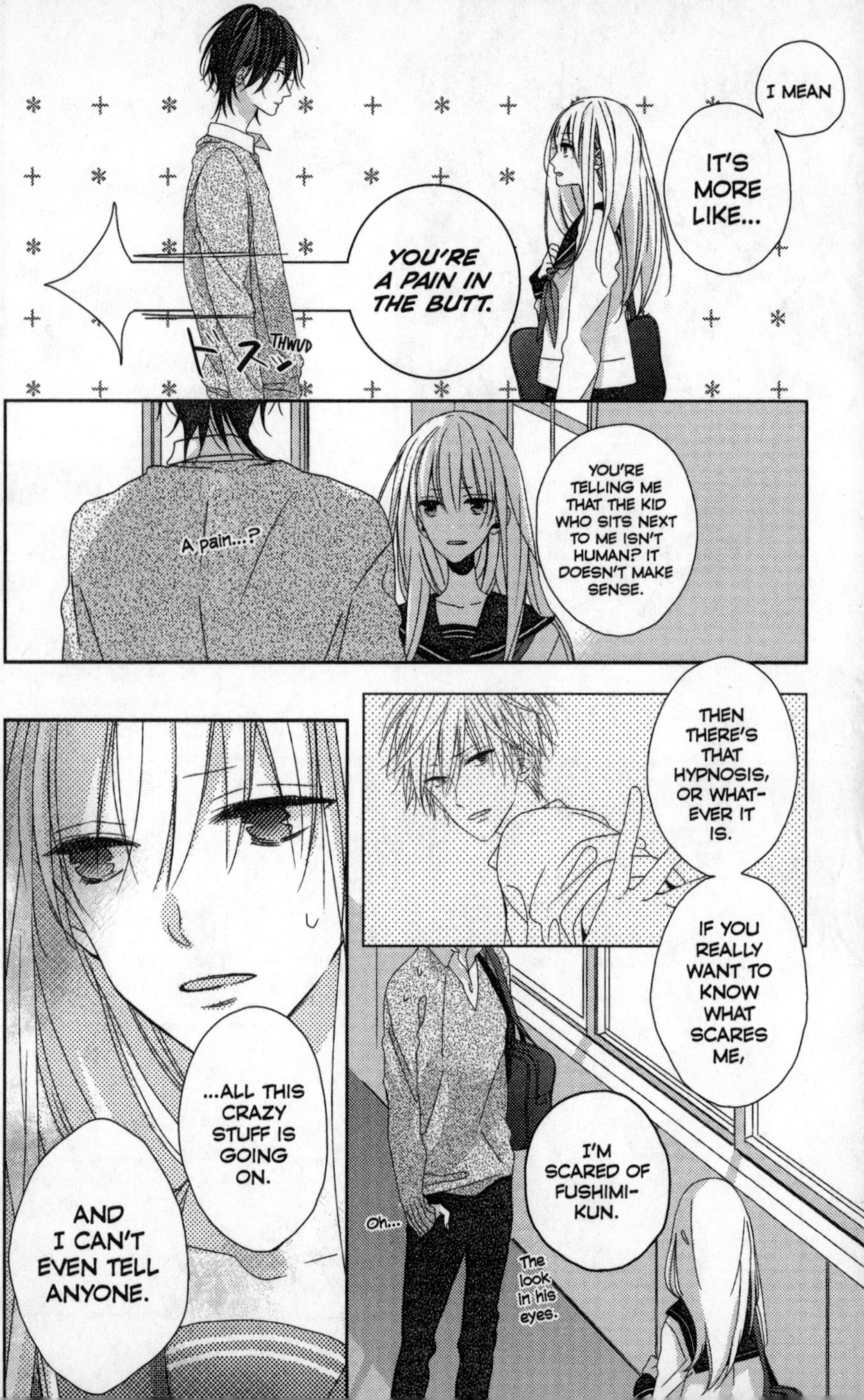
I MEAN
IT'S MORE LIKE...
YOU'RE A PAIN IN THE BUTT.
THWUD
YOU'RE TELLING ME THAT THE KID WHO SITS NEXT TO ME ISN'T HUMAN? IT DOESN'T MAKE SENSE.
A pain...?
THEN THERE'S THAT HYPNOSIS, OR WHAT-EVER IT IS.
IF YOU REALLY WANT TO KNOW WHAT SCARES ME,
I'M SCARED OF FUSHIMI-KUN.
The look in his eyes.
Oh...
...ALL THIS CRAZY STUFF IS GOING ON.
AND I CAN'T EVEN TELL ANYONE.

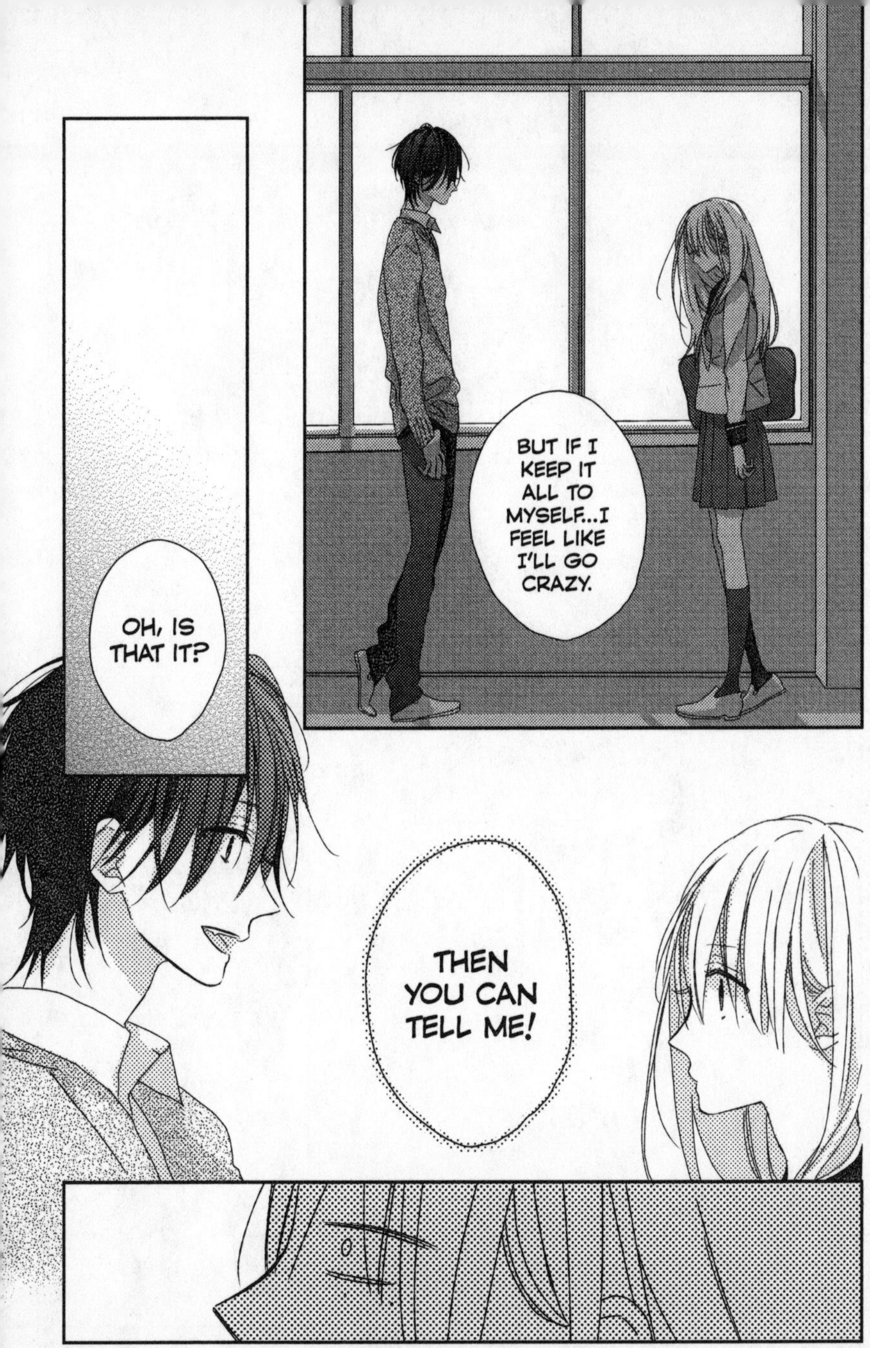
BUT IF I KEEP IT ALL TO MYSELF...I FEEL LIKE I'LL GO CRAZY.
OH, IS THAT IT?
THEN YOU CAN TELL ME!

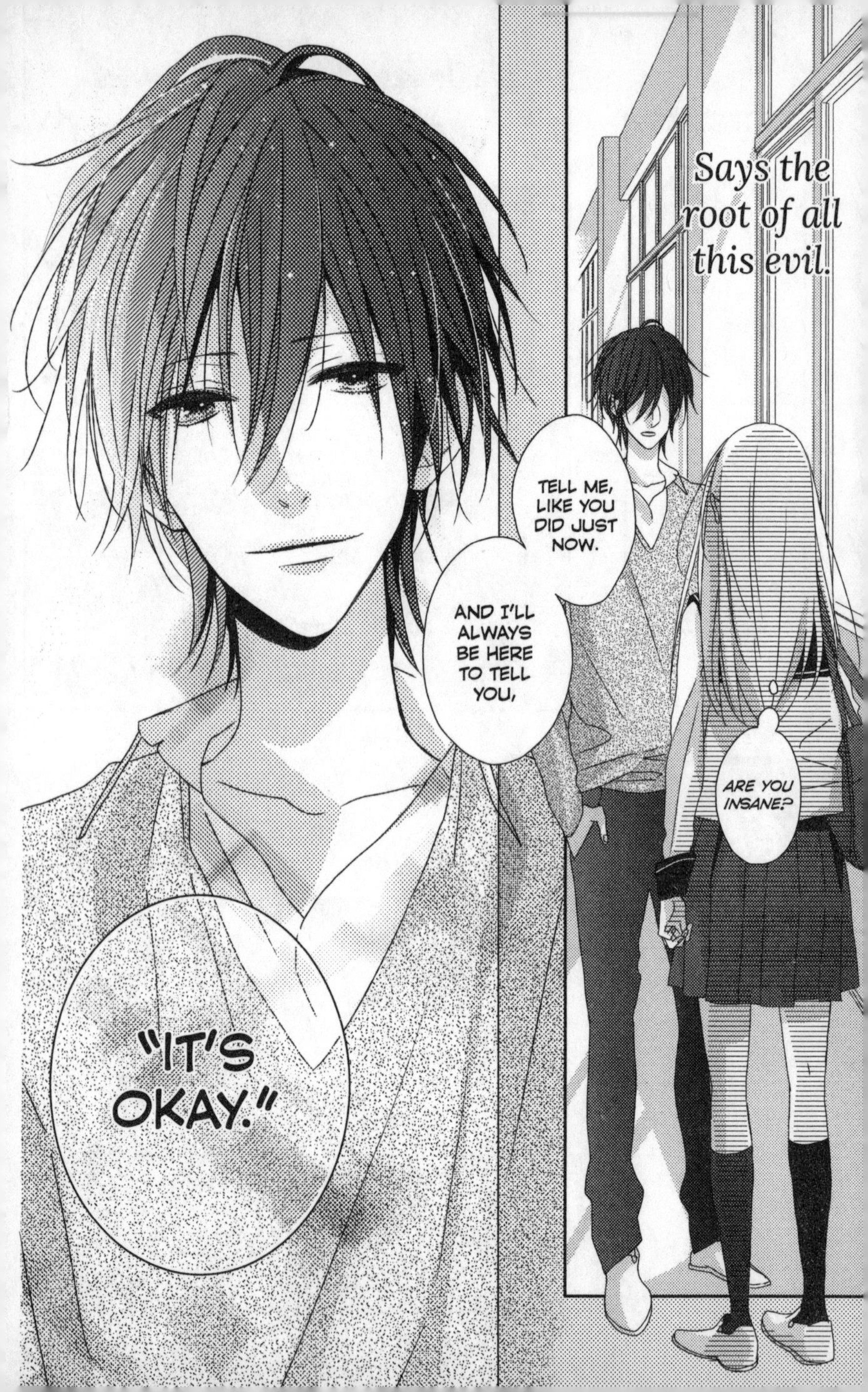

Says the root of all this evil.
TELL ME, LIKE YOU DID JUST NOW.
AND I'LL ALWAYS BE HERE TO TELL YOU,
ARE YOU INSANE?
"IT'S OKAY."

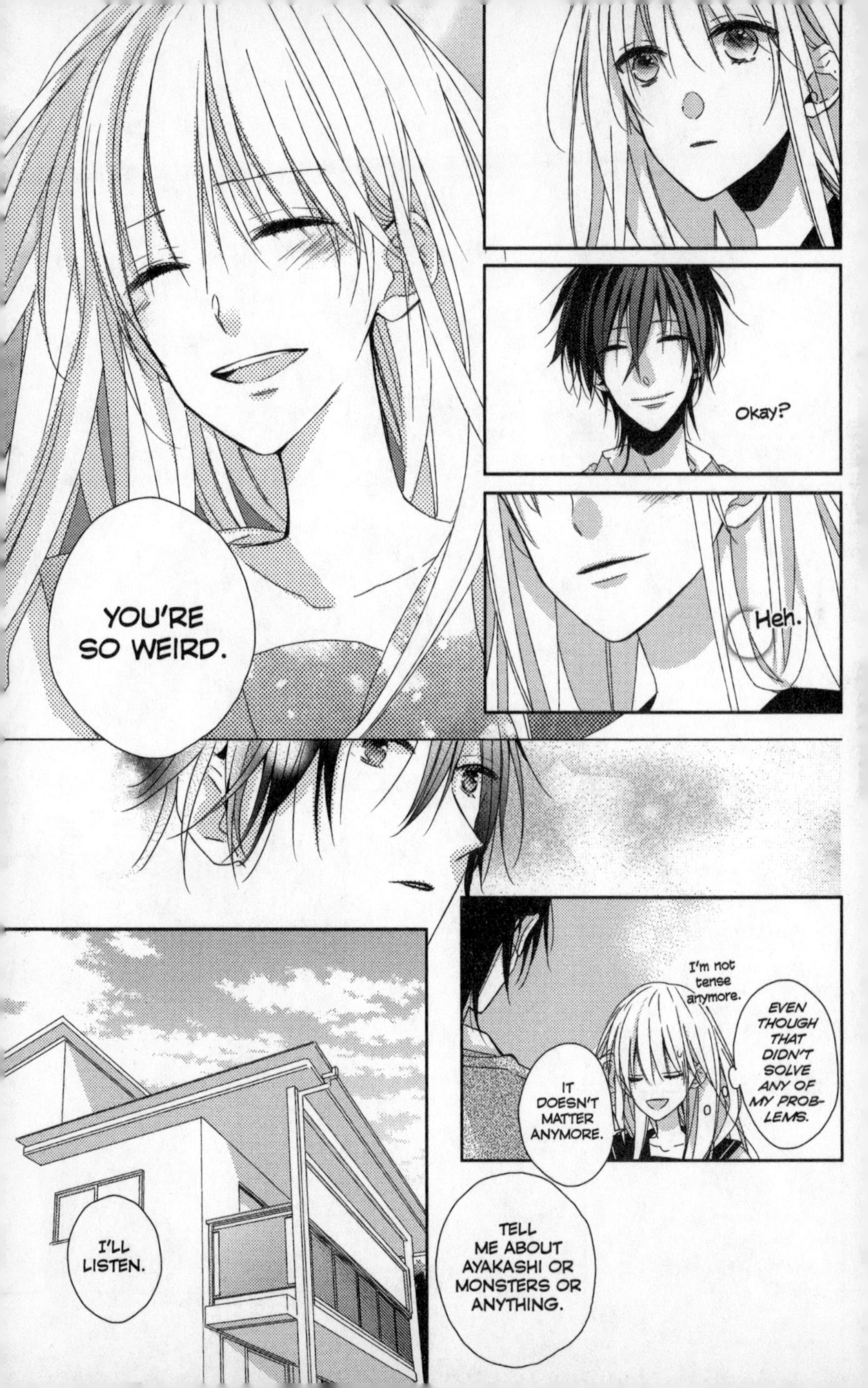
Okay?
Heh.
YOU'RE SO WEIRD.
I'm not tense anymore.
EVEN THOUGH THAT DIDN'T SOLVE ANY OF MY PROB-LEMS.
IT DOESN'T MATTER ANYMORE.
TELL ME ABOUT AYAKASHI OR MONSTERS OR ANYTHING.
I'LL LISTEN.

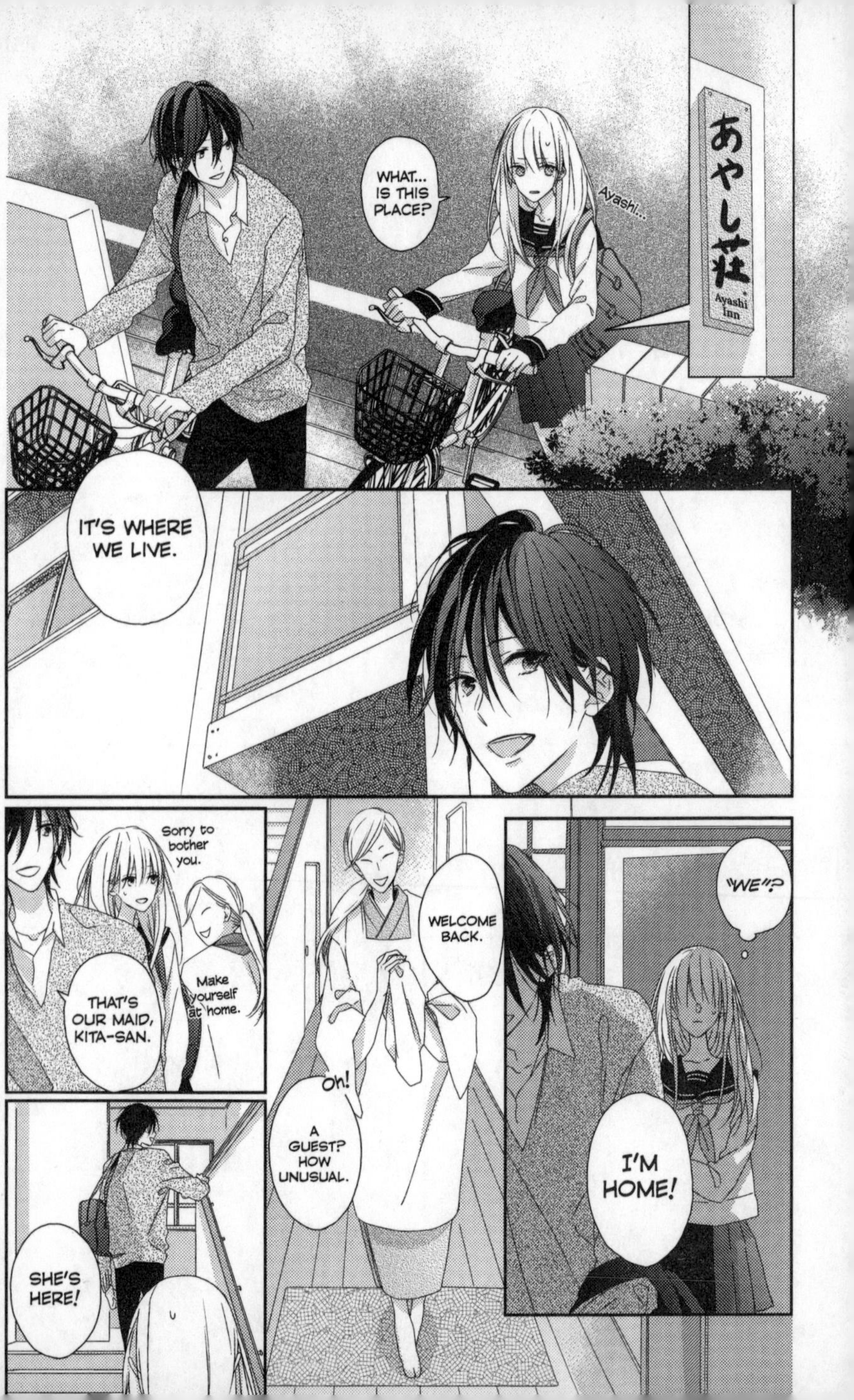
あやし荘
Ayashi Inn
Ayashi...
WHAT... IS THIS PLACE?
IT'S WHERE WE LIVE.
"WE"?
I'M HOME!
WELCOME BACK.
Oh!
A GUEST? HOW UNUSUAL.
Sorry to bother you.
Make yourself at home.
THAT'S OUR MAID, KITA-SAN.
SHE'S HERE!

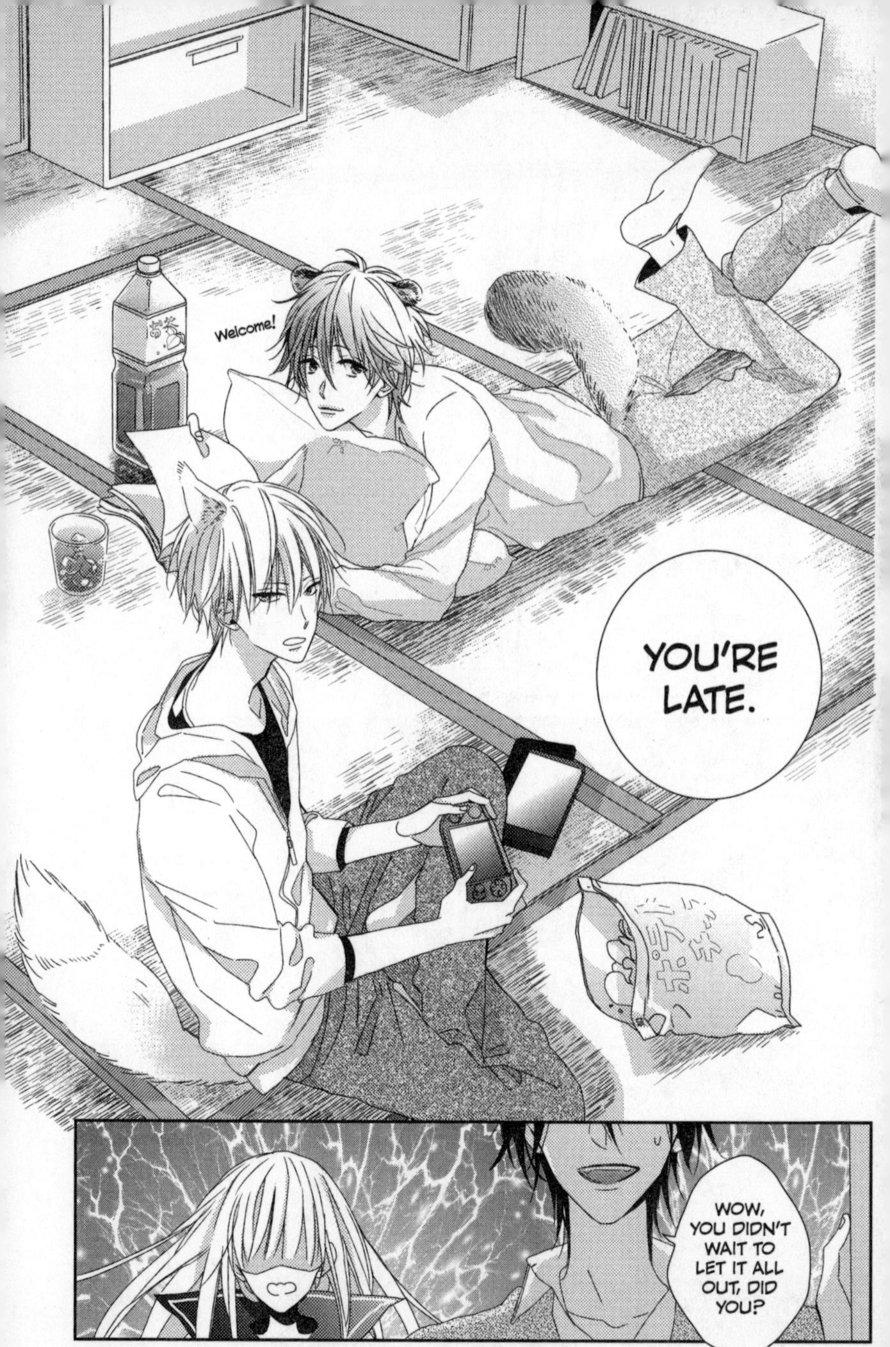
Welcome!
YOU'RE LATE.
WOW, YOU DIDN'T WAIT TO LET IT ALL OUT, DID YOU?

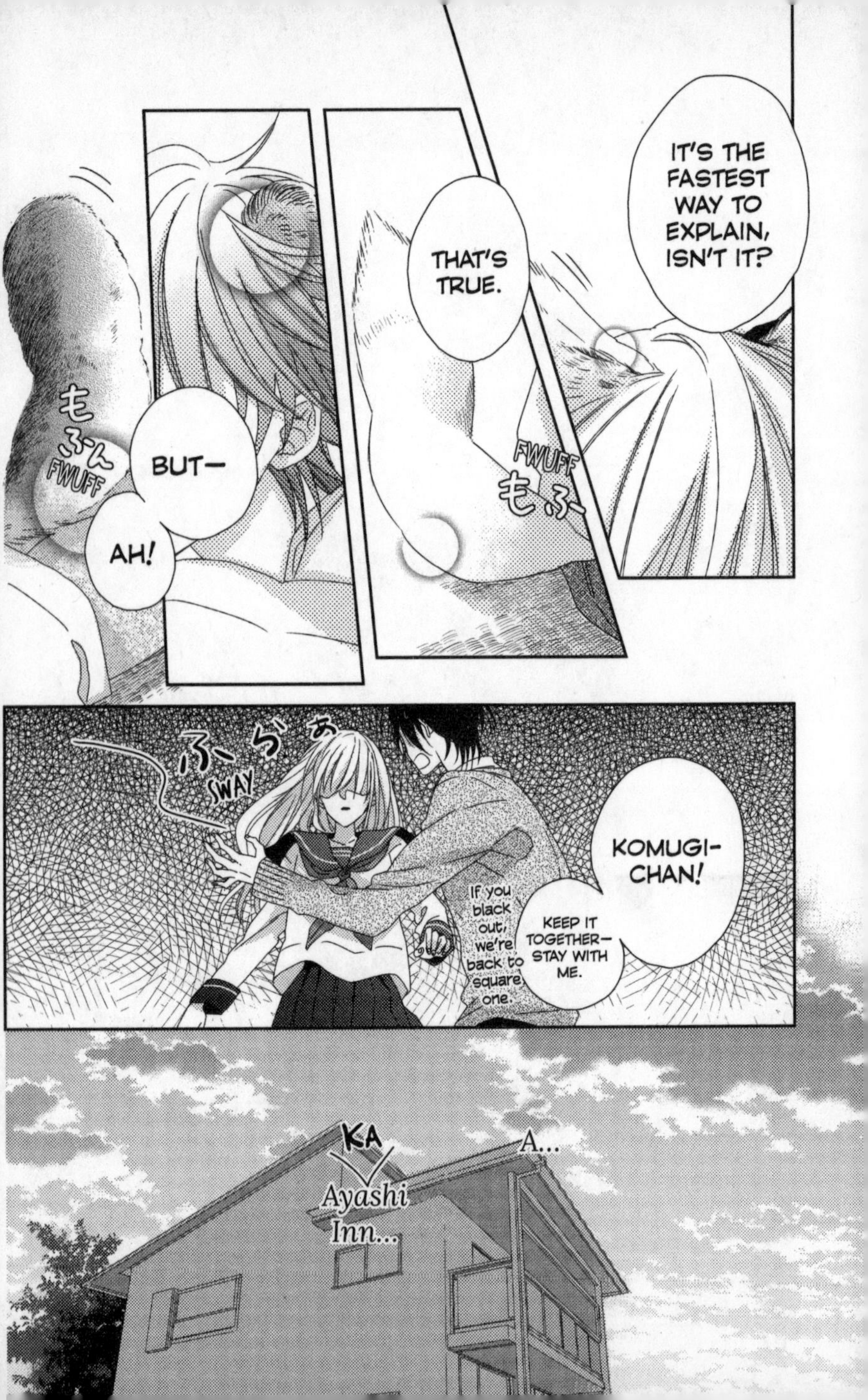
IT'S THE FASTEST WAY TO EXPLAIN, ISN'T IT?
THAT'S TRUE.
FWUFF
もふ~
BUT—
AH!
もふん
FWUFF
KOMUGI-CHAN!
KEEP IT TOGETHER—STAY WITH ME.
If you black out, we're back to square one.
ふらぁ
SWAY
A...
KA
Ayashi Inn...

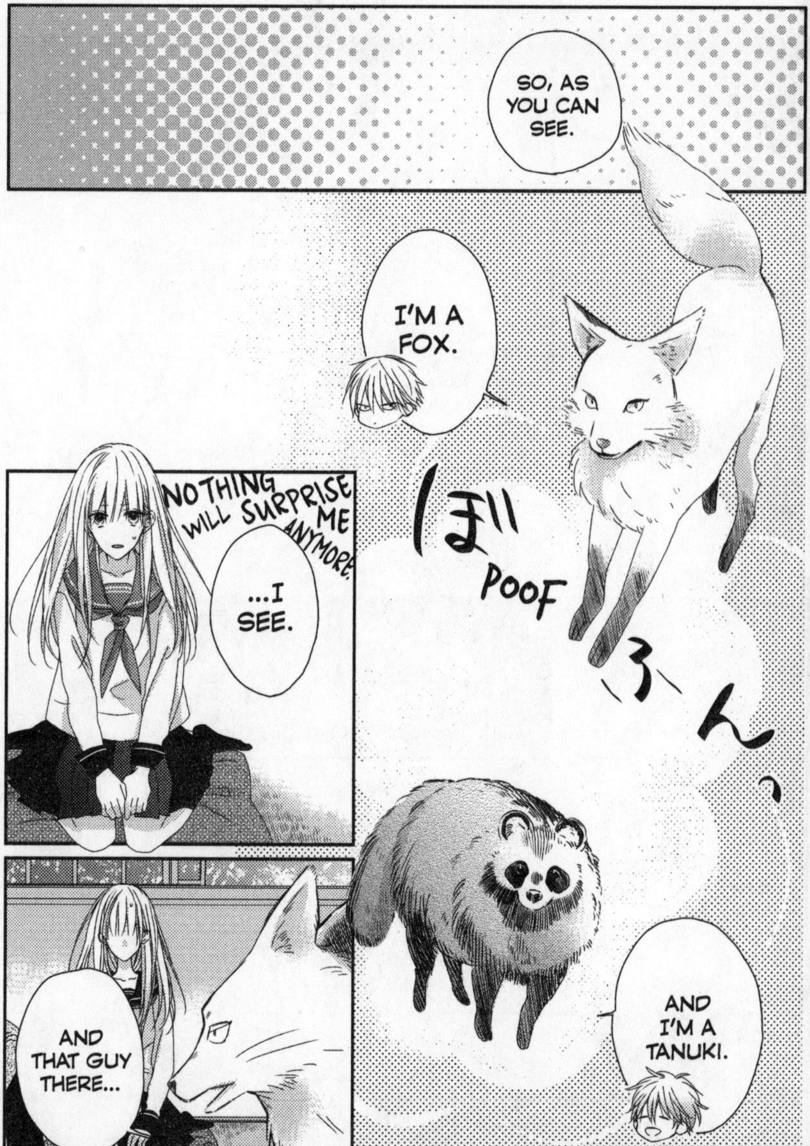
SO, AS YOU CAN SEE.
I'M A FOX.
ぼふん
POOF
AND I'M A TANUKI.
NOTHING WILL SURPRISE ME ANYMORE.
...I SEE.
AND THAT GUY THERE...

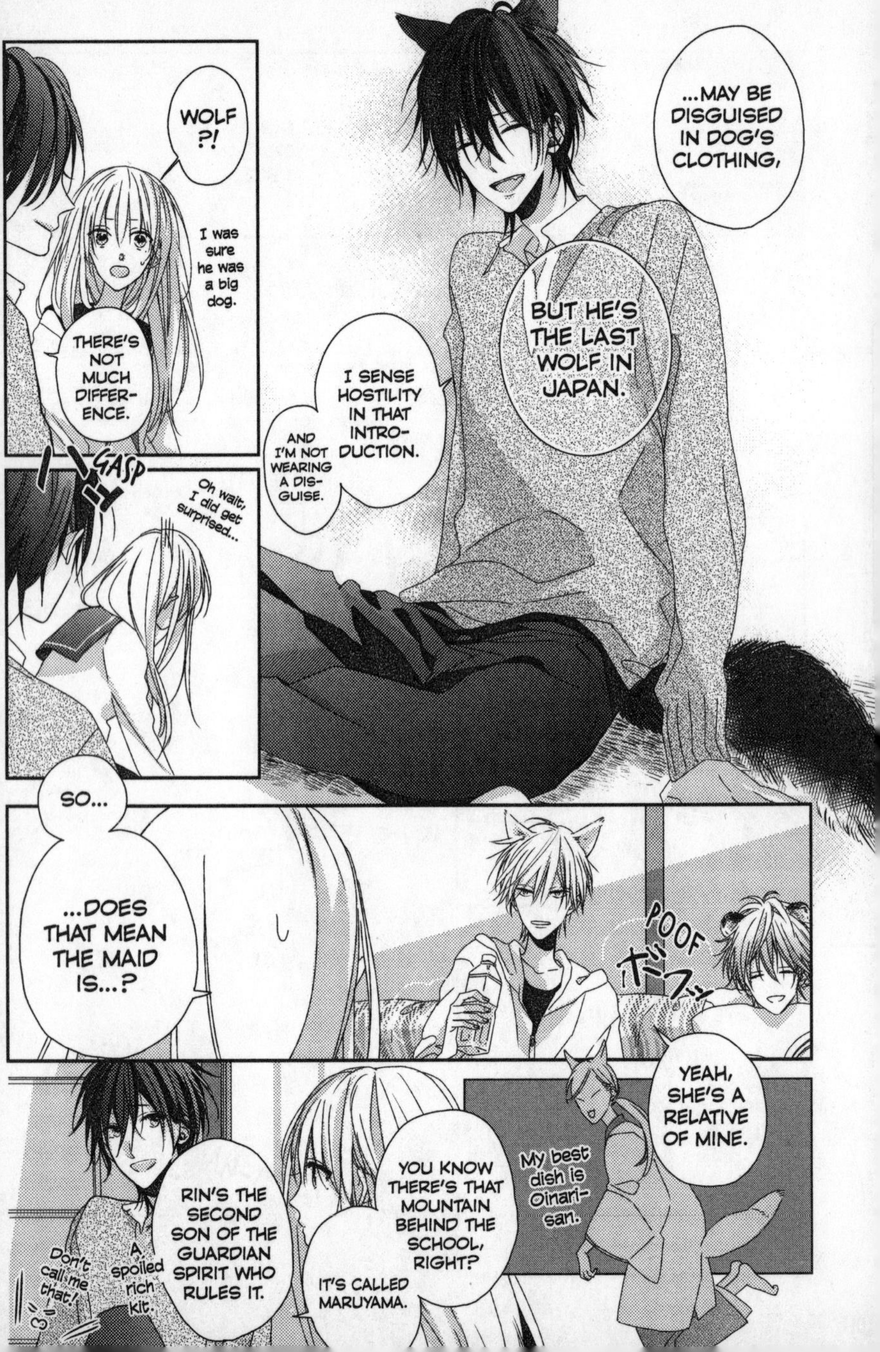
...MAY BE DISGUISED IN DOG'S CLOTHING,
BUT HE'S THE LAST WOLF IN JAPAN.
I SENSE HOSTILITY IN THAT INTRODUCTION.
AND I'M NOT WEARING A DISGUISE.
WOLF ?!
I was sure he was a big dog.
THERE'S NOT MUCH DIFFERENCE.
GASP
Oh wait, I did get surprised...
SO...
...DOES THAT MEAN THE MAID IS...?
POOF
YEAH, SHE'S A RELATIVE OF MINE.
My best dish is Oinari-san.
YOU KNOW THERE'S THAT MOUNTAIN BEHIND THE SCHOOL, RIGHT?
IT'S CALLED MARUYAMA.
RIN'S THE SECOND SON OF THE GUARDIAN SPIRIT WHO RULES IT.
A spoiled rich kit.
Don't call me that!

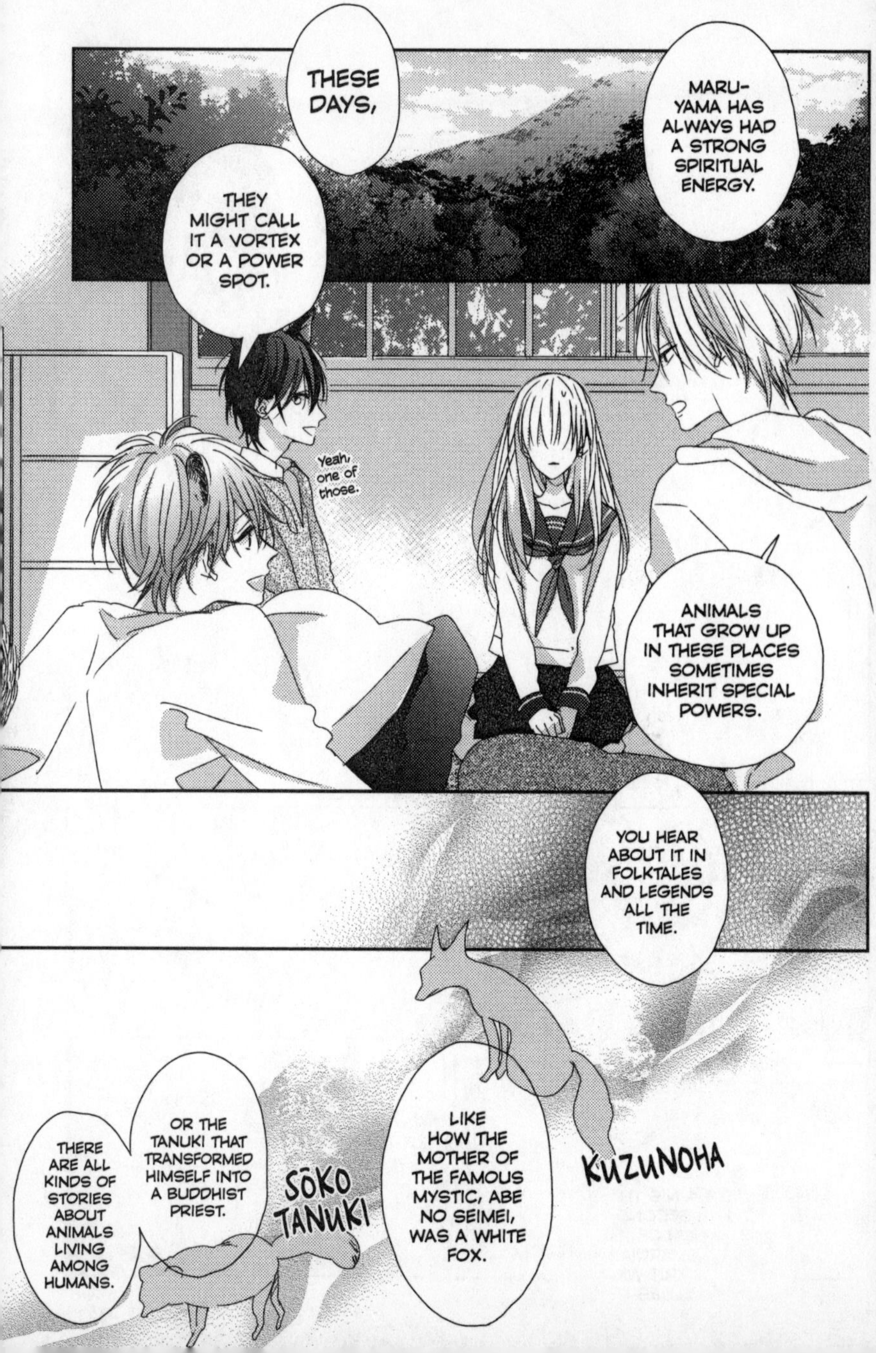
MARUYAMA HAS ALWAYS HAD A STRONG SPIRITUAL ENERGY.
THESE DAYS,
THEY MIGHT CALL IT A VORTEX OR A POWER SPOT.
Yeah, one of those.
ANIMALS THAT GROW UP IN THESE PLACES SOMETIMES INHERIT SPECIAL POWERS.
YOU HEAR ABOUT IT IN FOLKTALES AND LEGENDS ALL THE TIME.
KUZUNOHA
LIKE HOW THE MOTHER OF THE FAMOUS MYSTIC, ABE NO SEIMEI, WAS A WHITE FOX.
SŌKO TANUKI
OR THE TANUKI THAT TRANSFORMED HIMSELF INTO A BUDDHIST PRIEST.
THERE ARE ALL KINDS OF STORIES ABOUT ANIMALS LIVING AMONG HUMANS.

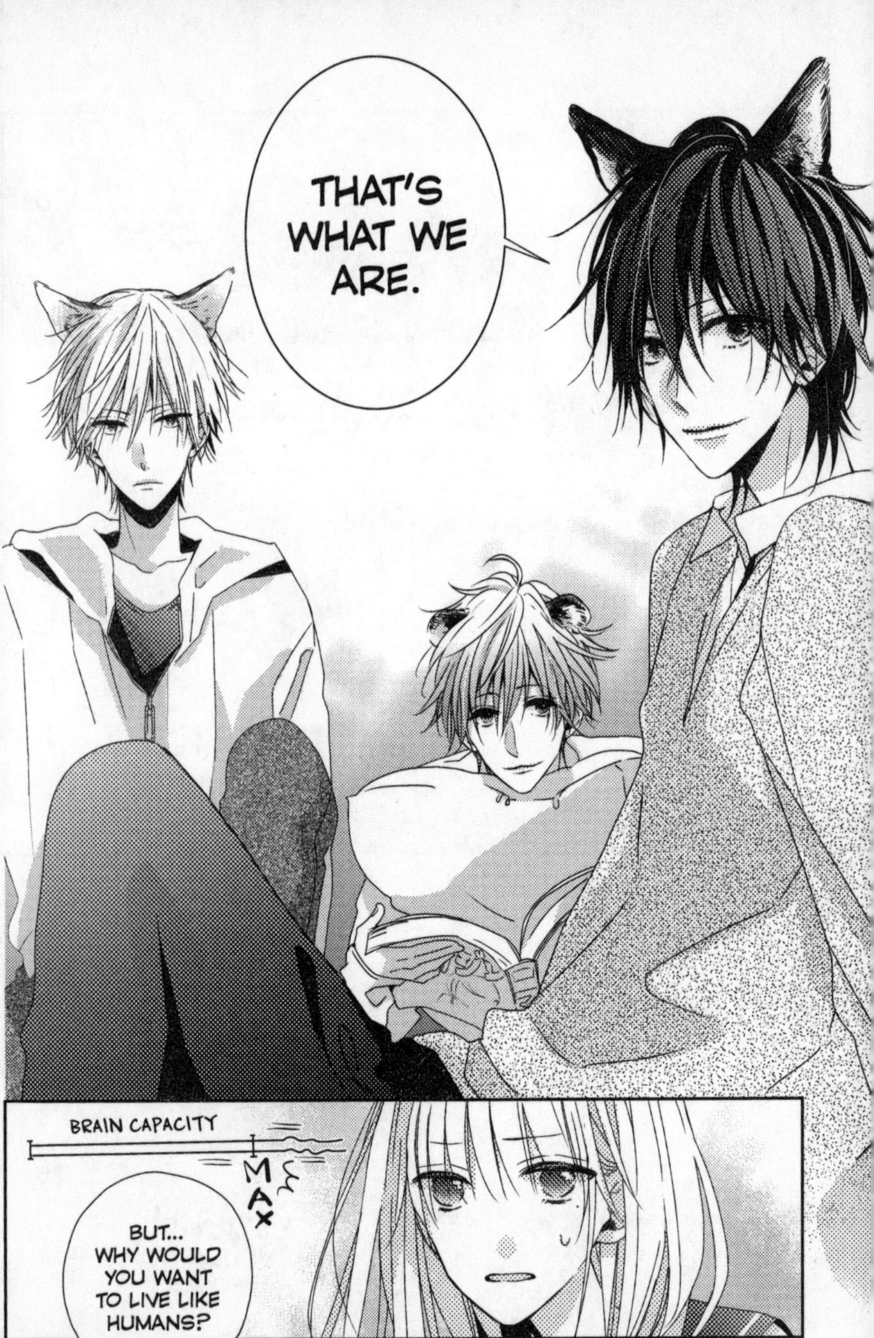
THAT'S WHAT WE ARE.
BRAIN CAPACITY
MAX
BUT... WHY WOULD YOU WANT TO LIVE LIKE HUMANS?

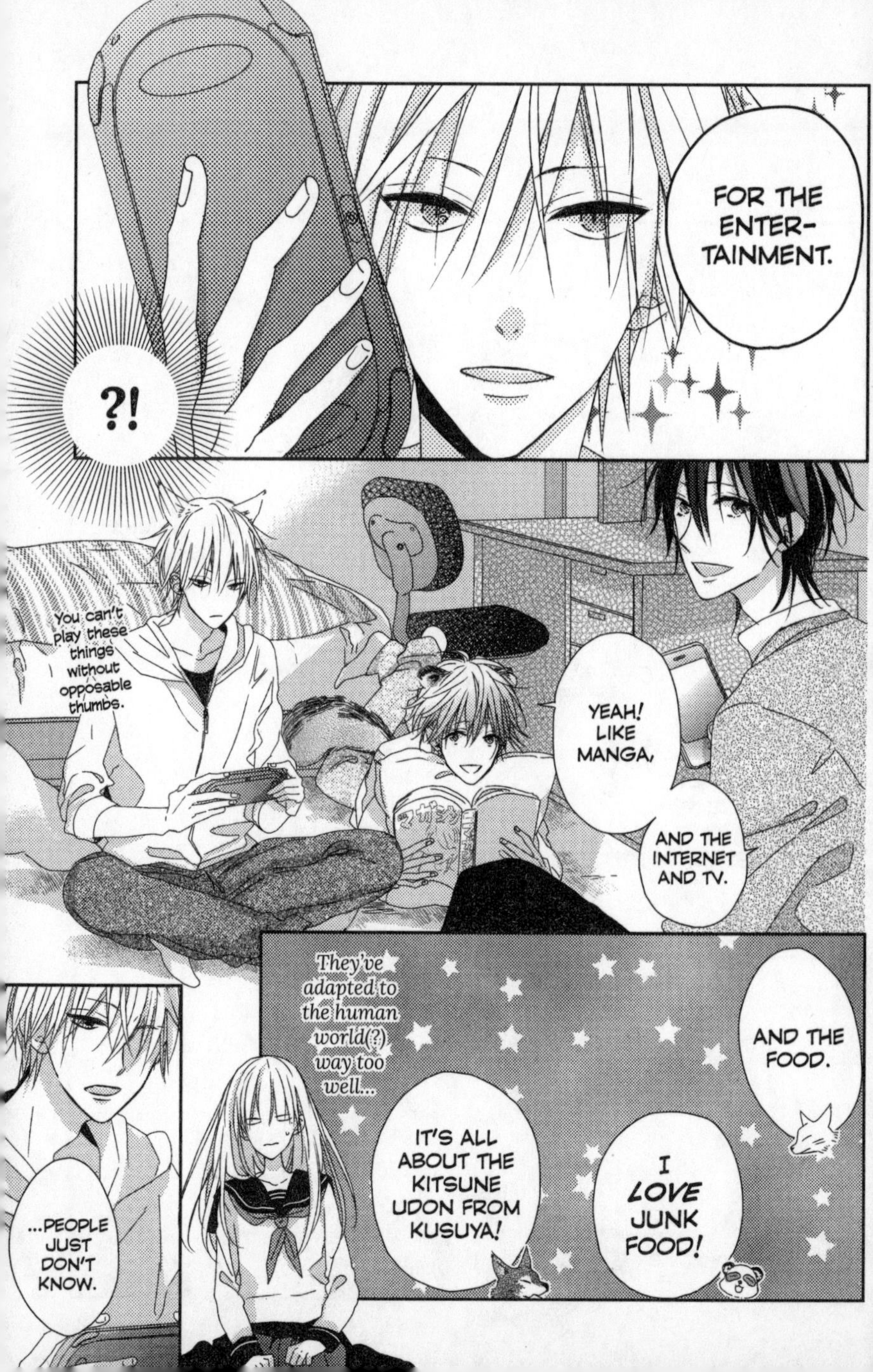
FOR THE ENTER-TAINMENT.
?!
YEAH! LIKE MANGA,
AND THE INTERNET AND TV.
You can't play these things without opposable thumbs.
AND THE FOOD.
I *LOVE* JUNK FOOD!
IT'S ALL ABOUT THE KITSUNE UDON FROM KUSUYA!
They've adapted to the human world(?) way too well...
...PEOPLE JUST DON'T KNOW.

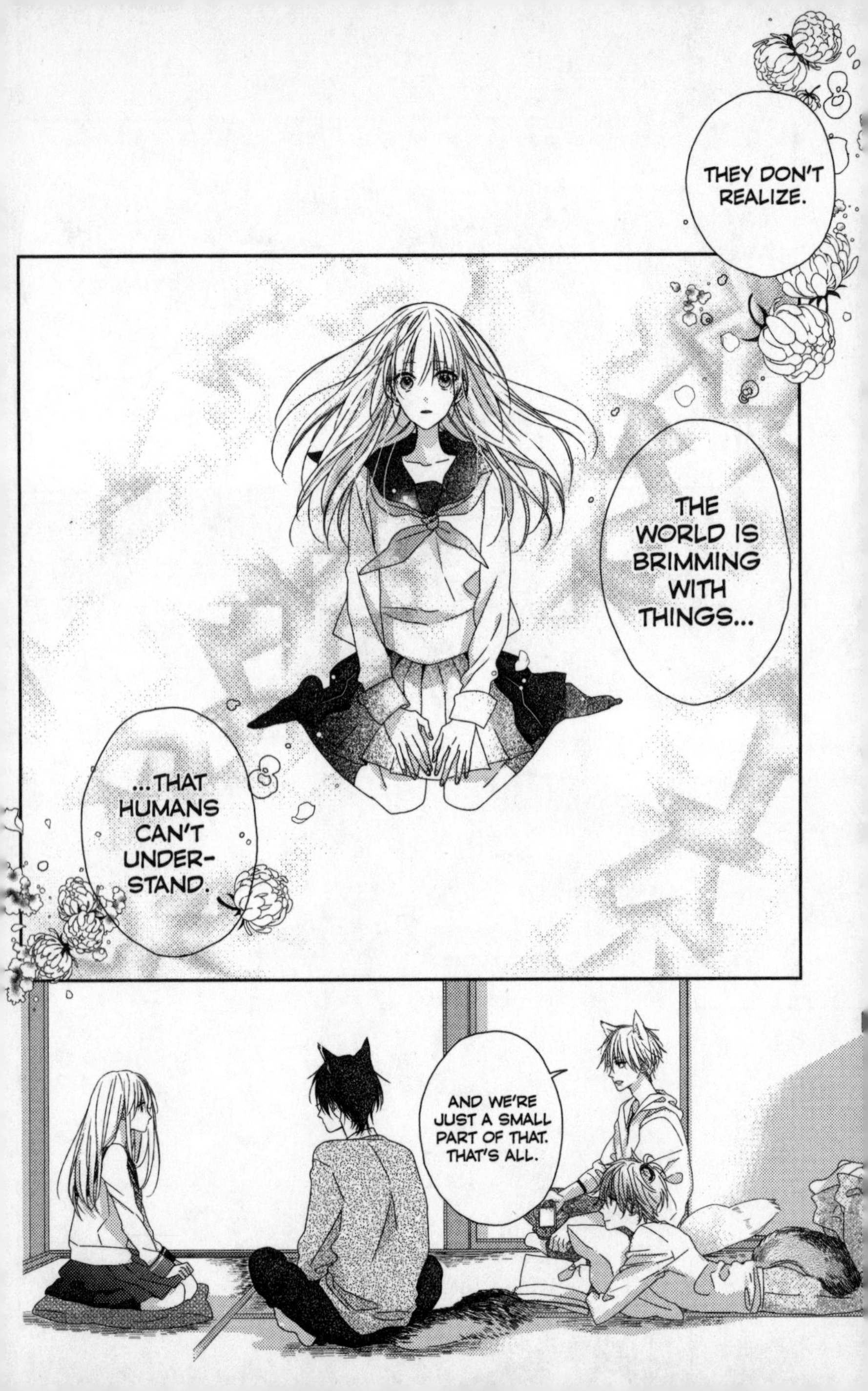
THEY DON'T REALIZE.
THE WORLD IS BRIMMING WITH THINGS...
...THAT HUMANS CAN'T UNDER-STAND.
AND WE'RE JUST A SMALL PART OF THAT. THAT'S ALL.

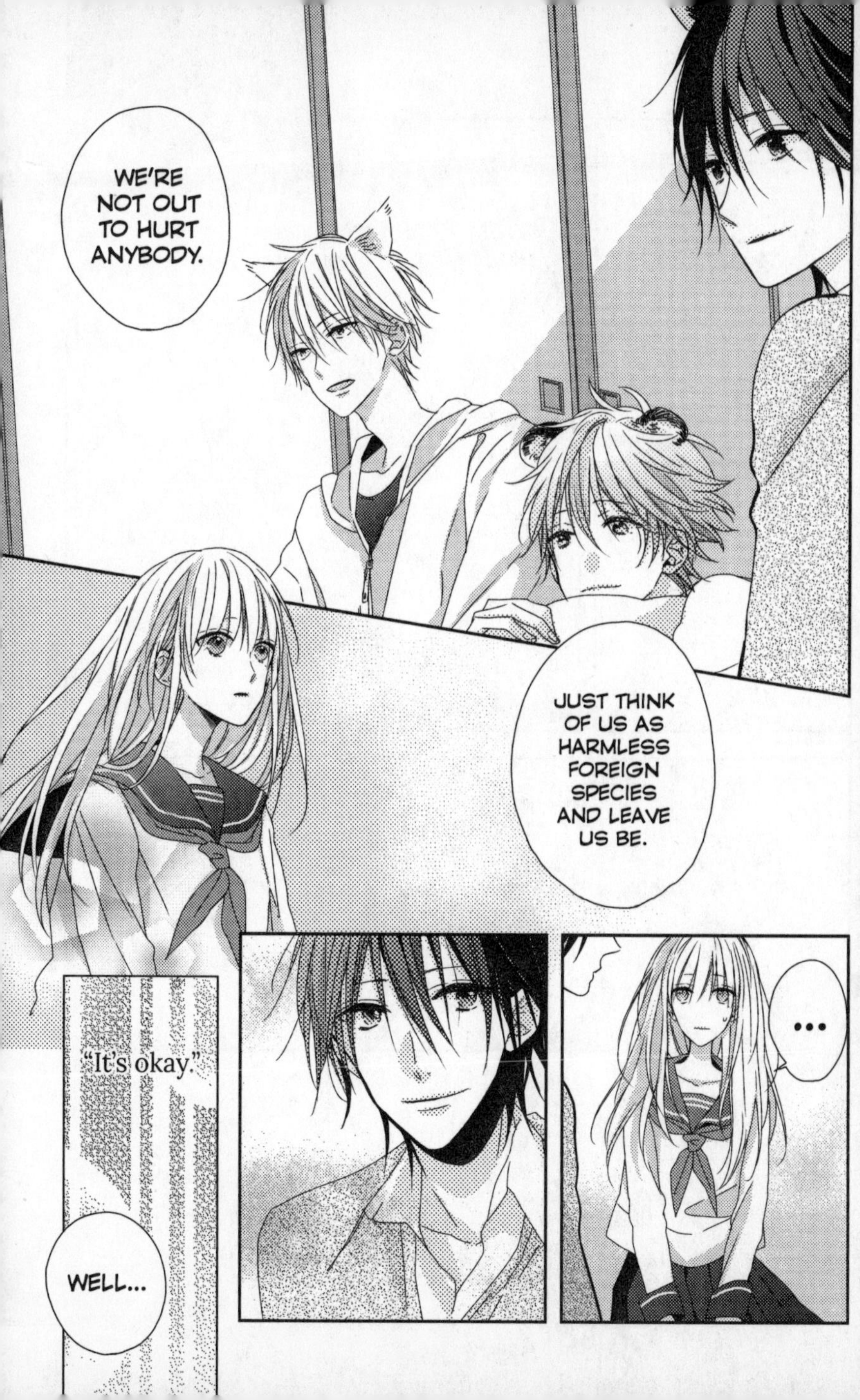
WE'RE NOT OUT TO HURT ANYBODY.
JUST THINK OF US AS HARMLESS FOREIGN SPECIES AND LEAVE US BE.
...
“It's okay.”
WELL...

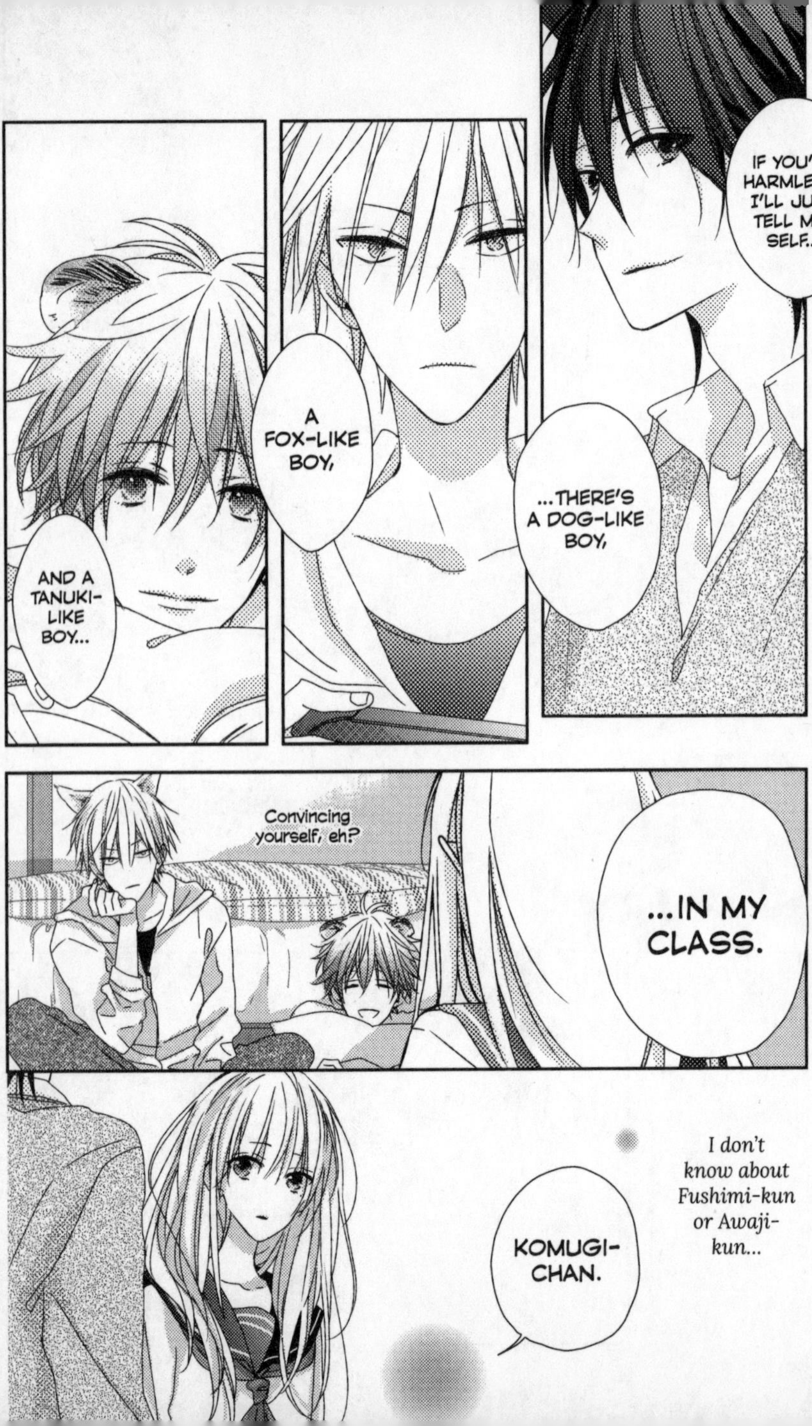
IF YOU'RE HARMLESS, I'LL JUST TELL MY-SELF...
...THERE'S A DOG-LIKE BOY,
A FOX-LIKE BOY,
AND A TANUKI-LIKE BOY...
...IN MY CLASS.
Convincing yourself, eh?
I don't know about Fushimi-kun or Awaji-kun...
KOMUGI-CHAN.

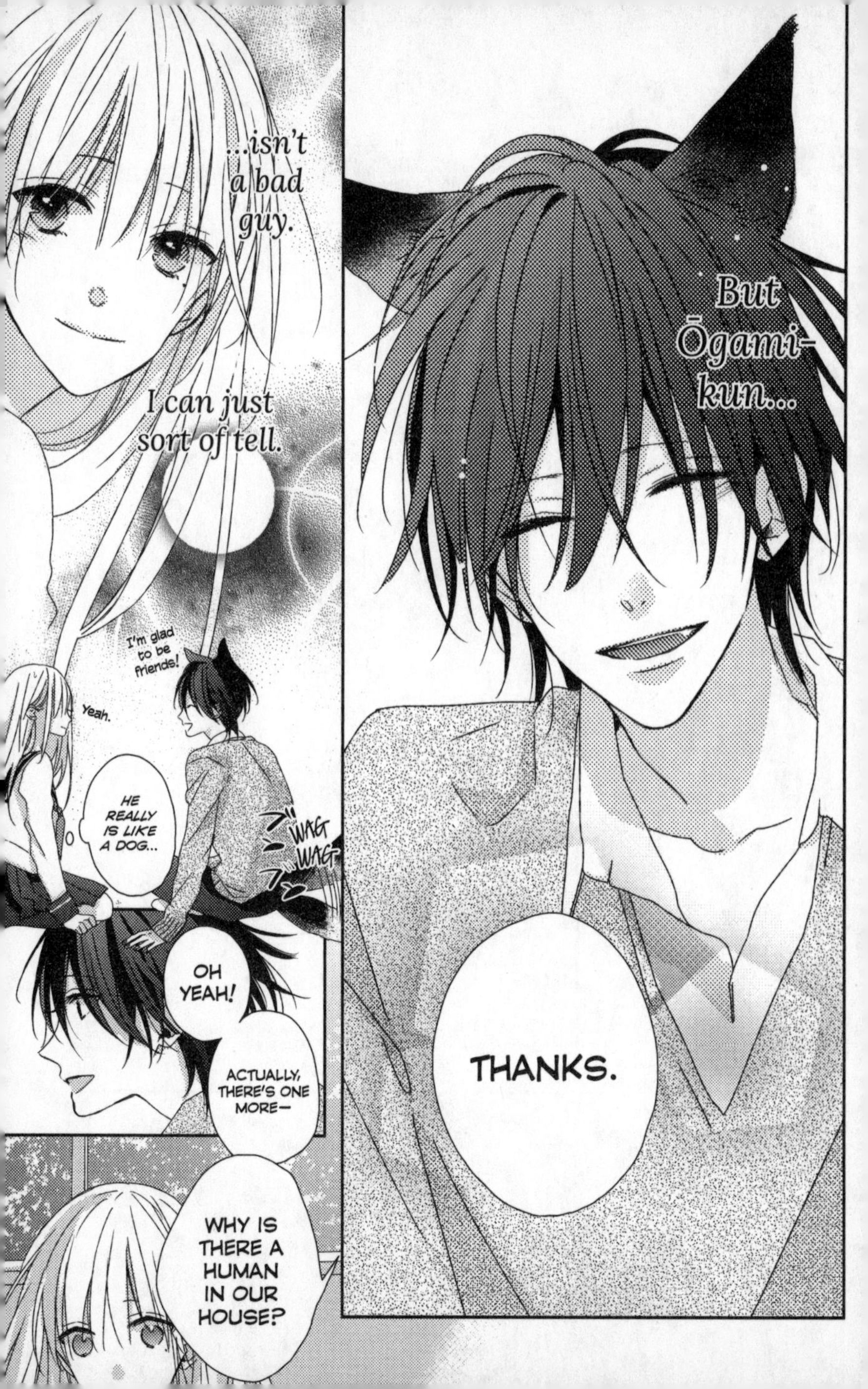
But Ōgami-kun...
THANKS.
...isn't a bad guy.
I can just sort of tell.
I'm glad to be friends!
Yeah.
HE REALLY IS LIKE A DOG...
WAG WAG
OH YEAH!
ACTUALLY, THERE'S ONE MORE—
WHY IS THERE A HUMAN IN OUR HOUSE?

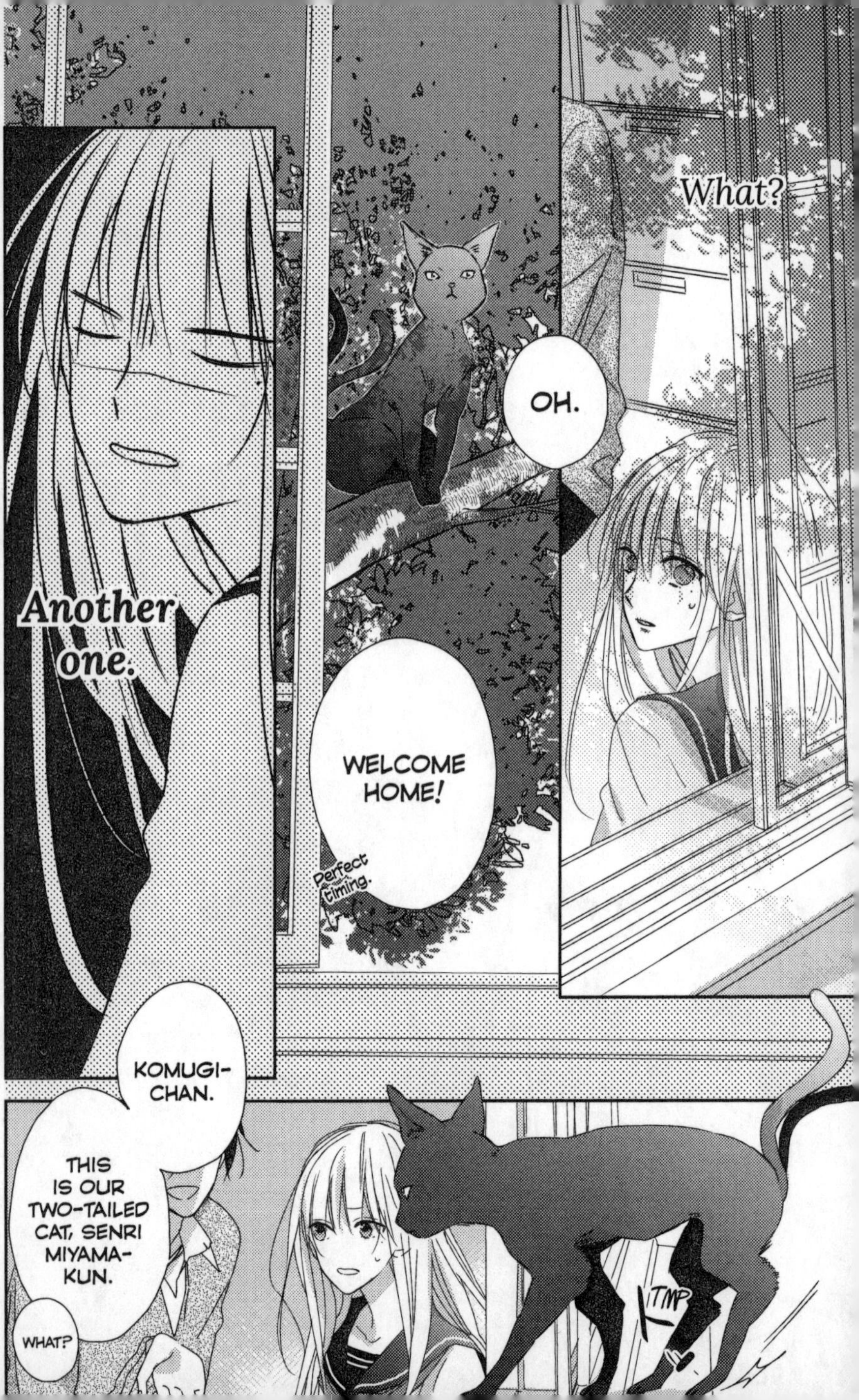
What?
OH.
WELCOME HOME!
Perfect timing.
Another one.
KOMUGI-CHAN.
THIS IS OUR TWO-TAILED CAT, SENRI MIYAMA-KUN.
TMP
WHAT?

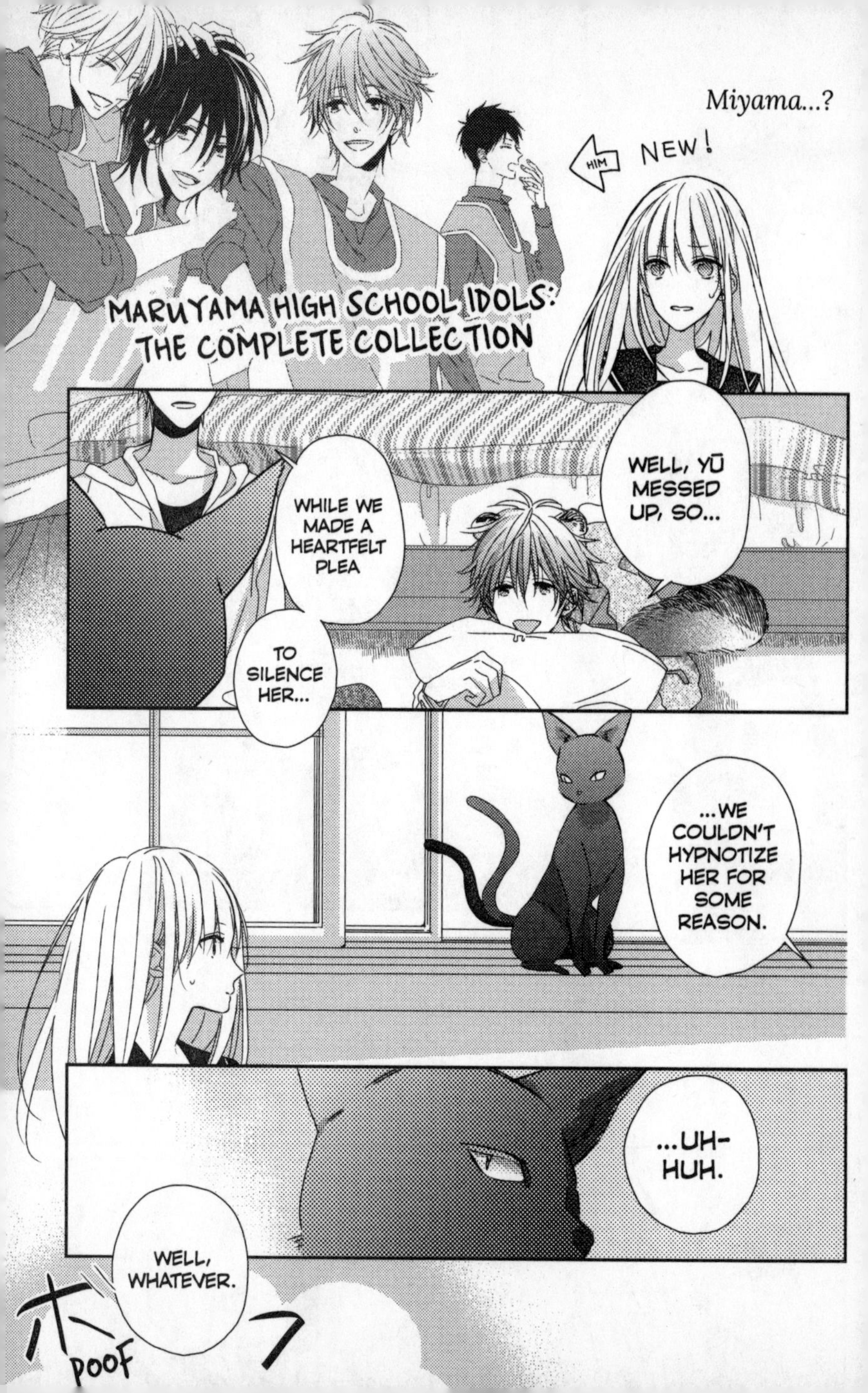
Miyama...?
NEW!
HIM
MARUYAMA HIGH SCHOOL IDOLS: THE COMPLETE COLLECTION
WELL, YŪ MESSED UP, SO...
WHILE WE MADE A HEARTFELT PLEA
TO SILENCE HER...
...WE COULDN'T HYPNOTIZE HER FOR SOME REASON.
...UH-HUH.
WELL, WHATEVER.
POOF

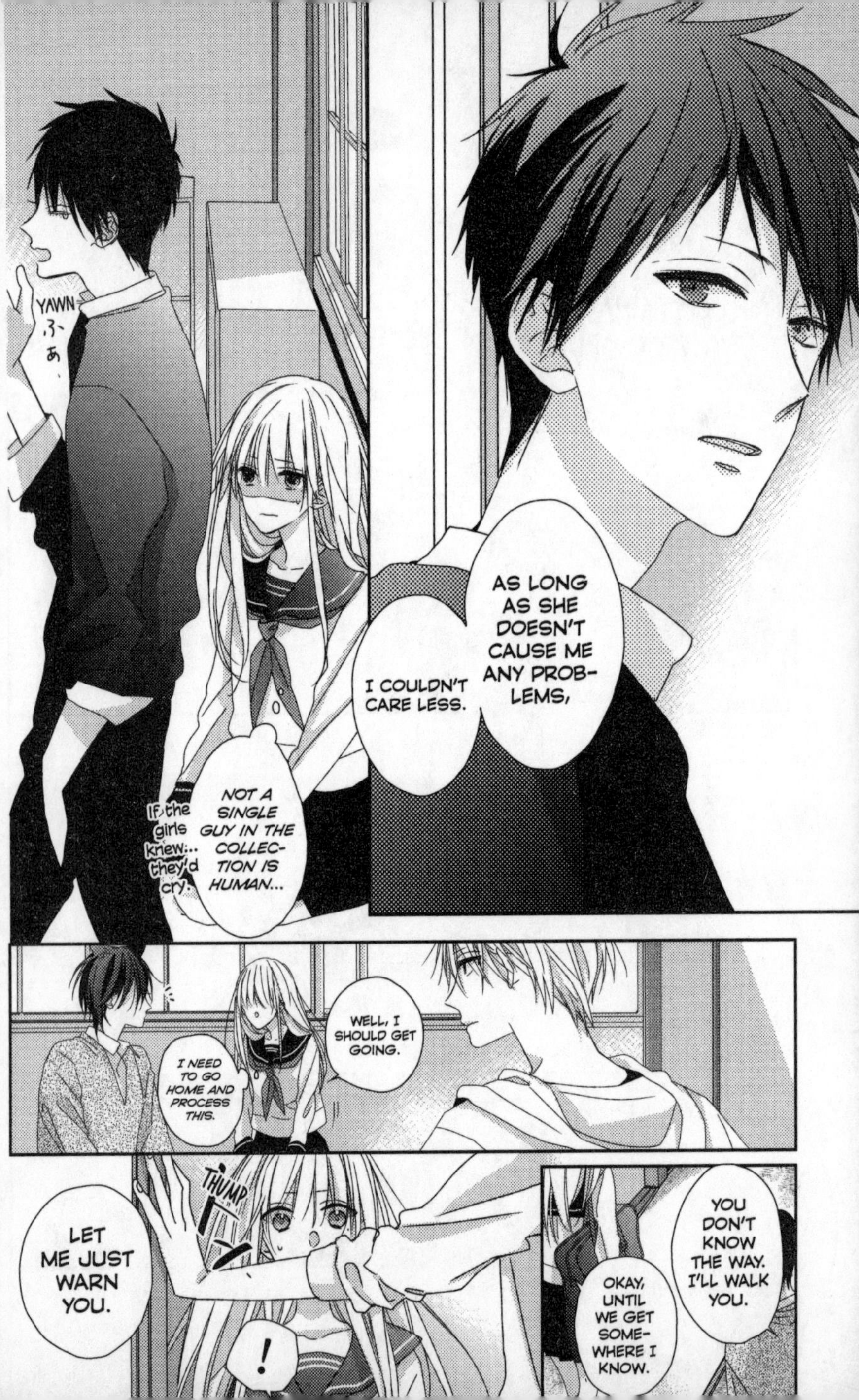
AS LONG AS SHE DOESN'T CAUSE ME ANY PROBLEMS,
I COULDN'T CARE LESS.
YAWN
ふあ、
NOT A SINGLE GUY IN THE COLLECTION IS HUMAN...
If the girls knew... they'd cry.
WELL, I SHOULD GET GOING.
I NEED TO GO HOME AND PROCESS THIS.
YOU DON'T KNOW THE WAY. I'LL WALK YOU.
OKAY, UNTIL WE GET SOMEWHERE I KNOW.
THUMP
LET ME JUST WARN YOU.
!

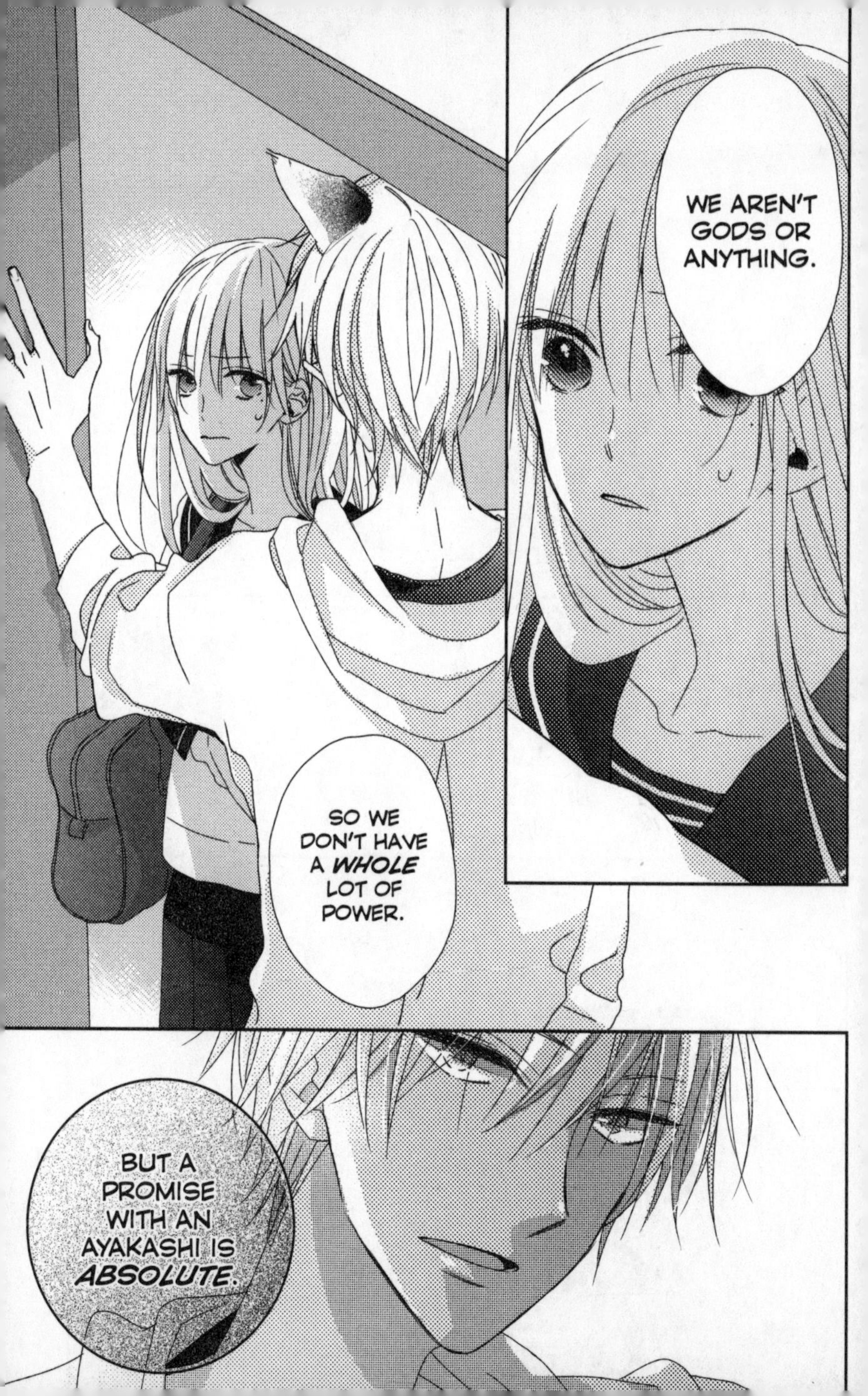
WE AREN'T GODS OR ANYTHING.
SO WE DON'T HAVE A *WHOLE* LOT OF POWER.
BUT A PROMISE WITH AN AYAKASHI IS *ABSOLUTE*.

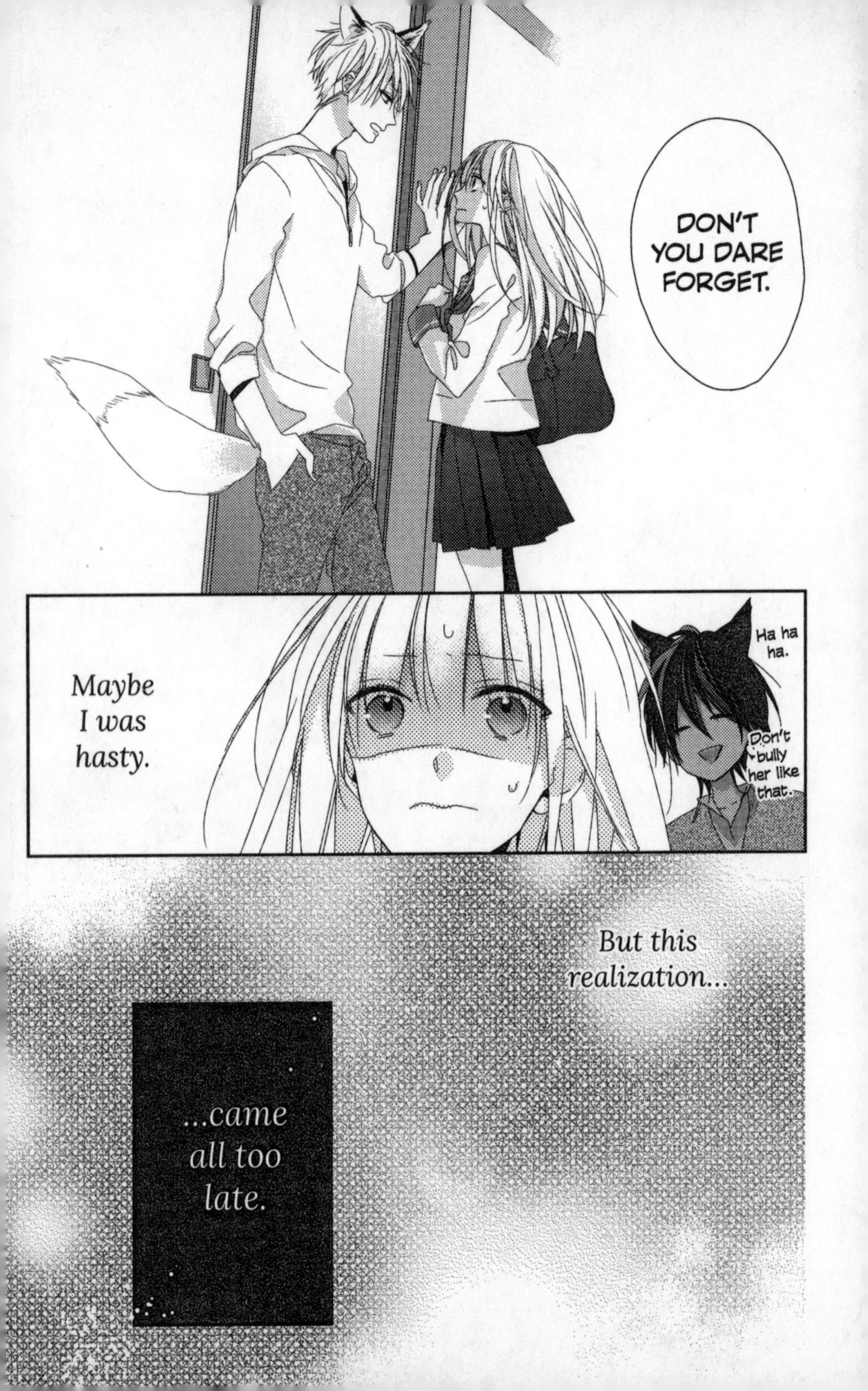
DON'T YOU DARE FORGET.
Ha ha ha.
Don't bully her like that.
Maybe I was hasty.
But this realization...
...came all too late.

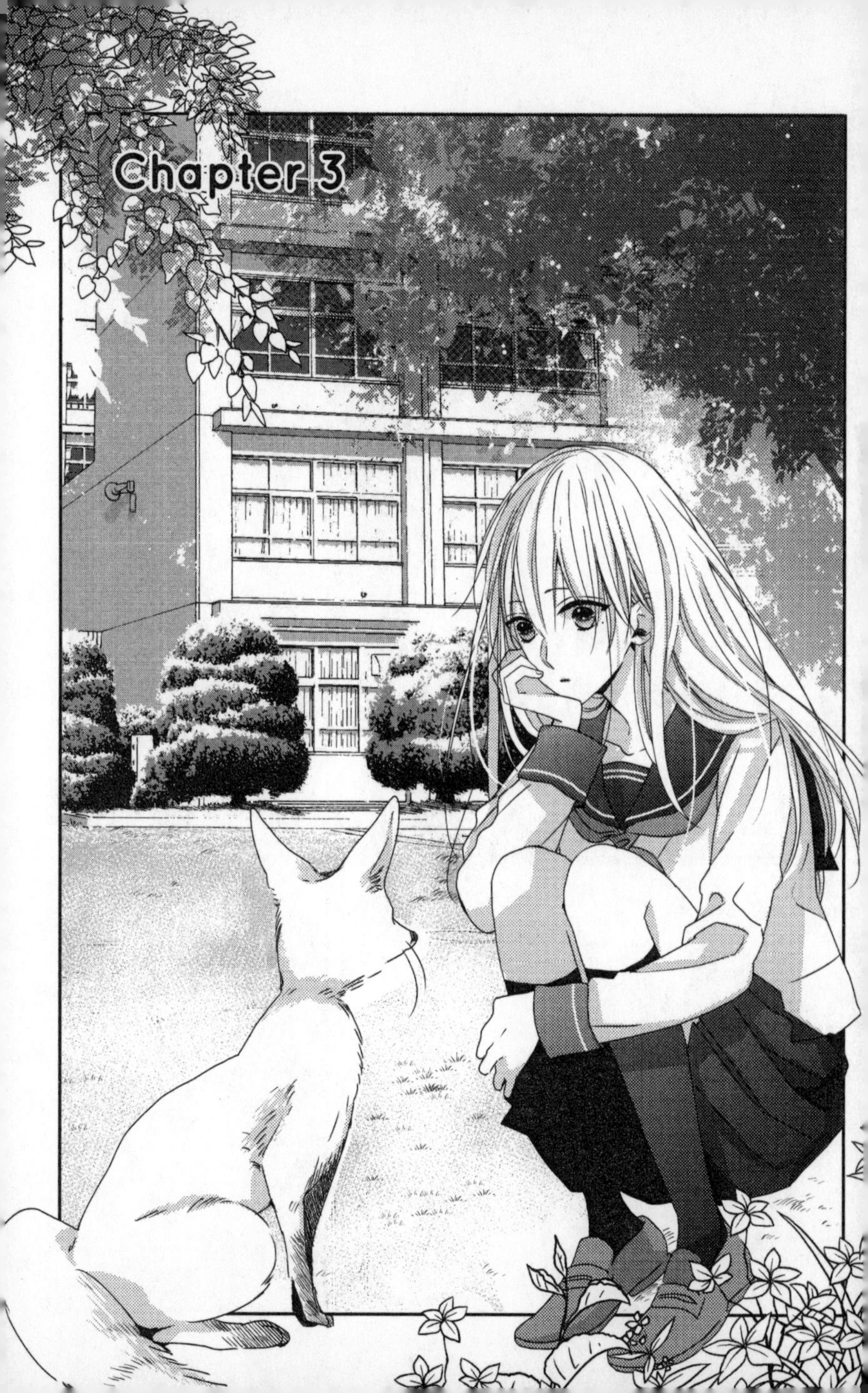
Chapter 3

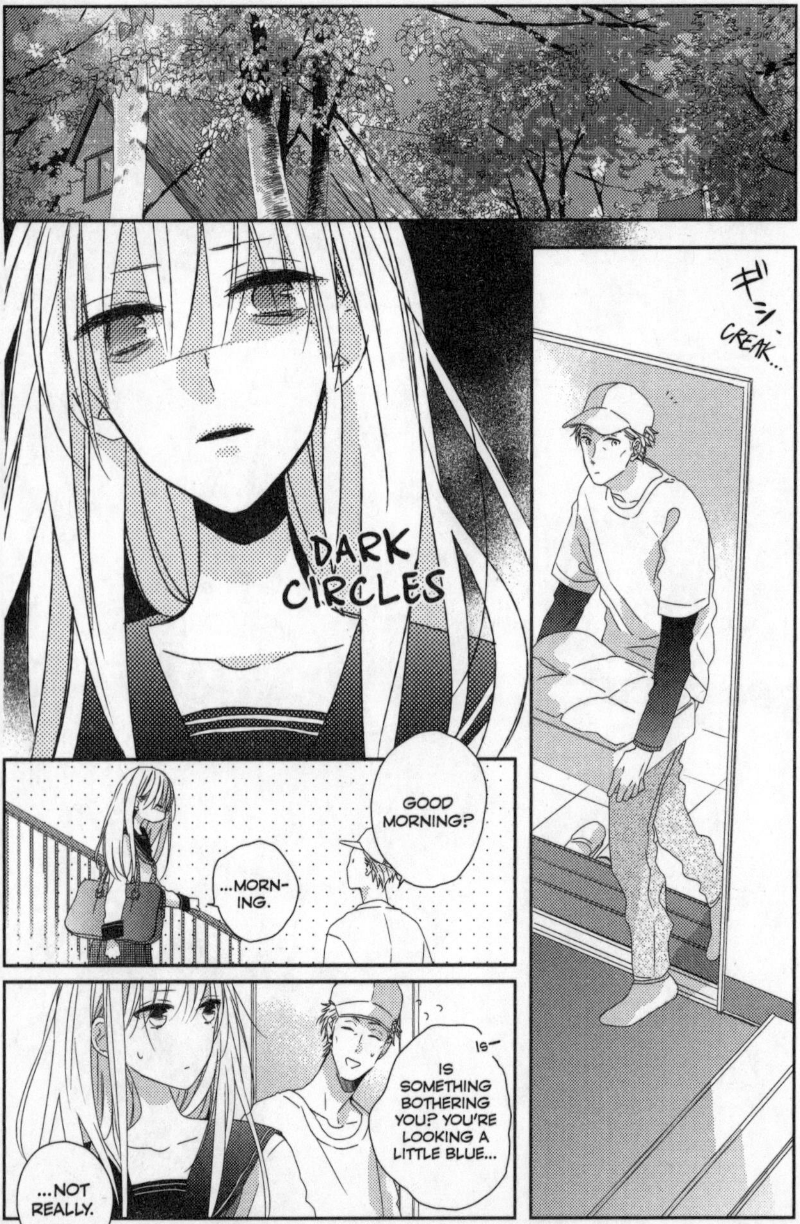
ギシ
CREAK...
DARK CIRCLES
GOOD MORNING?
...MORNING.
IS—
IS SOMETHING BOTHERING YOU? YOU'RE LOOKING A LITTLE BLUE...
...NOT REALLY.

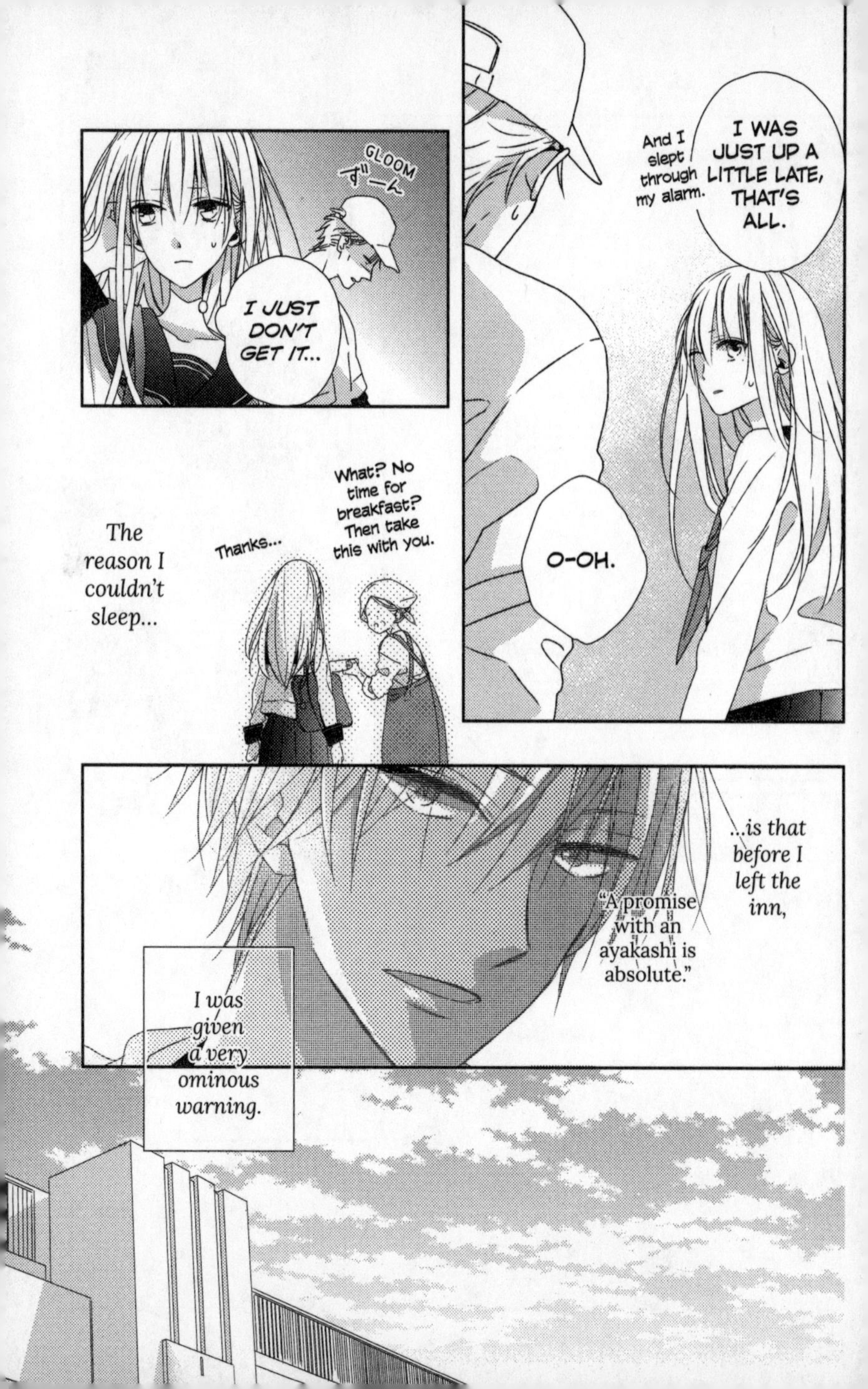

I WAS JUST UP A LITTLE LATE, THAT'S ALL.
And I slept through my alarm.
O-OH.
GLOOM
ずーん
I JUST DON'T GET IT...
What? No time for breakfast? Then take this with you.
Thanks...
The reason I couldn't sleep...
...is that before I left the inn,
"A promise with an ayakashi is absolute."
I was given a very ominous warning.

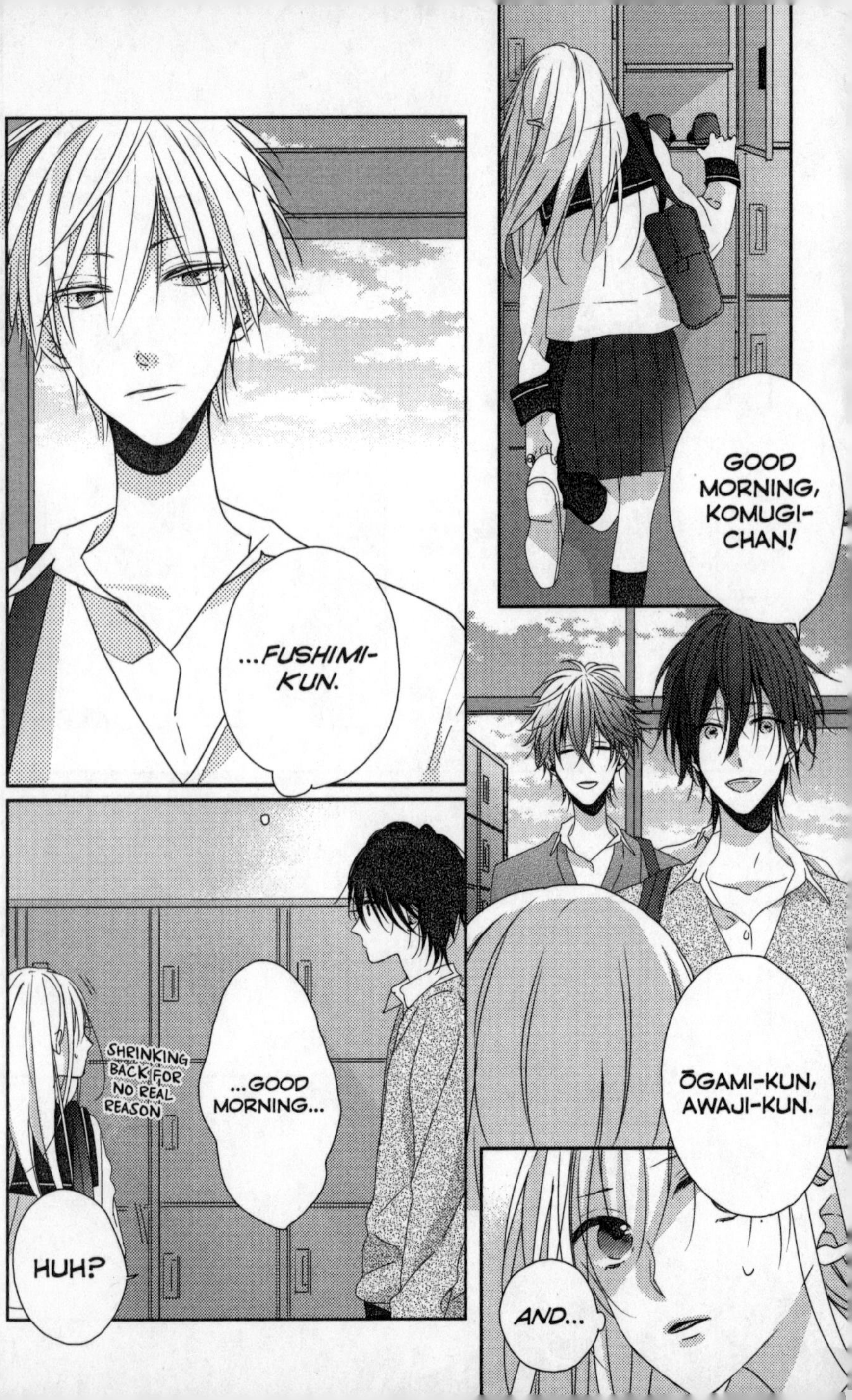
GOOD MORNING, KOMUGI-CHAN!
ŌGAMI-KUN, AWAJI-KUN.
AND...
...FUSHIMI-KUN.
...GOOD MORNING...
SHRINKING BACK FOR NO REAL REASON
HUH?

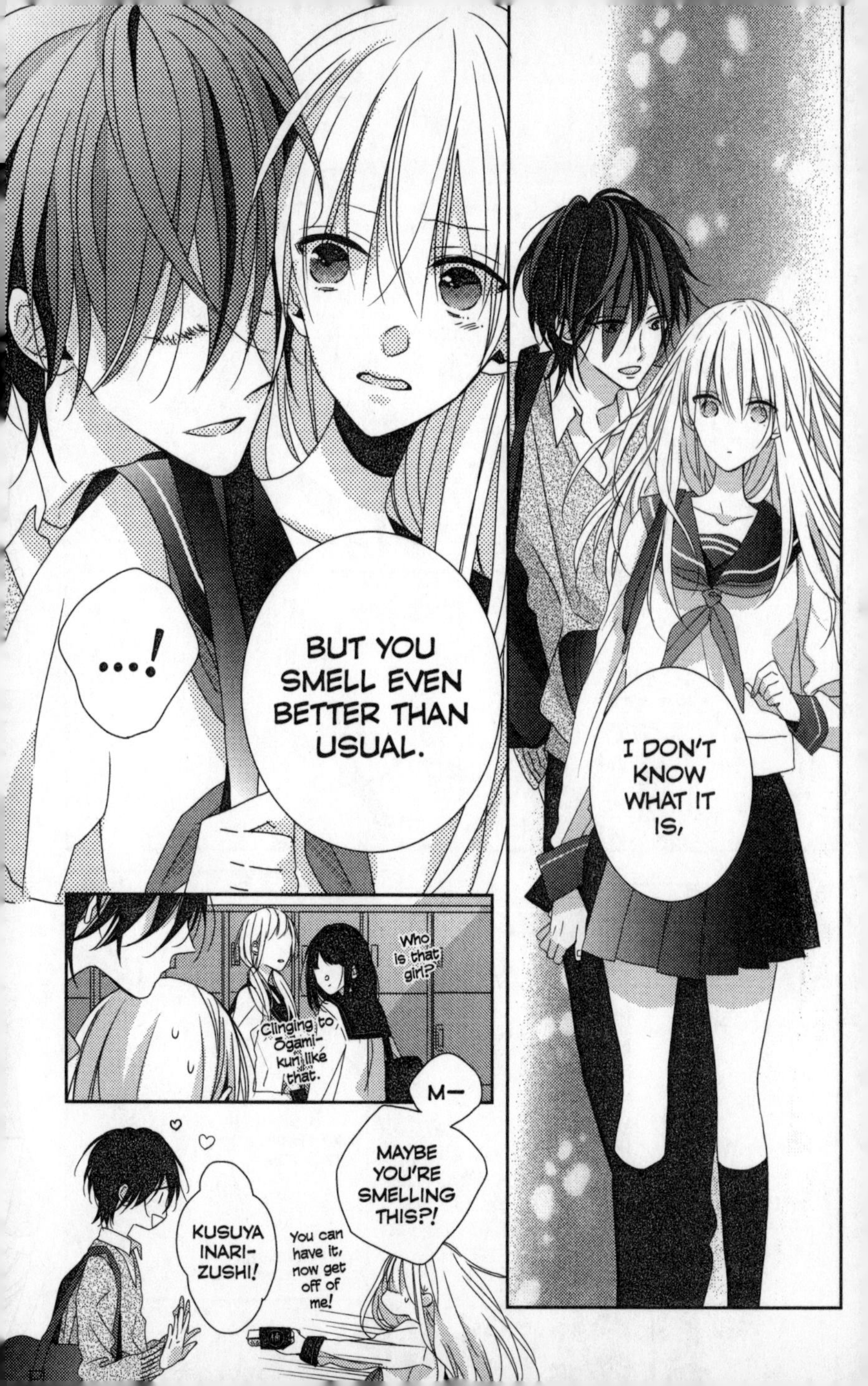
I DON'T KNOW WHAT IT IS,
BUT YOU SMELL EVEN BETTER THAN USUAL.
...!
Who is that girl?
Clinging to Ōgami-kun like that.
M—
MAYBE YOU'RE SMELLING THIS?!
You can have it, now get off of me!
KUSUYA INARI-ZUSHI!

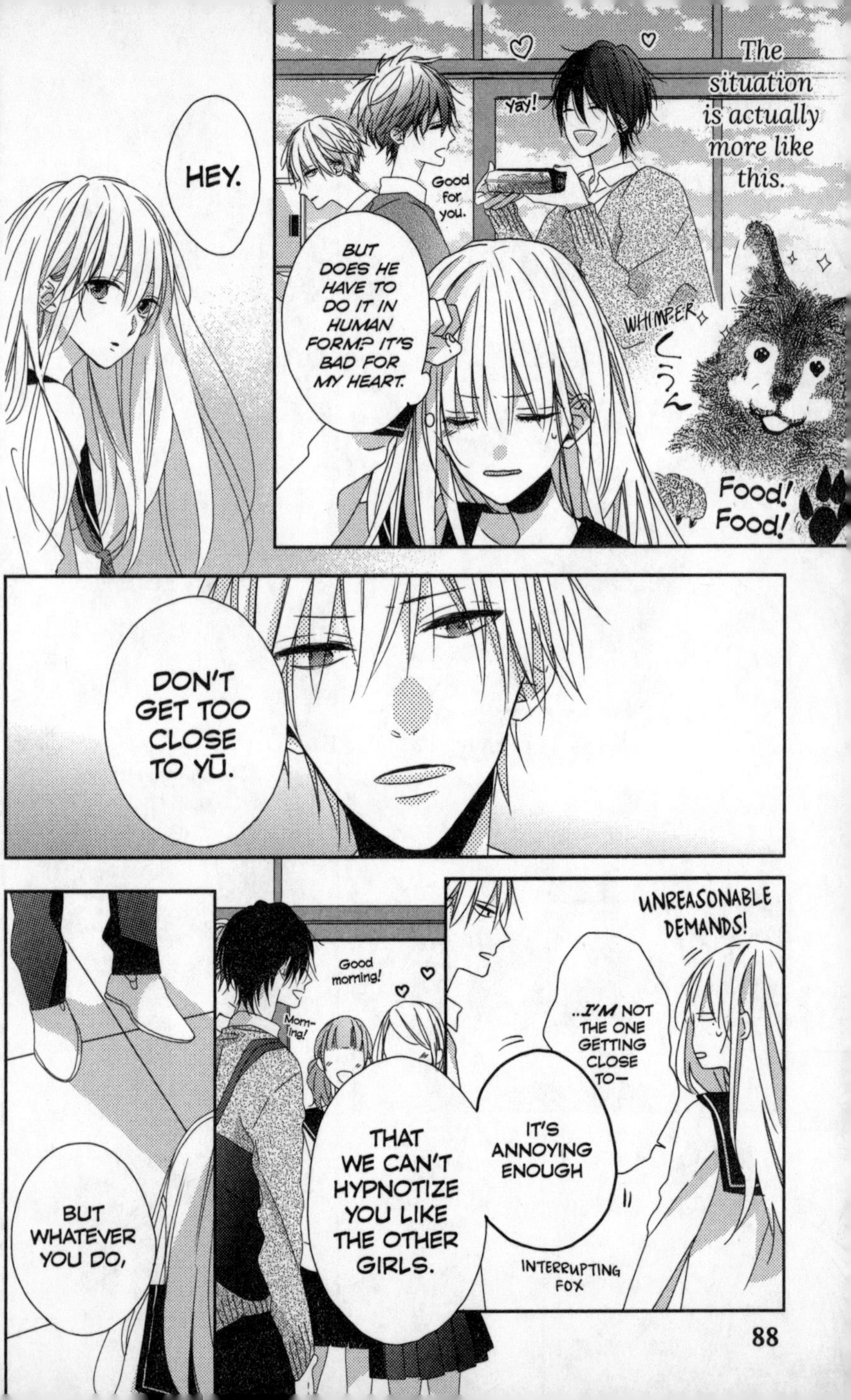
The situation is actually more like this.
Yay!
Good for you.
BUT DOES HE HAVE TO DO IT IN HUMAN FORM? IT'S BAD FOR MY HEART.
WHIMPER
Food! Food!
HEY.
DON'T GET TOO CLOSE TO YŪ.
UNREASONABLE DEMANDS!
...I'M NOT THE ONE GETTING CLOSE TO—
IT'S ANNOYING ENOUGH
INTERRUPTING FOX
THAT WE CAN'T HYPNOTIZE YOU LIKE THE OTHER GIRLS.
Good morning!
Morn-ing!
BUT WHATEVER YOU DO,

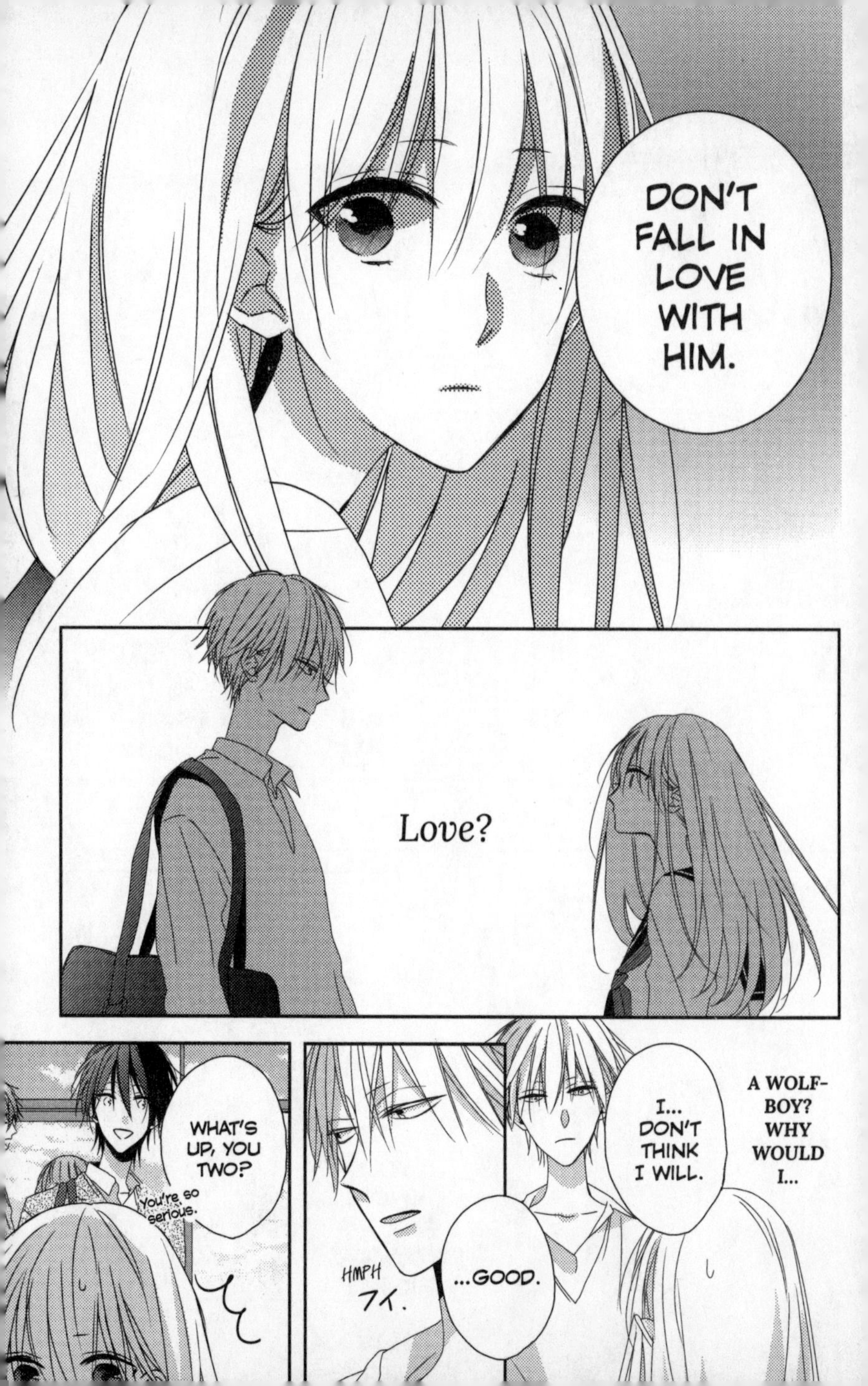
DON'T FALL IN LOVE WITH HIM.
Love?
A WOLF-BOY? WHY WOULD I...
I... DON'T THINK I WILL.
HMPH
フイ.
...GOOD.
WHAT'S UP, YOU TWO?
You're so serious.

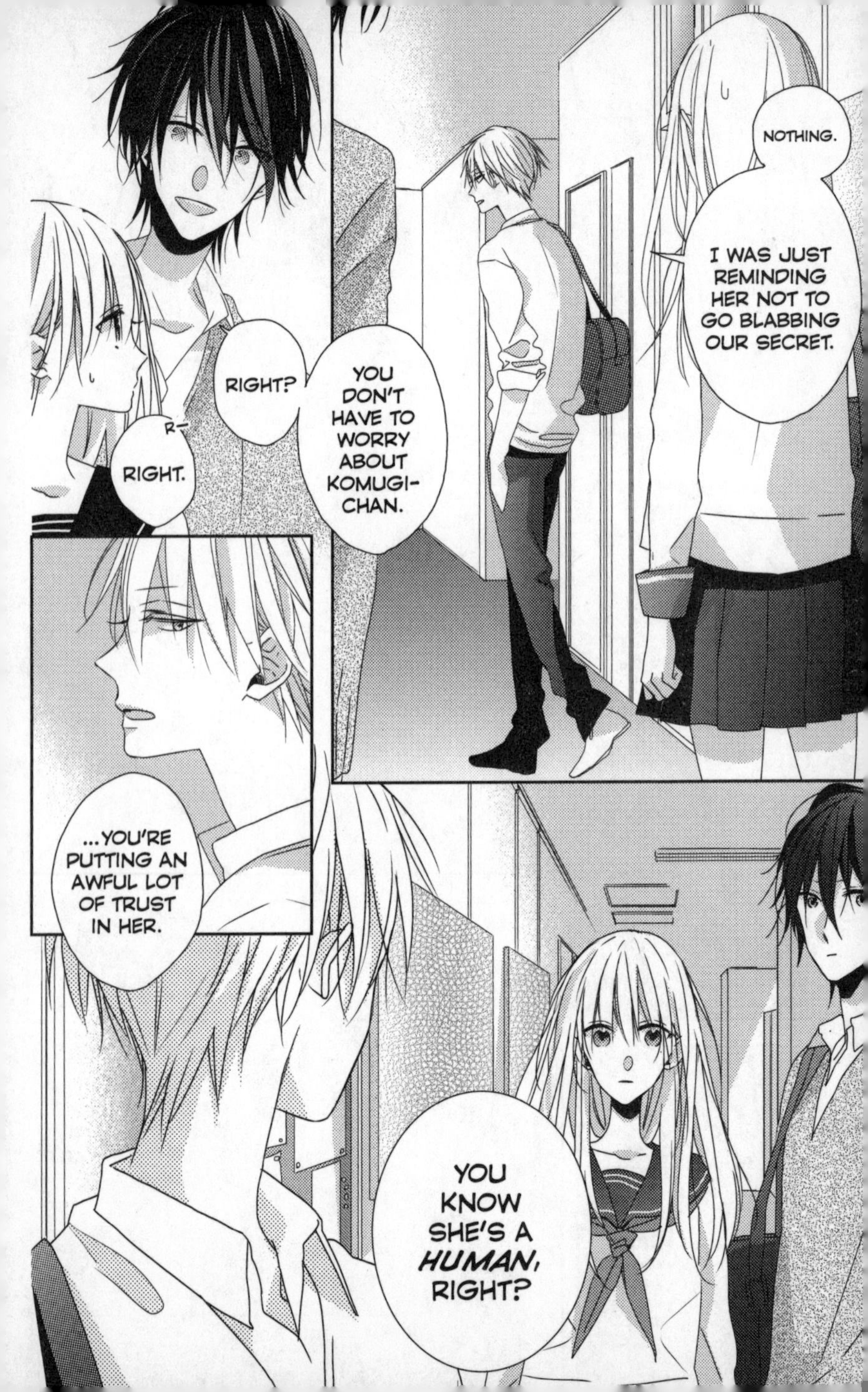
NOTHING.
I WAS JUST REMINDING HER NOT TO GO BLABBING OUR SECRET.
YOU DON'T HAVE TO WORRY ABOUT KOMUGI-CHAN.
RIGHT?
R— RIGHT.
...YOU'RE PUTTING AN AWFUL LOT OF TRUST IN HER.
YOU KNOW SHE'S A *HUMAN*, RIGHT?

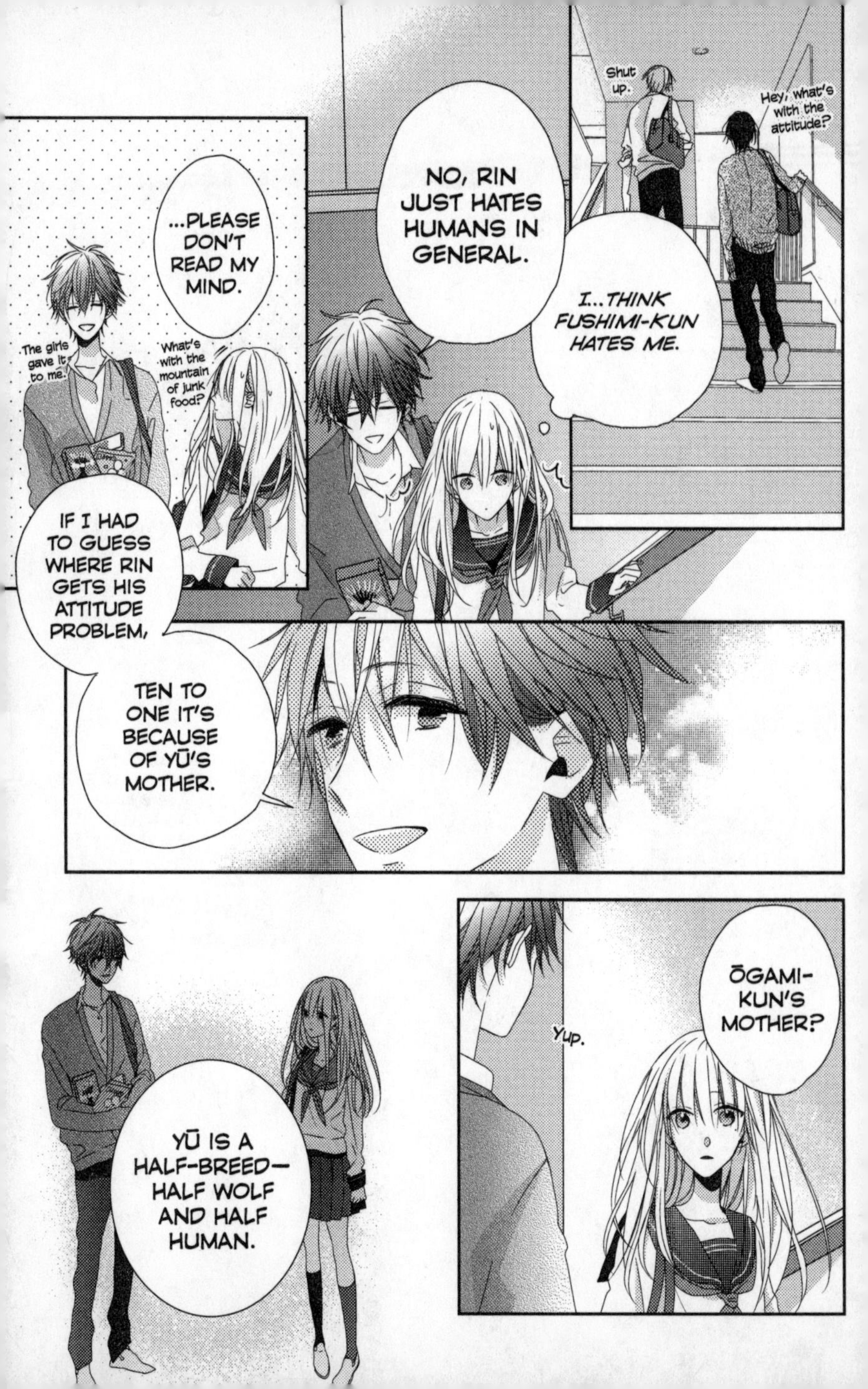
Hey, what's with the attitude?
Shut up.
I...THINK FUSHIMI-KUN HATES ME.
NO, RIN JUST HATES HUMANS IN GENERAL.
...PLEASE DON'T READ MY MIND.
What's with the mountain of junk food?
The girls gave it to me.
IF I HAD TO GUESS WHERE RIN GETS HIS ATTITUDE PROBLEM,
TEN TO ONE IT'S BECAUSE OF YŪ'S MOTHER.
ŌGAMI-KUN'S MOTHER?
Yup.
YŪ IS A HALF-BREED—HALF WOLF AND HALF HUMAN.

APPARENTLY YŪ'S FATHER DIED BEFORE HE WAS BORN.

BUT MIXED BREEDS ARE UNSTABLE

UNTIL THEY LEARN HOW TO CONTROL THEIR FORM.

THEY KEEP SWITCHING BACK AND FORTH.

AND HIS MOTHER WAS HUMAN,

SO A LITTLE SHAPESHIFTER LIKE YŪ WOULD HAVE BEEN TOO MUCH FOR HER.

...I'm sorry.

I'm sorry.

IF RIN HADN'T FOUND HIM,

YŪ COULD HAVE DIED.

"We're not out to hurt anybody."

...YEAH, RIGHT.

If you're harmless.

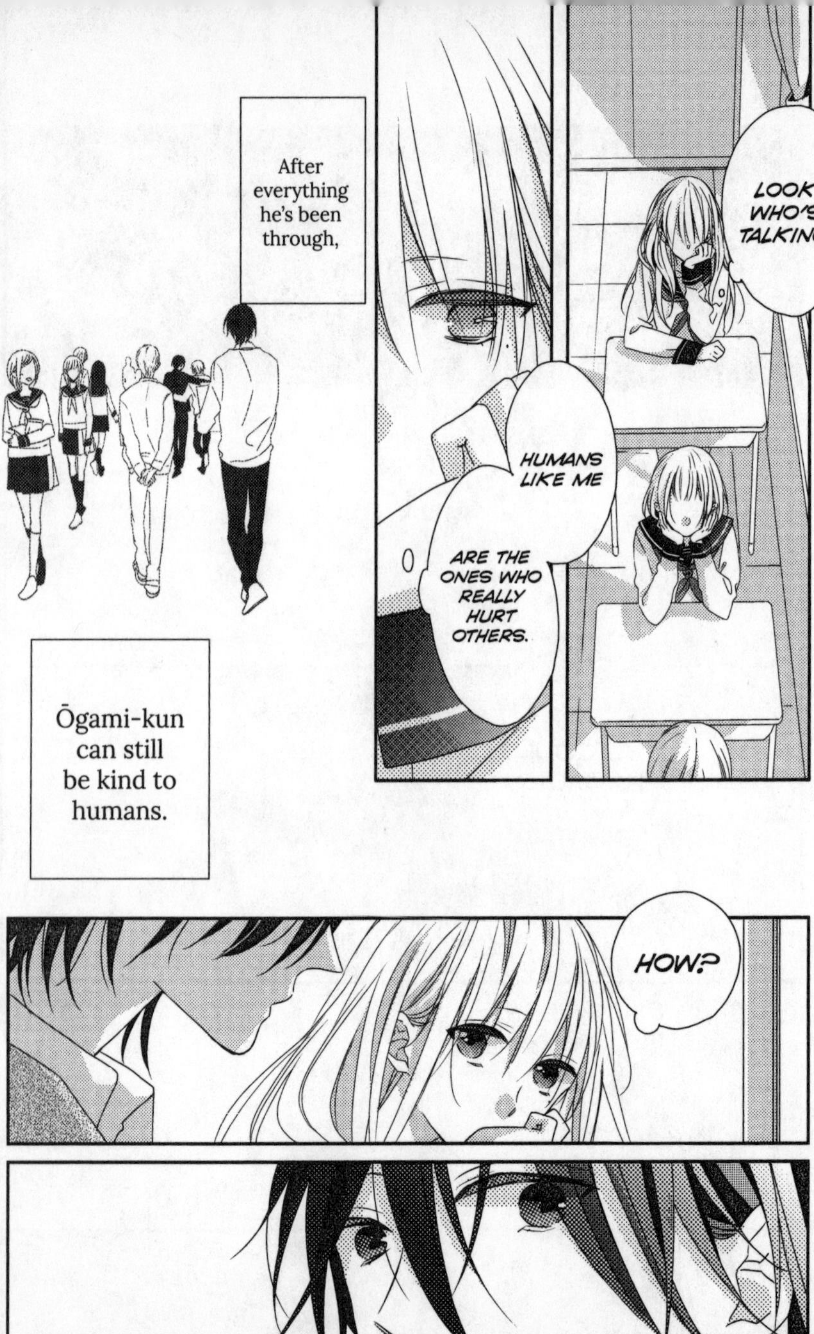
LOOK WHO'S TALKING.
HUMANS LIKE ME
ARE THE ONES WHO REALLY HURT OTHERS.
After everything he's been through,
Ōgami-kun can still be kind to humans.
HOW?

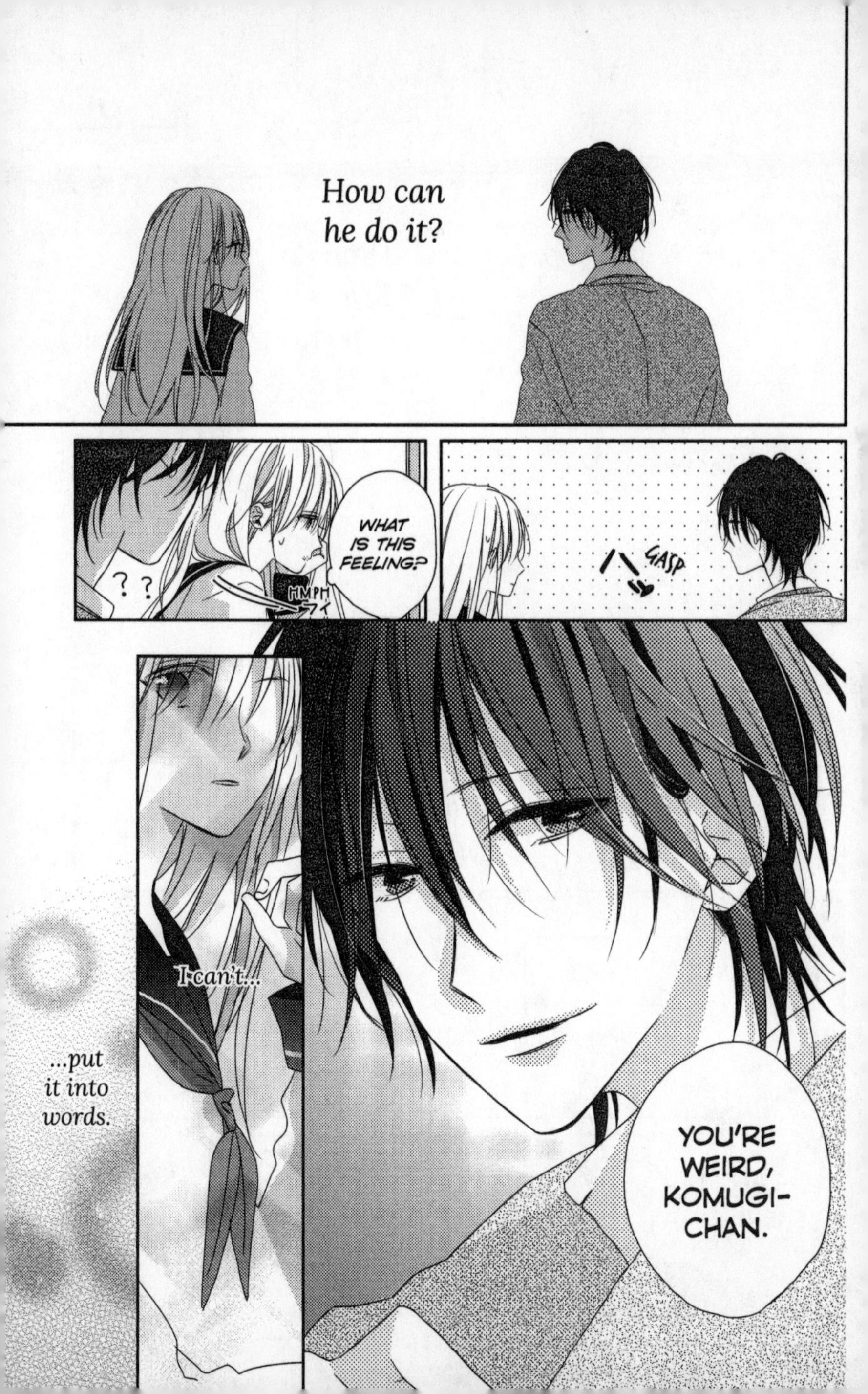
How can he do it?
GASP
WHAT IS THIS FEELING?
HMPH
? ?
YOU'RE WEIRD, KOMUGI-CHAN.
I can't...
...put it into words.

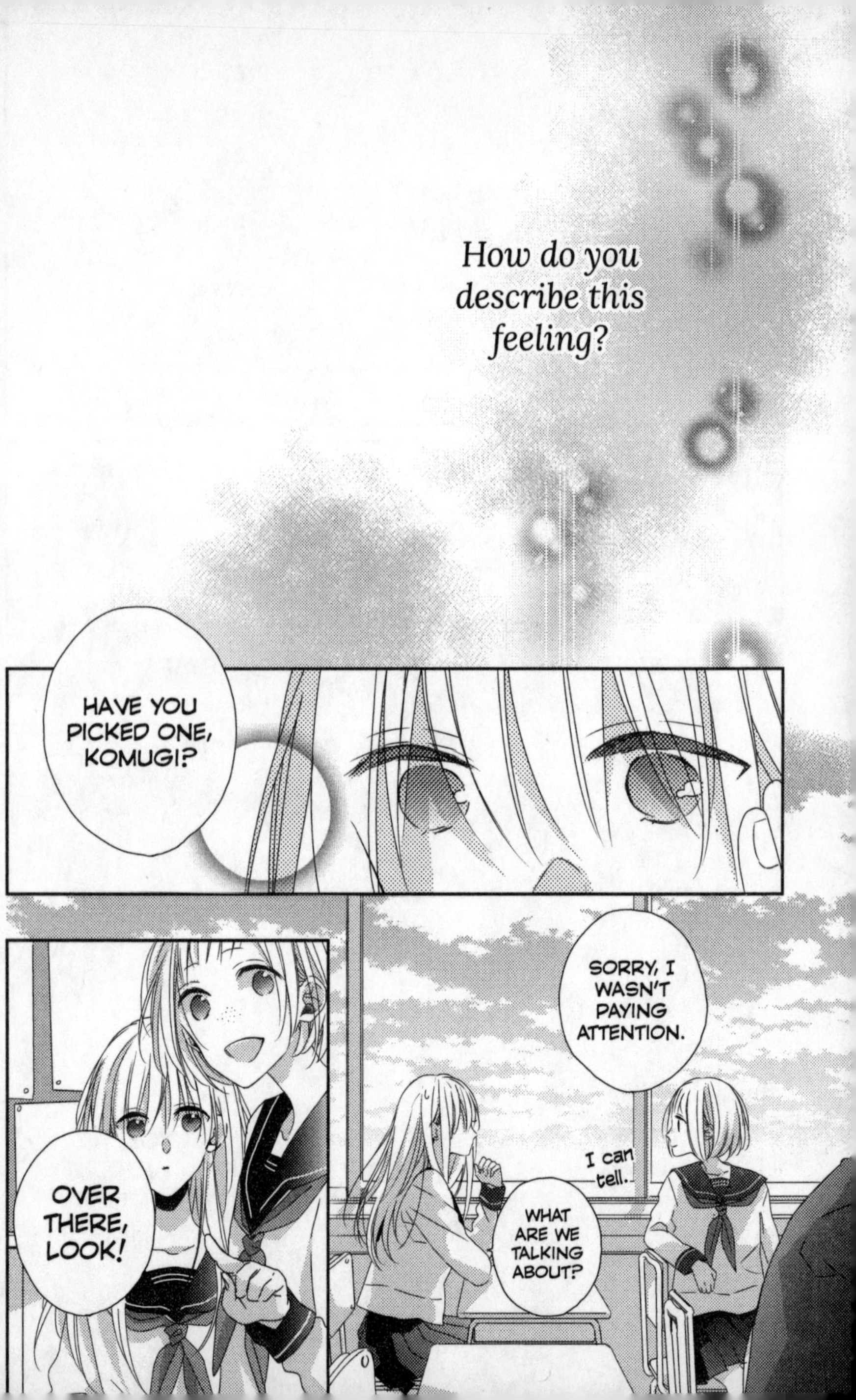
How do you describe this feeling?
HAVE YOU PICKED ONE, KOMUGI?
SORRY, I WASN'T PAYING ATTENTION.
I can tell.
WHAT ARE WE TALKING ABOUT?
OVER THERE, LOOK!

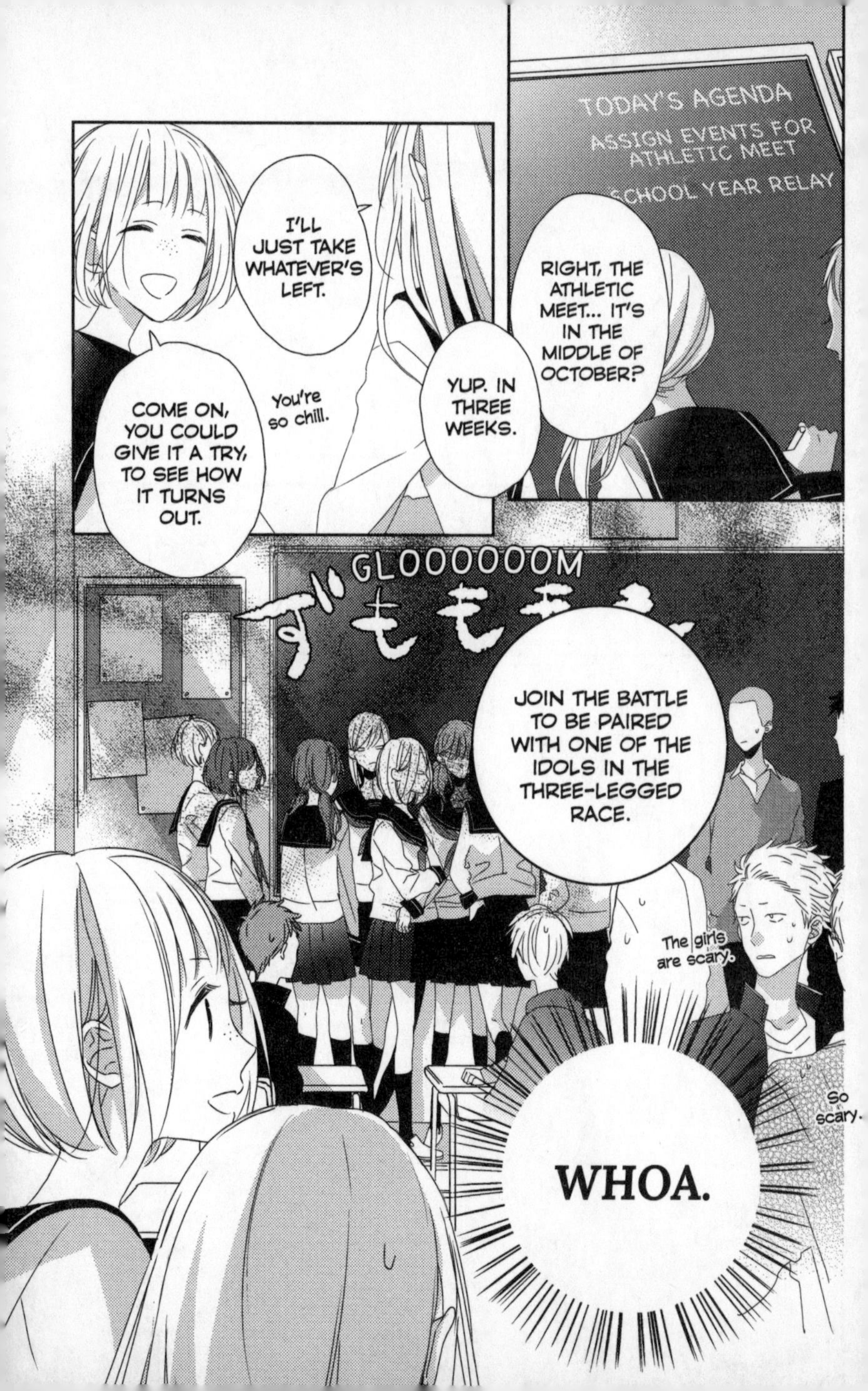
TODAY'S AGENDA
ASSIGN EVENTS FOR ATHLETIC MEET
SCHOOL YEAR RELAY
RIGHT, THE ATHLETIC MEET... IT'S IN THE MIDDLE OF OCTOBER?
YUP. IN THREE WEEKS.
I'LL JUST TAKE WHATEVER'S LEFT.
You're so chill.
COME ON, YOU COULD GIVE IT A TRY, TO SEE HOW IT TURNS OUT.
GLOOOOOOM
JOIN THE BATTLE TO BE PAIRED WITH ONE OF THE IDOLS IN THE THREE-LEGGED RACE.
The girls are scary.
So scary.
WHOA.

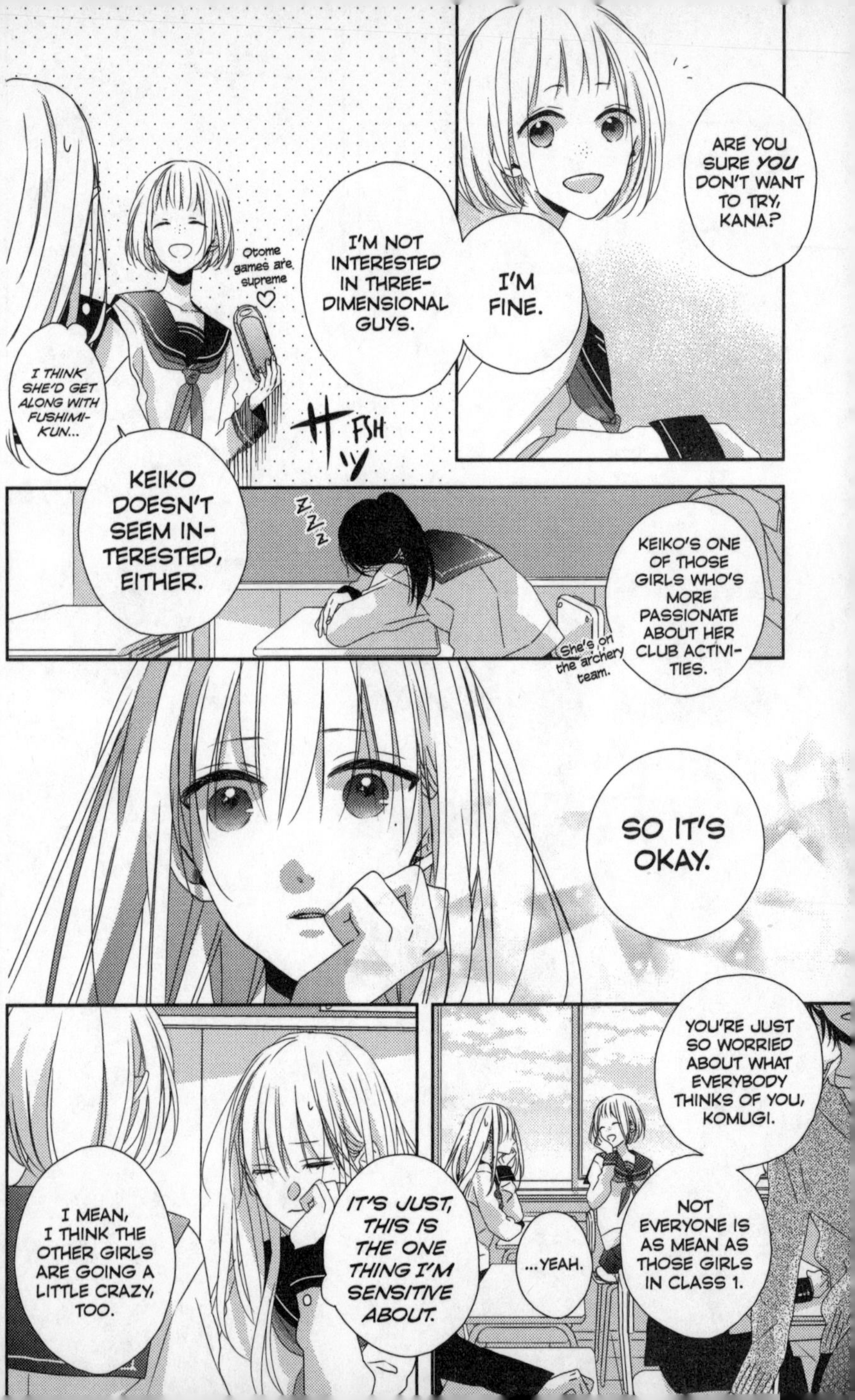
ARE YOU SURE *YOU* DON'T WANT TO TRY, KANA?
I'M FINE.
I'M NOT INTERESTED IN THREE-DIMENSIONAL GUYS.
Otome games are supreme ♡
FSH
I THINK SHE'D GET ALONG WITH FUSHIMI-KUN...
KEIKO DOESN'T SEEM INTERESTED, EITHER.
KEIKO'S ONE OF THOSE GIRLS WHO'S MORE PASSIONATE ABOUT HER CLUB ACTIVITIES.
She's on the archery team.
SO IT'S OKAY.
YOU'RE JUST SO WORRIED ABOUT WHAT EVERYBODY THINKS OF YOU, KOMUGI.
NOT EVERYONE IS AS MEAN AS THOSE GIRLS IN CLASS 1.
...YEAH.
IT'S JUST, THIS IS THE ONE THING I'M SENSITIVE ABOUT.
I MEAN, I THINK THE OTHER GIRLS ARE GOING A LITTLE CRAZY, TOO.

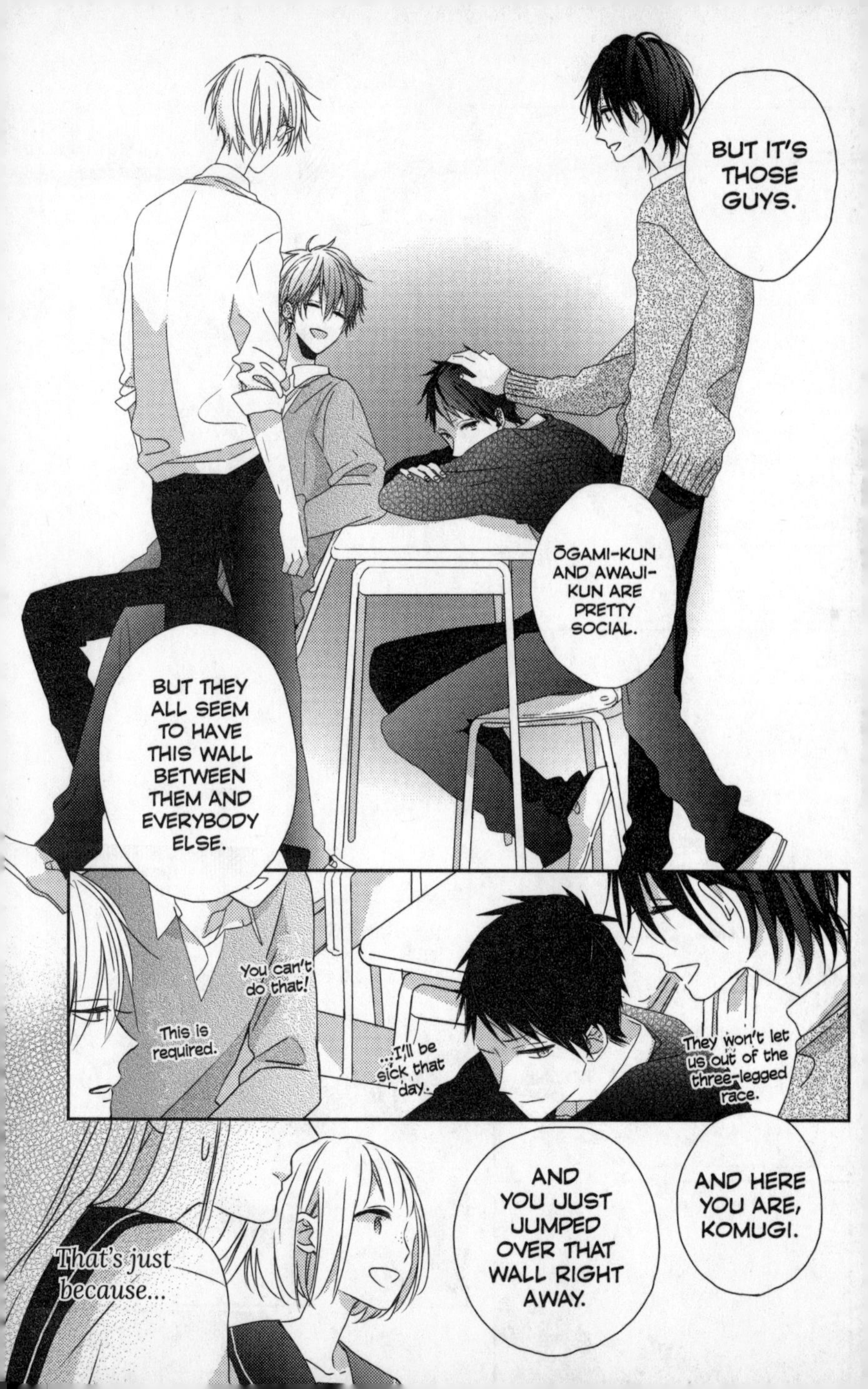
BUT IT'S THOSE GUYS.
ŌGAMI-KUN AND AWAJI-KUN ARE PRETTY SOCIAL.
BUT THEY ALL SEEM TO HAVE THIS WALL BETWEEN THEM AND EVERYBODY ELSE.
They won't let us out of the three-legged race.
...I'll be sick that day.
You can't do that!
This is required.
AND HERE YOU ARE, KOMUGI.
AND YOU JUST JUMPED OVER THAT WALL RIGHT AWAY.
That's just because...

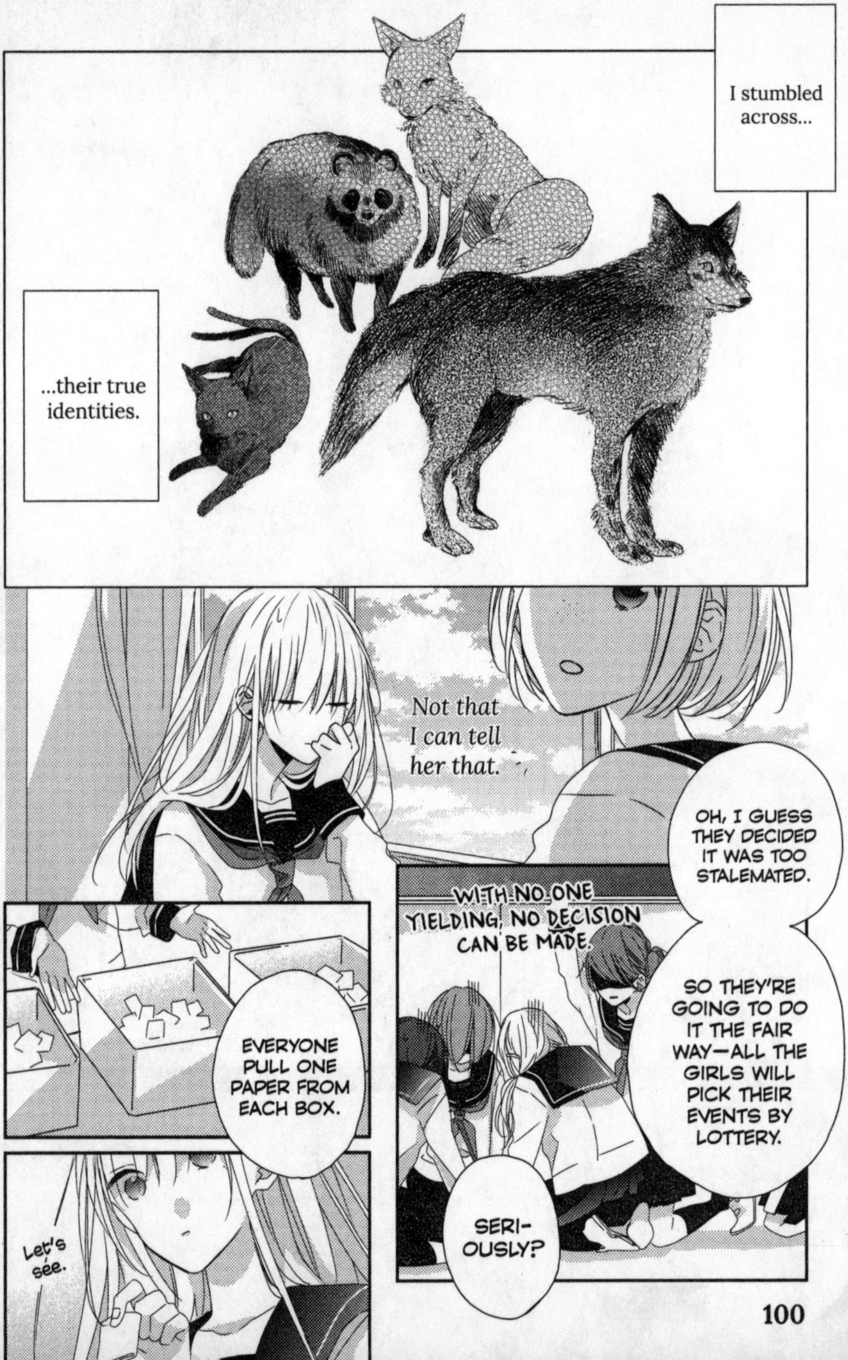
I stumbled across...
...their true identities.
Not that I can tell her that.
OH, I GUESS THEY DECIDED IT WAS TOO STALEMATED.
WITH NO ONE YIELDING, NO DECISION CAN BE MADE.
SO THEY'RE GOING TO DO IT THE FAIR WAY—ALL THE GIRLS WILL PICK THEIR EVENTS BY LOTTERY.
SERI-OUSLY?
EVERYONE PULL ONE PAPER FROM EACH BOX.
Let's see.

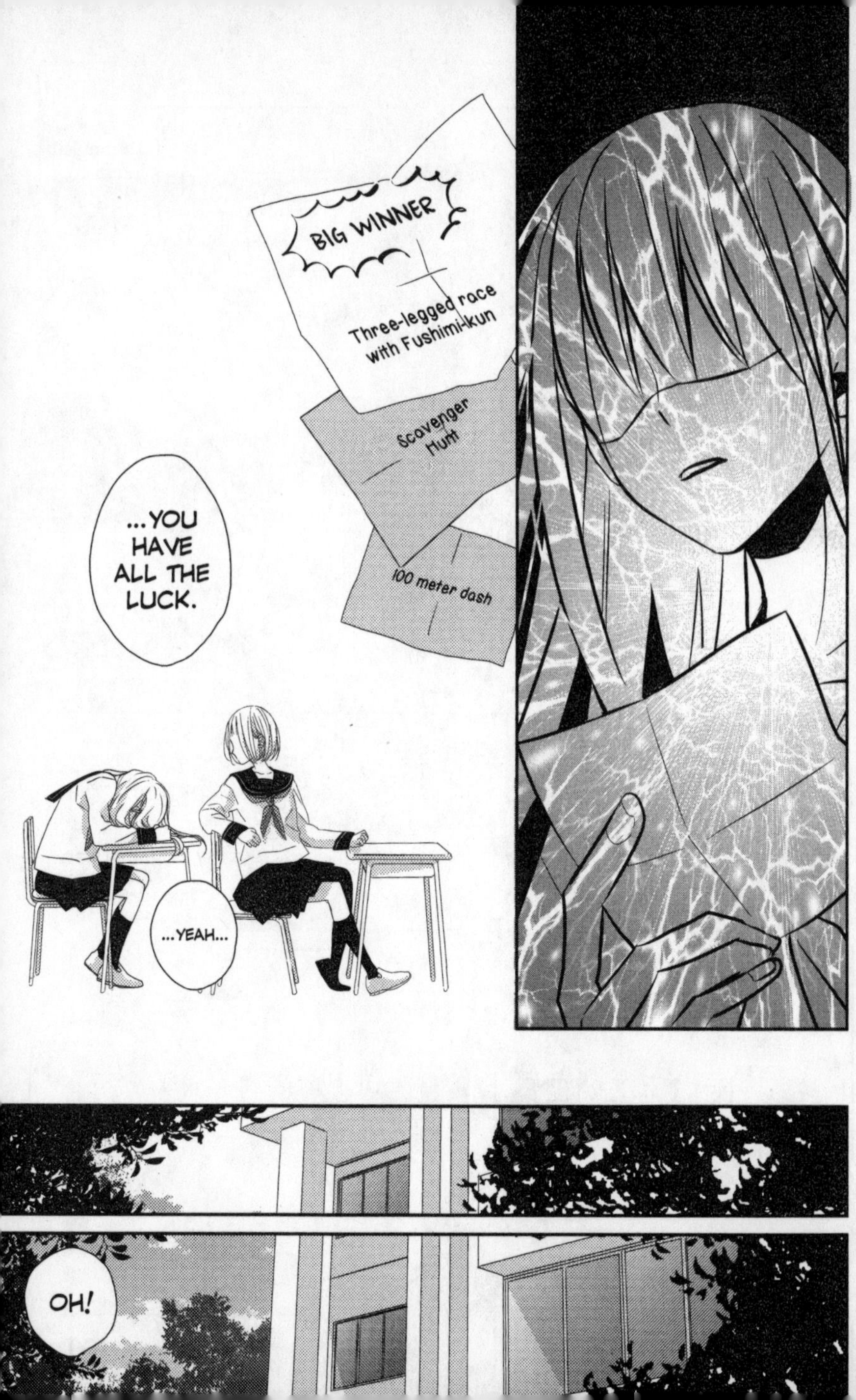
BIG WINNER
Three-legged race with Fushimi-kun
Scavenger Hunt
100 meter dash
...YOU HAVE ALL THE LUCK.
...YEAH...
OH!

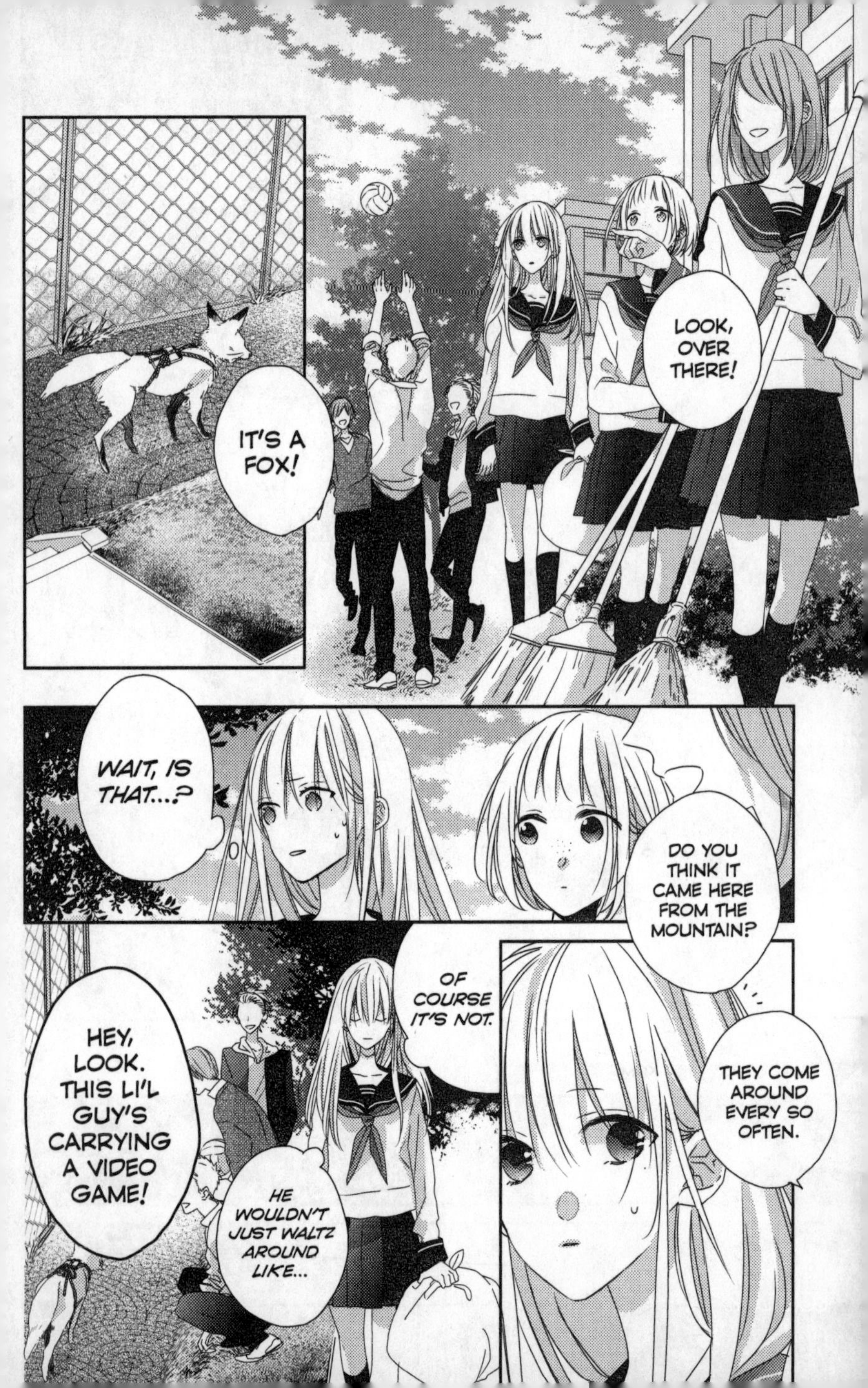
LOOK, OVER THERE!
IT'S A FOX!
WAIT, IS THAT...?
DO YOU THINK IT CAME HERE FROM THE MOUNTAIN?
...
THEY COME AROUND EVERY SO OFTEN.
OF COURSE IT'S NOT.
HEY, LOOK. THIS LI'L GUY'S CARRYING A VIDEO GAME!
HE WOULDN'T JUST WALTZ AROUND LIKE...

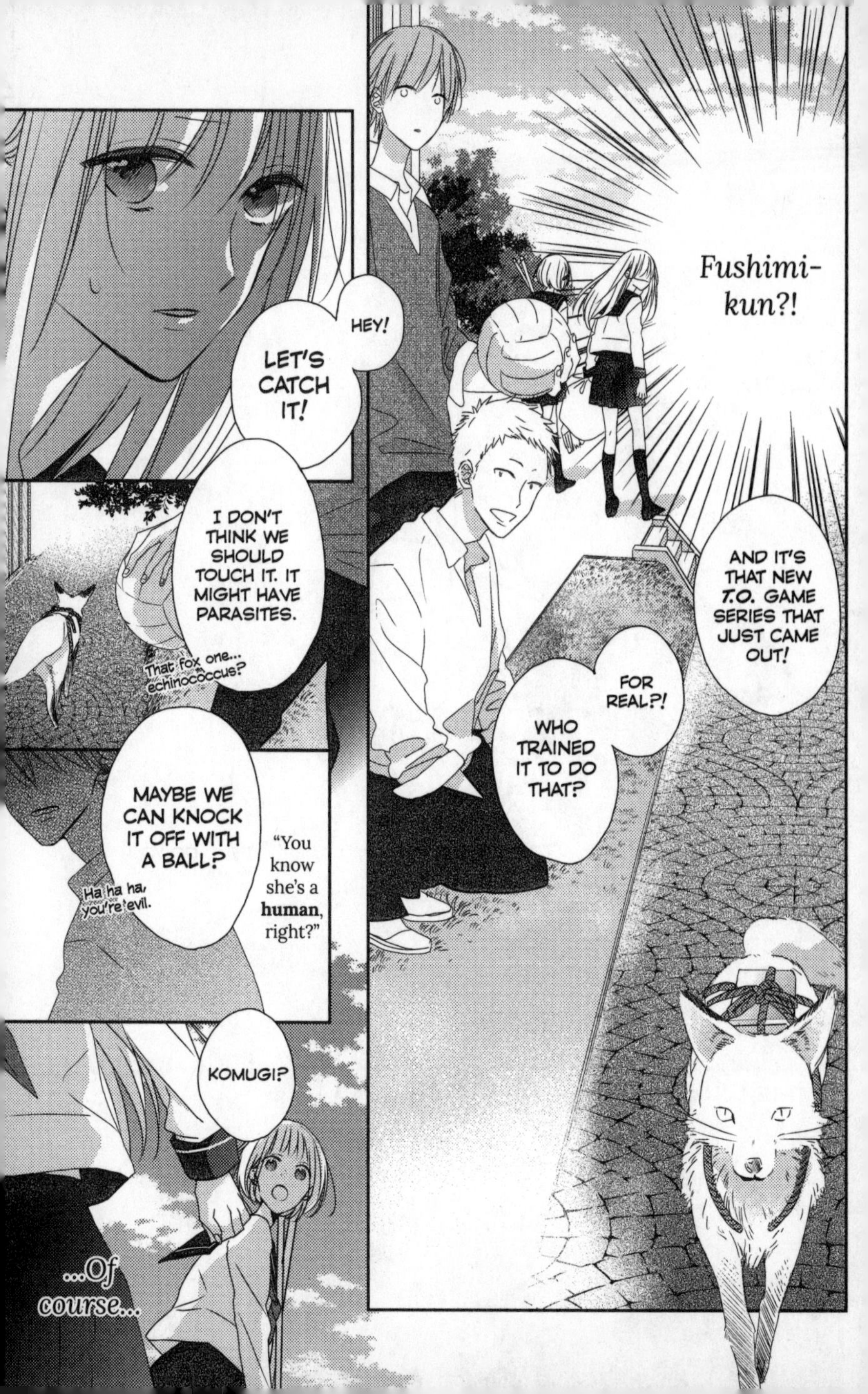
Fushimi-kun?!
AND IT'S THAT NEW T.O. GAME SERIES THAT JUST CAME OUT!
FOR REAL?!
WHO TRAINED IT TO DO THAT?
HEY!
LET'S CATCH IT!
I DON'T THINK WE SHOULD TOUCH IT. IT MIGHT HAVE PARASITES.
That fox one... echinococcus?
"You know she's a human, right?"
MAYBE WE CAN KNOCK IT OFF WITH A BALL?
Ha ha ha, you're evil.
KOMUGI?
...Of course...

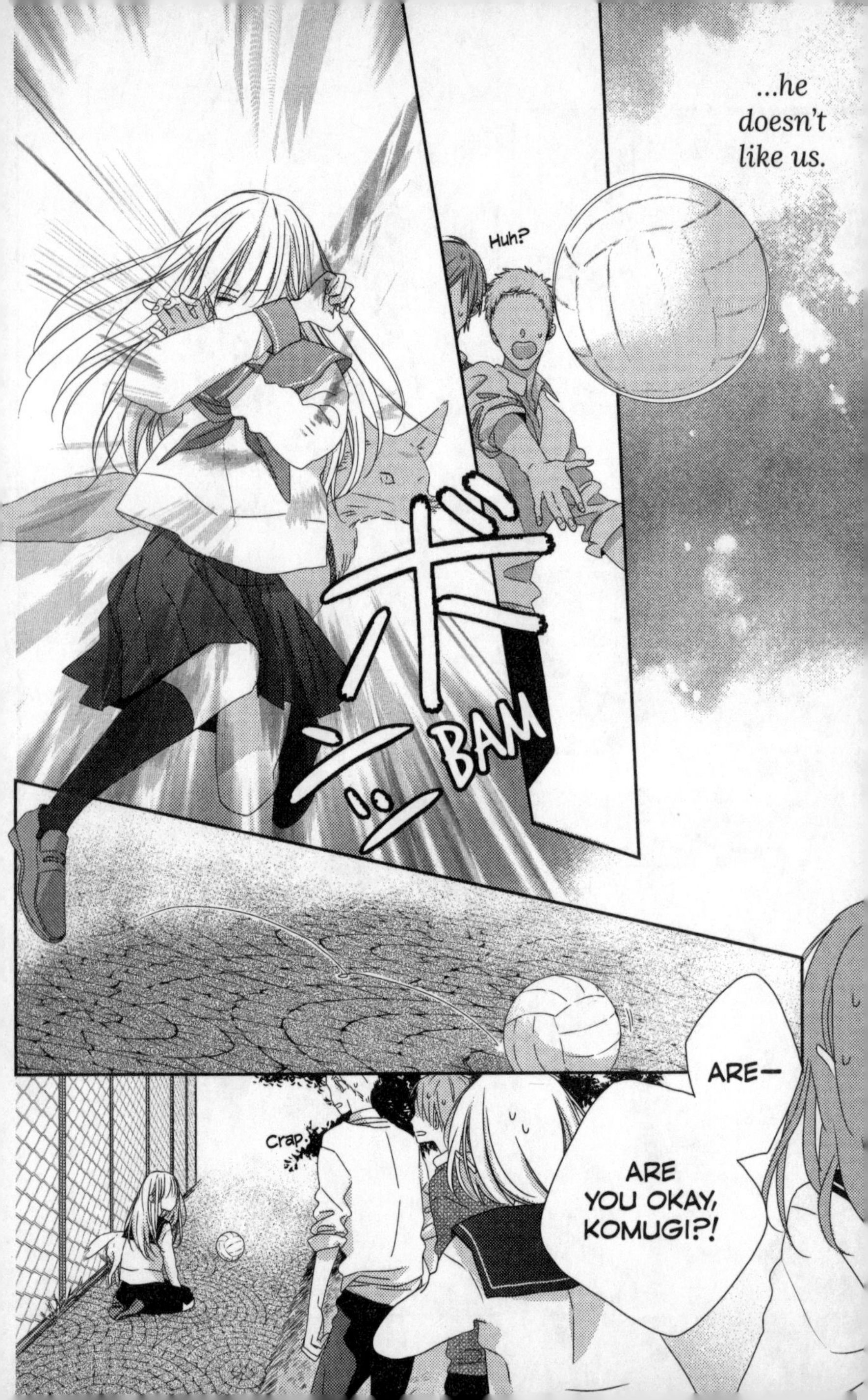
...he doesn't like us.
Huh?
BAM
ARE—
ARE YOU OKAY, KOMUGI?!
Crap.

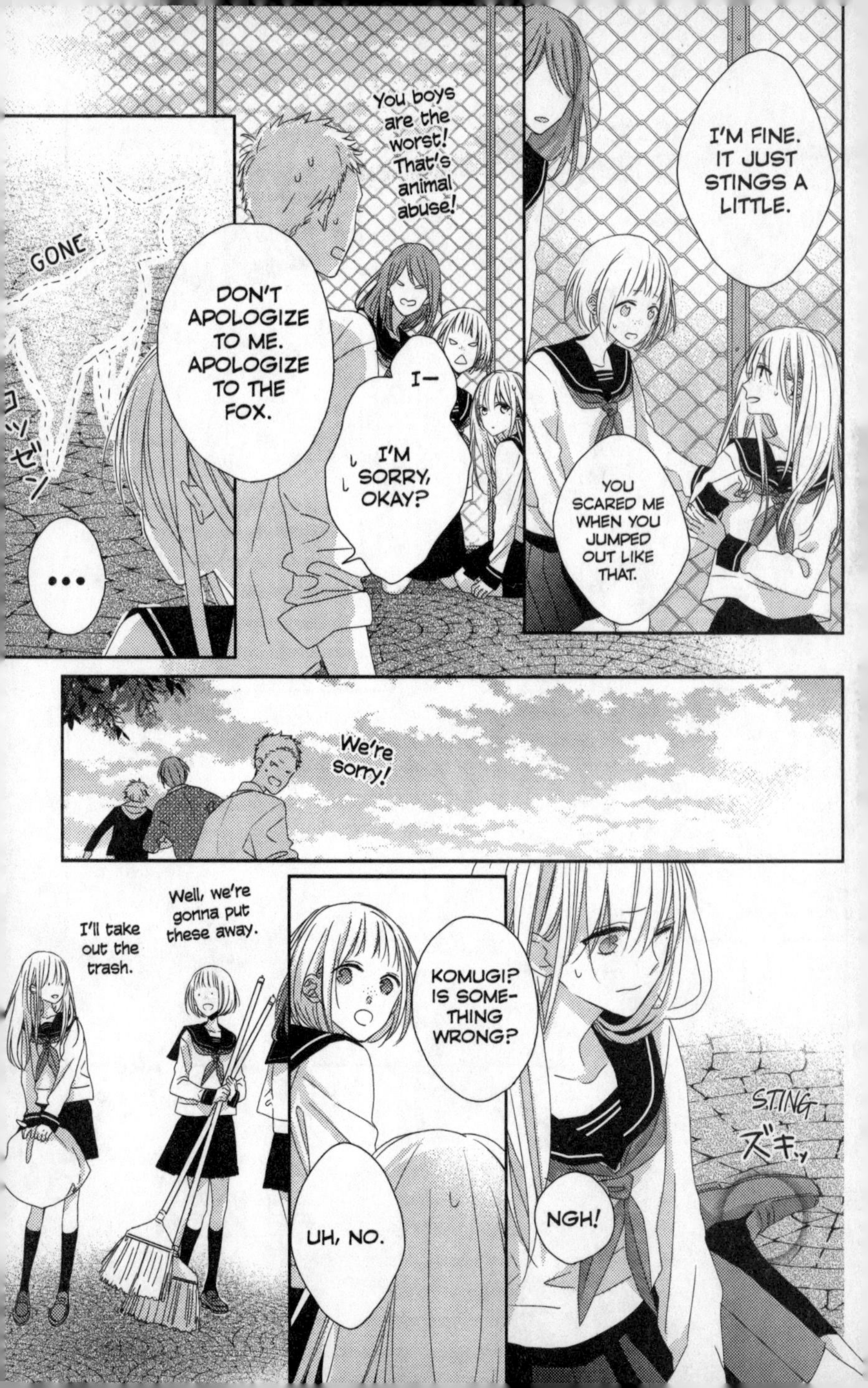
I'M FINE. IT JUST STINGS A LITTLE.
YOU SCARED ME WHEN YOU JUMPED OUT LIKE THAT.
You boys are the worst! That's animal abuse!
I—
I'M SORRY, OKAY?
DON'T APOLOGIZE TO ME. APOLOGIZE TO THE FOX.
GONE
...
We're sorry!
STING
ズキッ
NGH!
KOMUGI? IS SOME-THING WRONG?
UH, NO.
Well, we're gonna put these away.
I'll take out the trash.

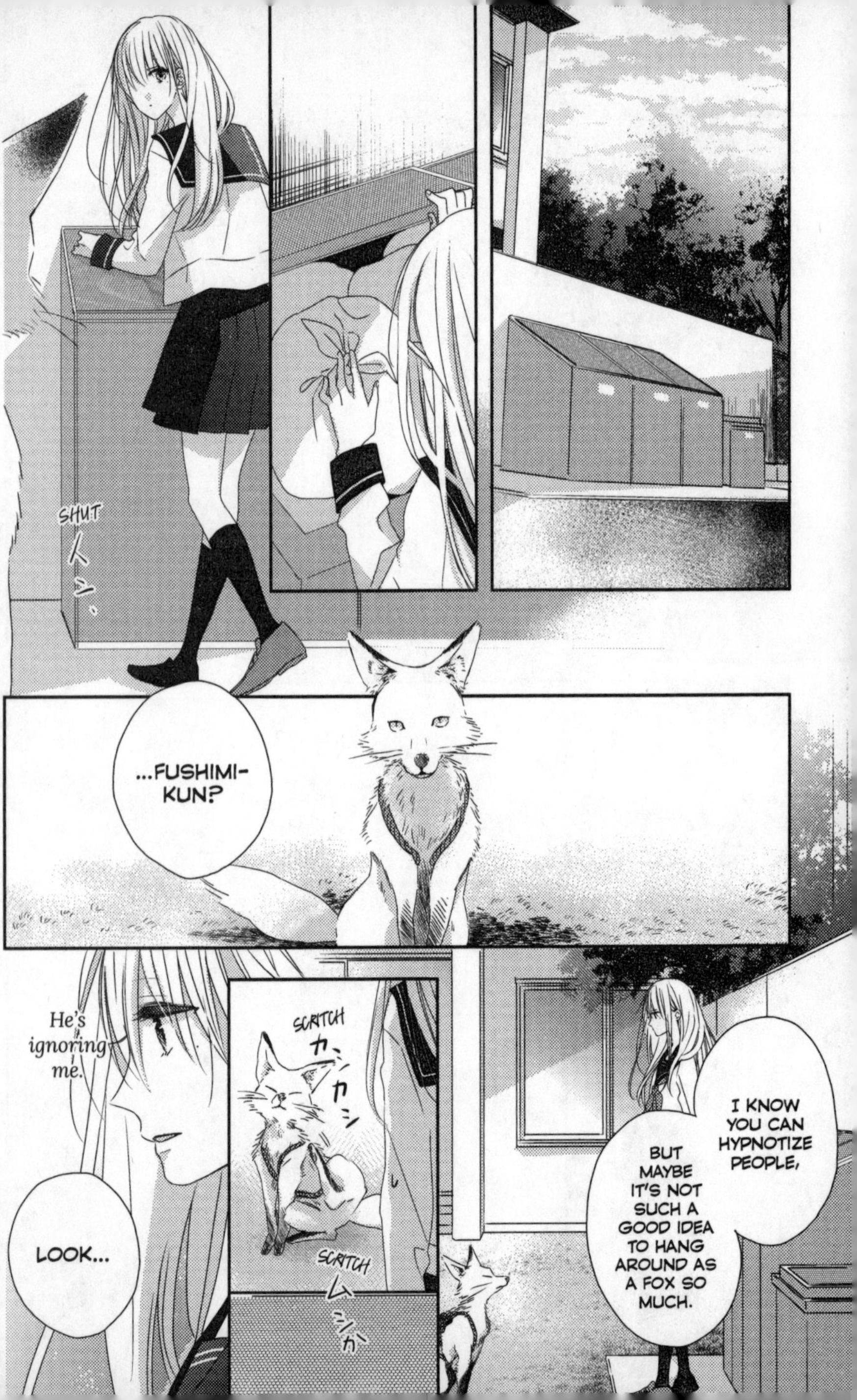
SHUT
...FUSHIMI-KUN?
I KNOW YOU CAN HYPNOTIZE PEOPLE,
BUT MAYBE IT'S NOT SUCH A GOOD IDEA TO HANG AROUND AS A FOX SO MUCH.
SCRITCH
SCRITCH
He's ignoring me.
LOOK...

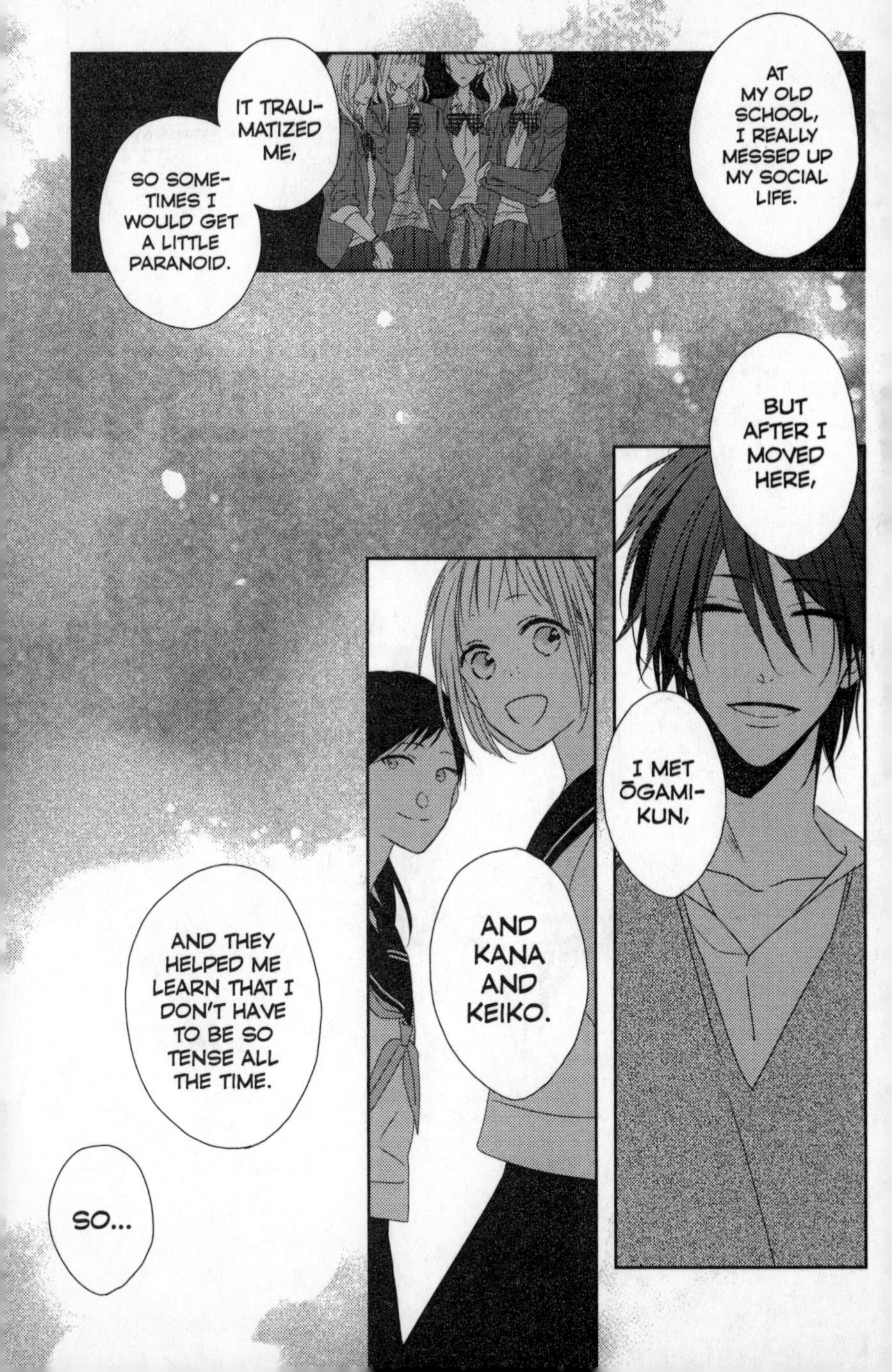
AT MY OLD SCHOOL, I REALLY MESSED UP MY SOCIAL LIFE.
IT TRAUMATIZED ME,
SO SOMETIMES I WOULD GET A LITTLE PARANOID.
BUT AFTER I MOVED HERE,
I MET ŌGAMI-KUN,
AND KANA AND KEIKO.
AND THEY HELPED ME LEARN THAT I DON'T HAVE TO BE SO TENSE ALL THE TIME.
SO...

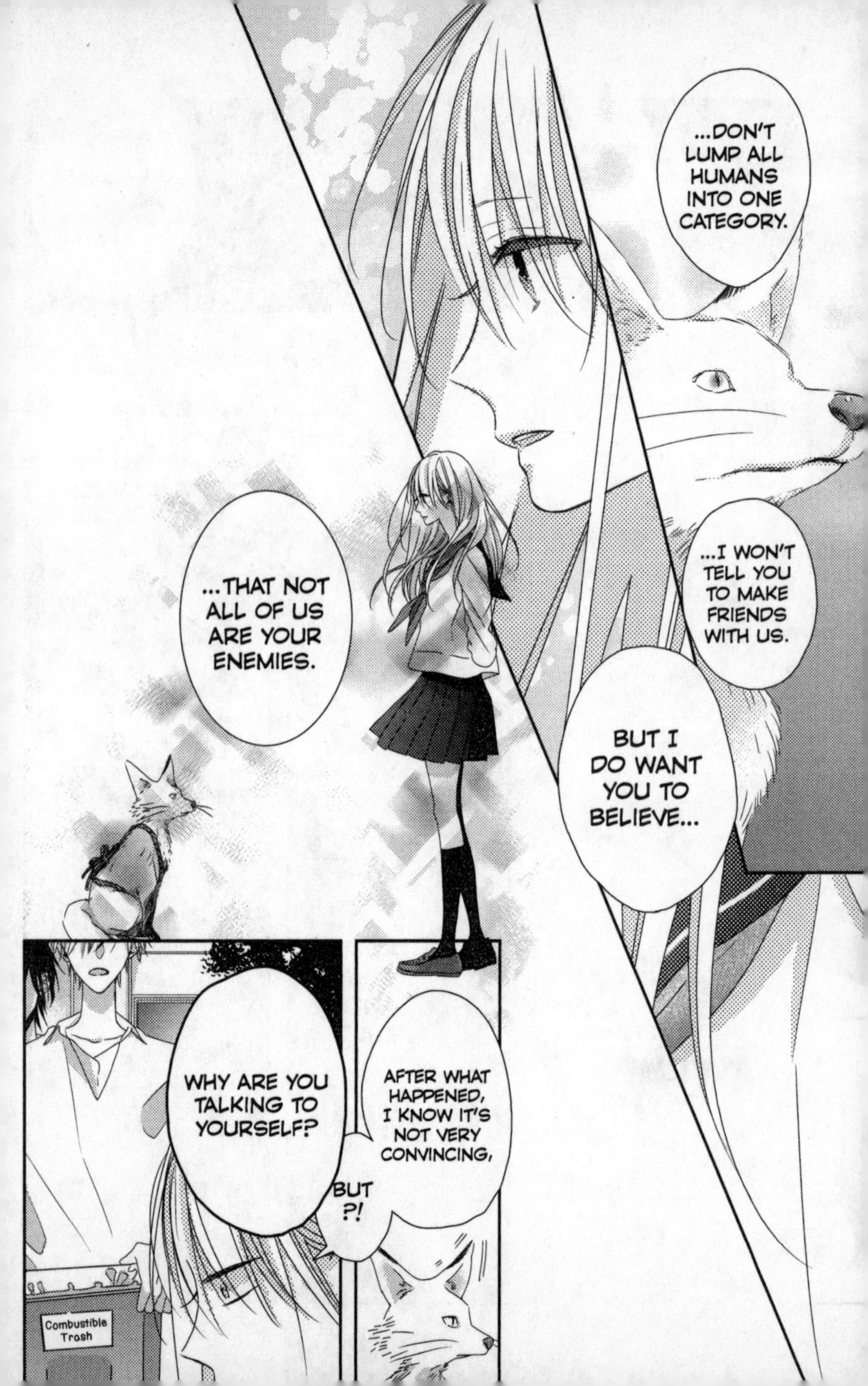
...DON'T LUMP ALL HUMANS INTO ONE CATEGORY.
...I WON'T TELL YOU TO MAKE FRIENDS WITH US.
BUT I DO WANT YOU TO BELIEVE...
...THAT NOT ALL OF US ARE YOUR ENEMIES.
AFTER WHAT HAPPENED, I KNOW IT'S NOT VERY CONVINCING,
BUT ?!
WHY ARE YOU TALKING TO YOURSELF?
Combustible Trash

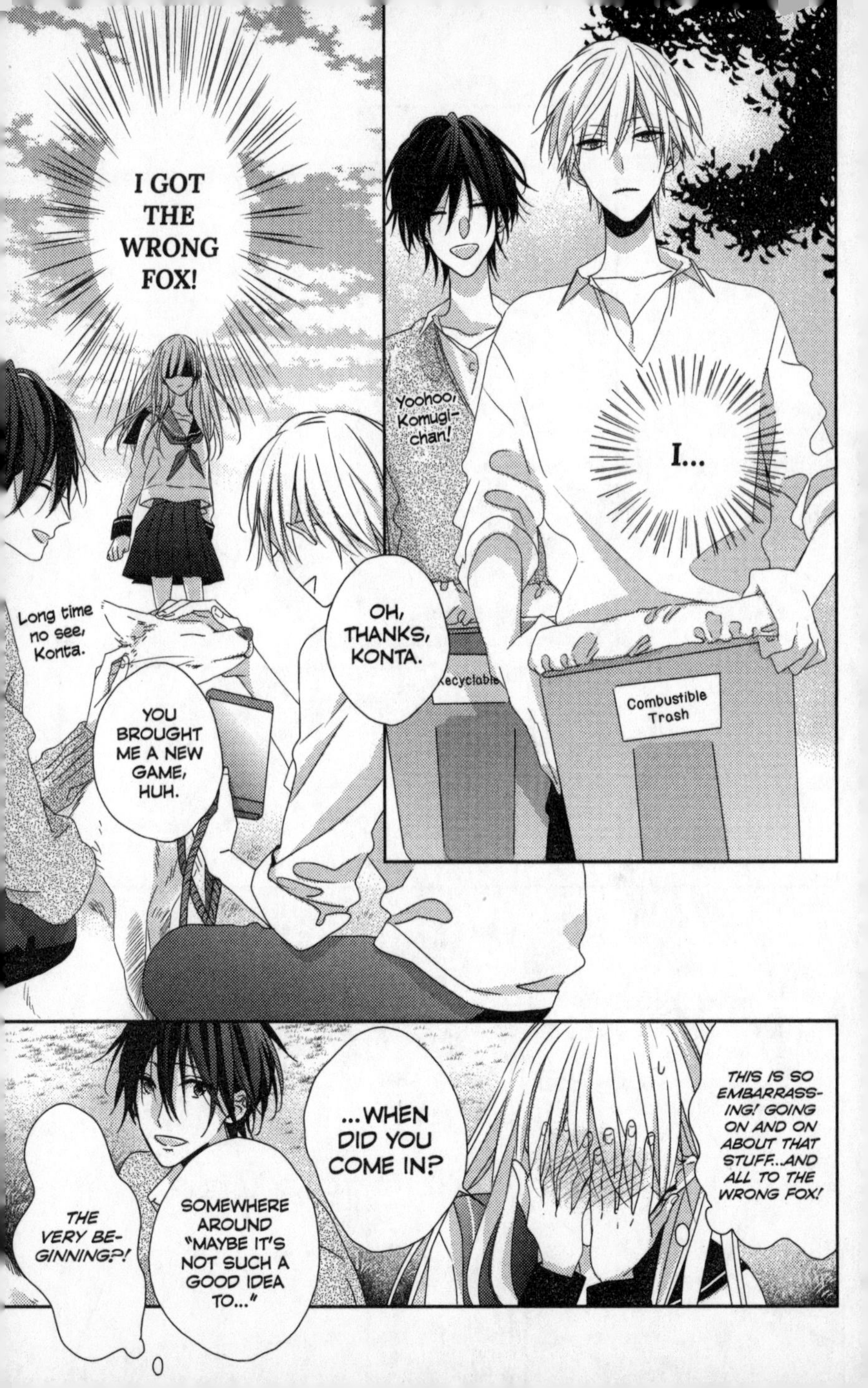

Yoohoo, Komugi-chan!
I...
Recyclable
Combustible Trash
I GOT THE WRONG FOX!
OH, THANKS, KONTA.
Long time no see, Konta.
YOU BROUGHT ME A NEW GAME, HUH.
THIS IS SO EMBARRASSING! GOING ON AND ON ABOUT THAT STUFF...AND ALL TO THE WRONG FOX!
...WHEN DID YOU COME IN?
SOMEWHERE AROUND "MAYBE IT'S NOT SUCH A GOOD IDEA TO..."
THE VERY BEGINNING?!

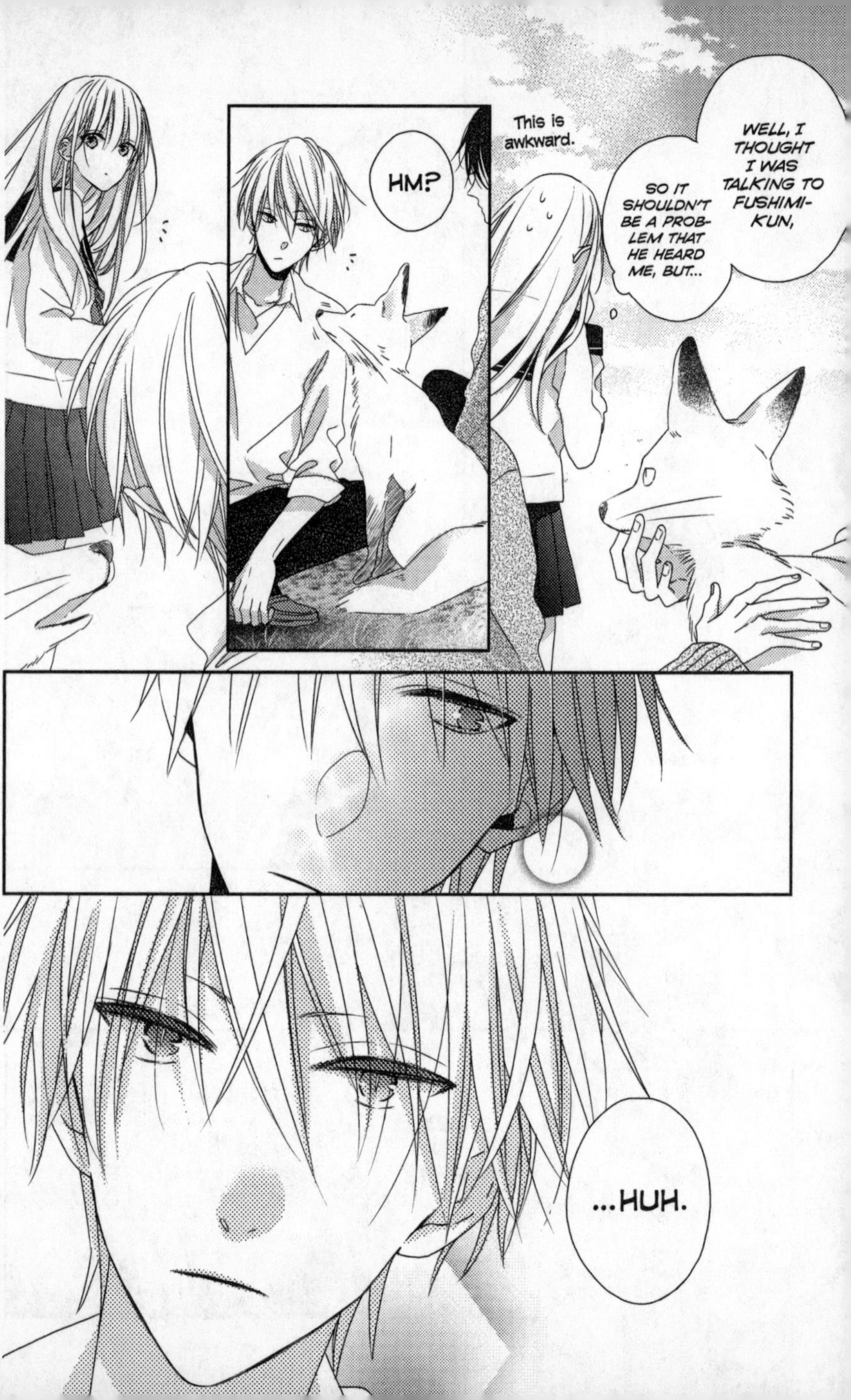
WELL, I THOUGHT I WAS TALKING TO FUSHIMI-KUN,
SO IT SHOULDN'T BE A PROB-LEM THAT HE HEARD ME, BUT...
This is awkward.
HM?
...HUH.

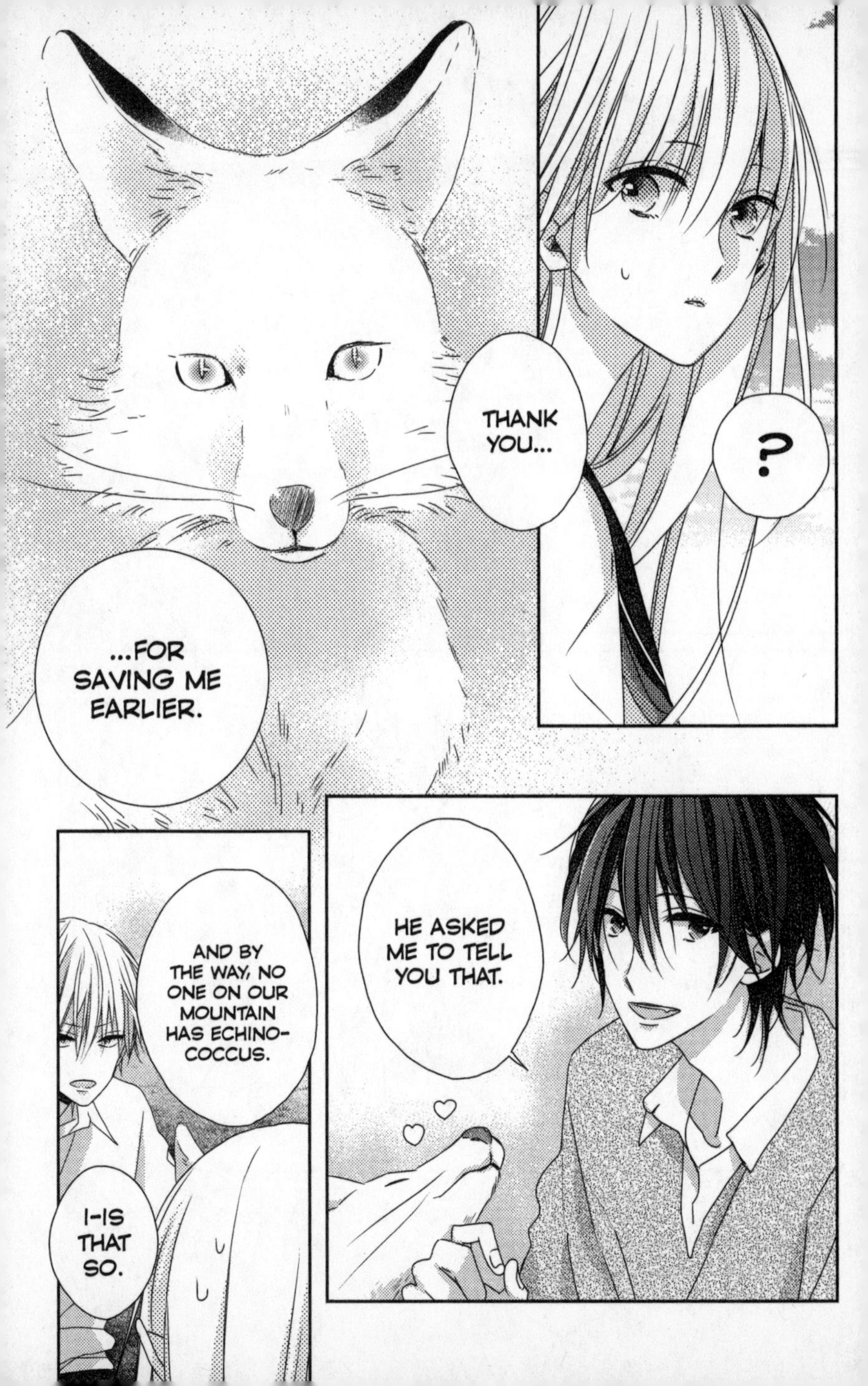
THANK YOU...
?
...FOR SAVING ME EARLIER.
HE ASKED ME TO TELL YOU THAT.
AND BY THE WAY, NO ONE ON OUR MOUNTAIN HAS ECHINO-COCCUS.
I-IS THAT SO.

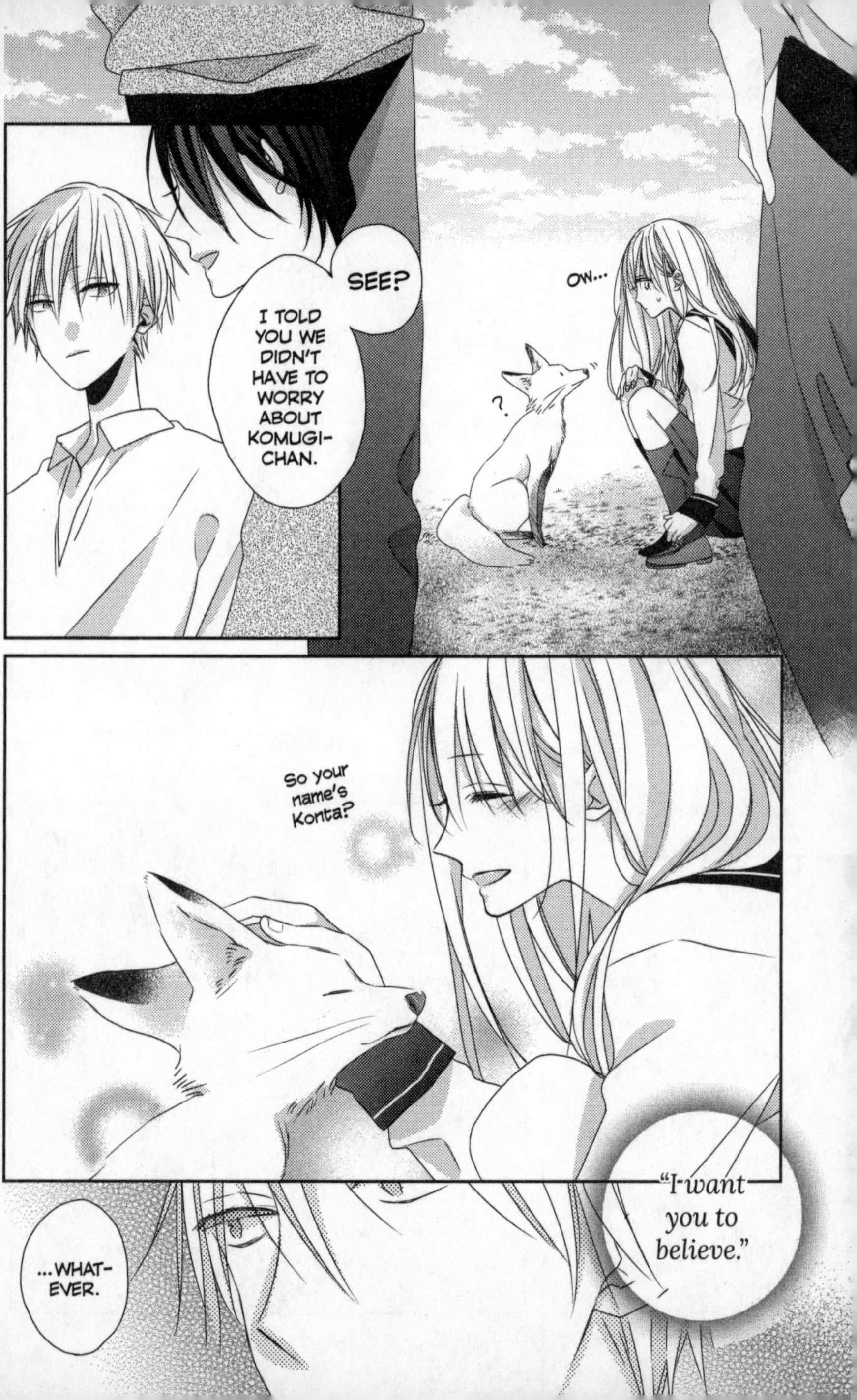
OW...
SEE?
I TOLD YOU WE DIDN'T HAVE TO WORRY ABOUT KOMUGI-CHAN.
So your name's Konta?
"I want you to believe."
...WHAT-EVER.

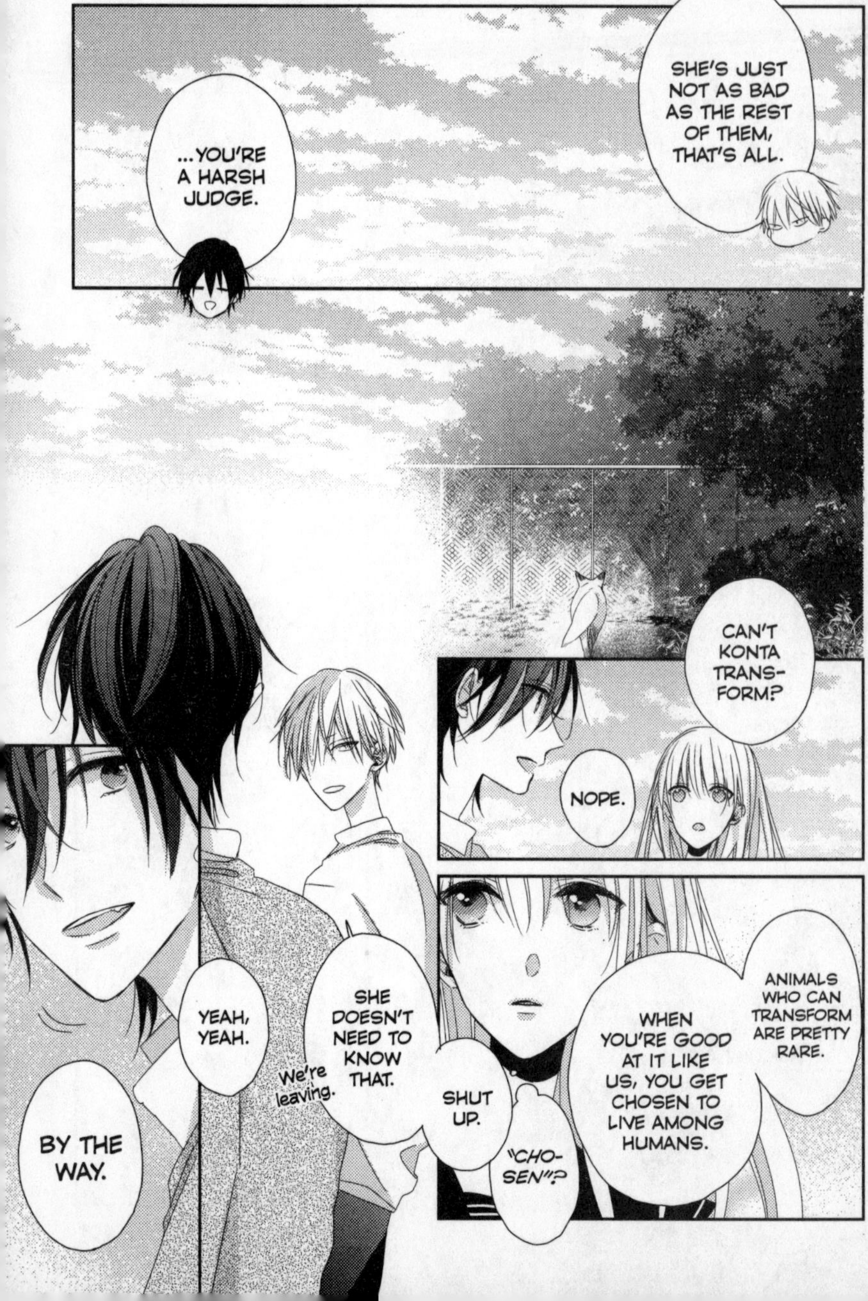
SHE'S JUST NOT AS BAD AS THE REST OF THEM, THAT'S ALL.
...YOU'RE A HARSH JUDGE.
CAN'T KONTA TRANS-FORM?
NOPE.
ANIMALS WHO CAN TRANSFORM ARE PRETTY RARE.
WHEN YOU'RE GOOD AT IT LIKE US, YOU GET CHOSEN TO LIVE AMONG HUMANS.
"CHO-SEN"?
SHUT UP.
SHE DOESN'T NEED TO KNOW THAT.
We're leaving.
YEAH, YEAH.
BY THE WAY.

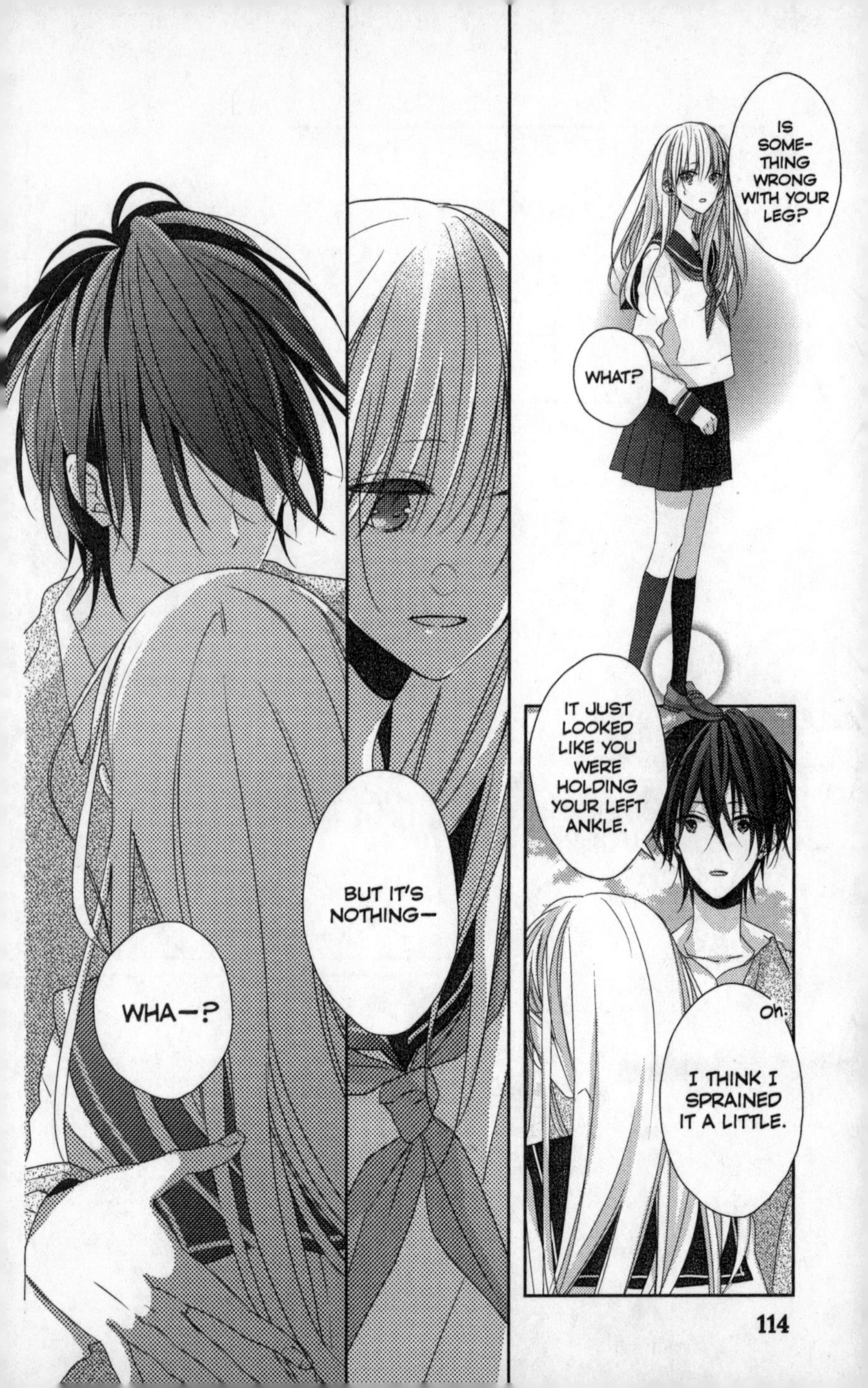
IS SOME-THING WRONG WITH YOUR LEG?
WHAT?
IT JUST LOOKED LIKE YOU WERE HOLDING YOUR LEFT ANKLE.
Oh.
I THINK I SPRAINED IT A LITTLE.
BUT IT'S NOTHING—
WHA—?

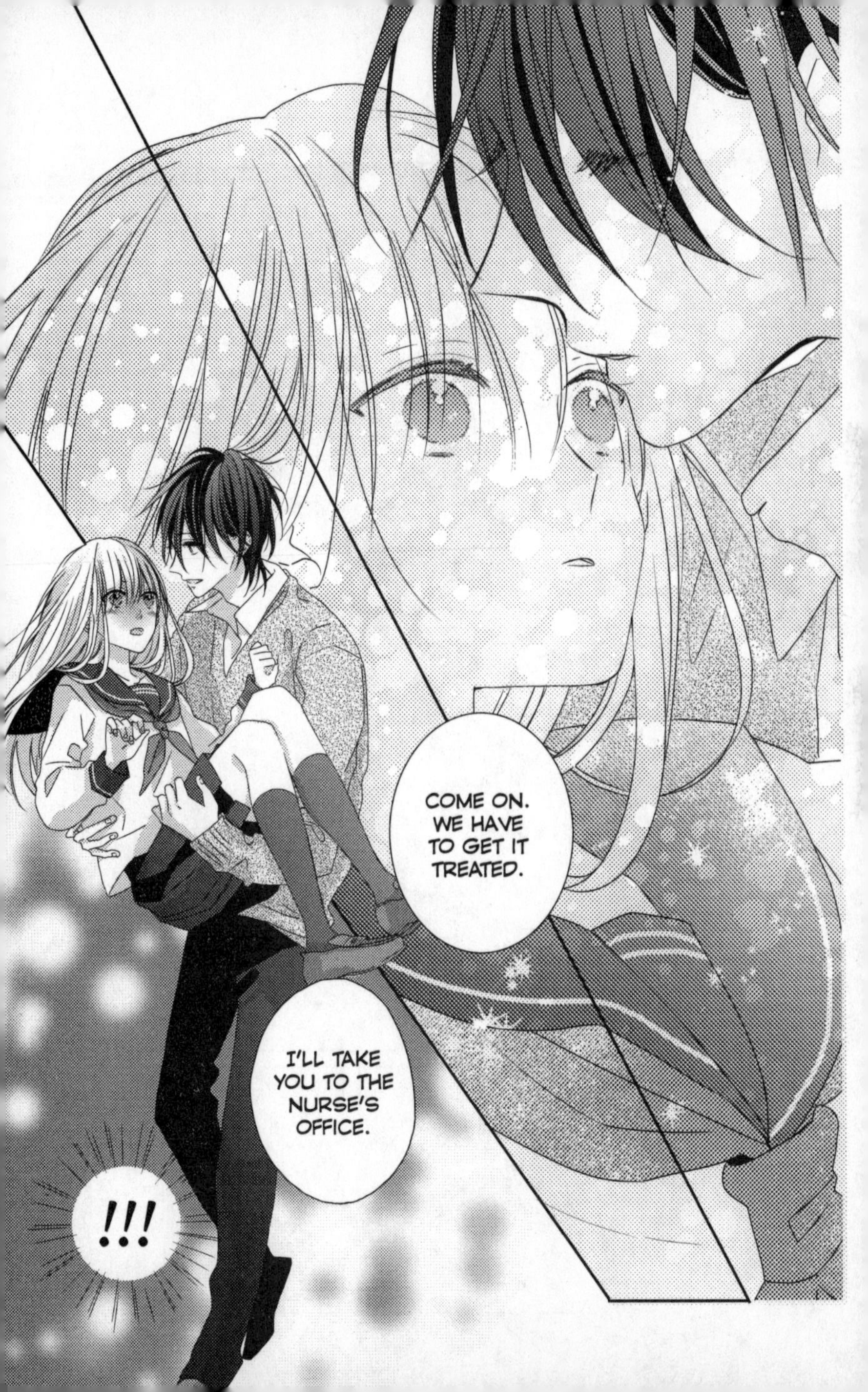
COME ON. WE HAVE TO GET IT TREATED.
I'LL TAKE YOU TO THE NURSE'S OFFICE.
!!!

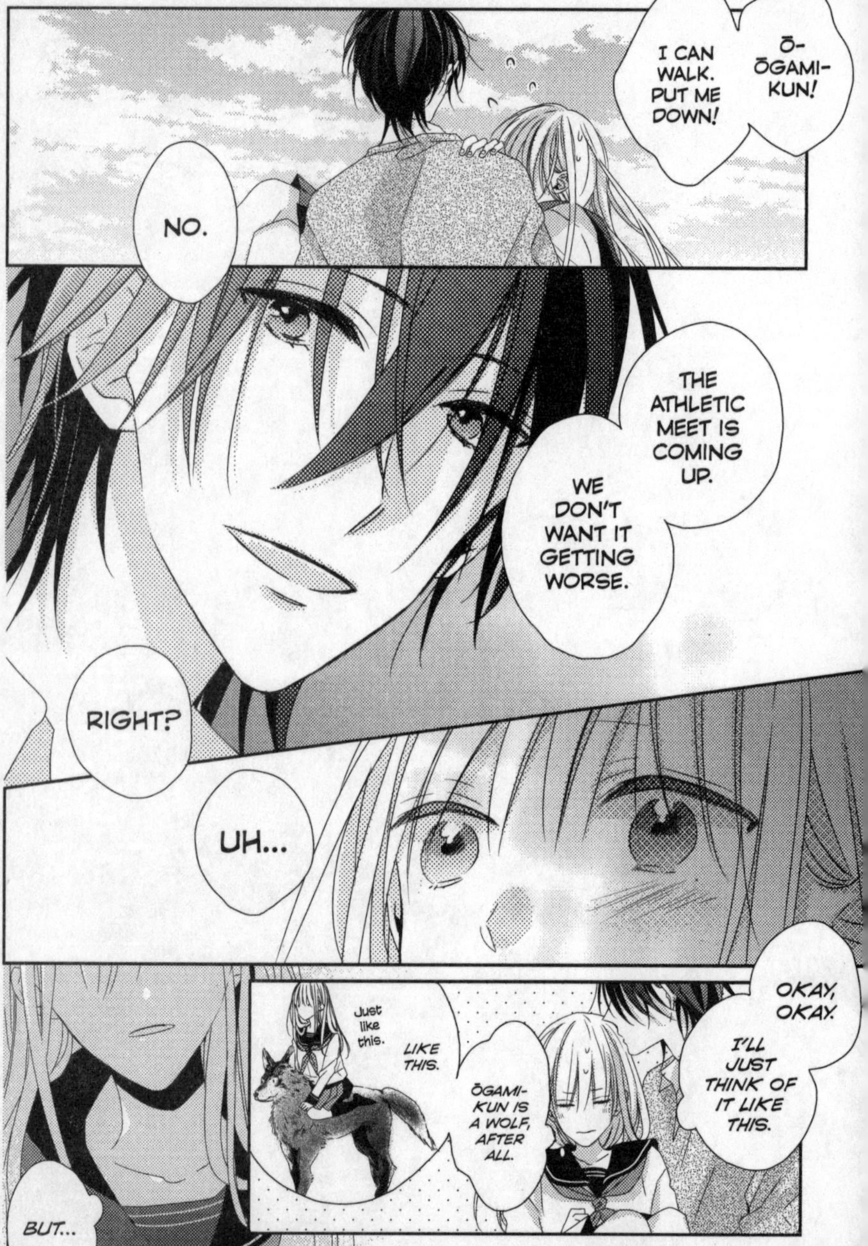
Ō-ŌGAMI-KUN!
I CAN WALK. PUT ME DOWN!
NO.
THE ATHLETIC MEET IS COMING UP.
WE DON'T WANT IT GETTING WORSE.
RIGHT?
UH...
OKAY, OKAY.
I'LL JUST THINK OF IT LIKE THIS.
ŌGAMI-KUN IS A WOLF, AFTER ALL.
LIKE THIS.
Just like this.
BUT...

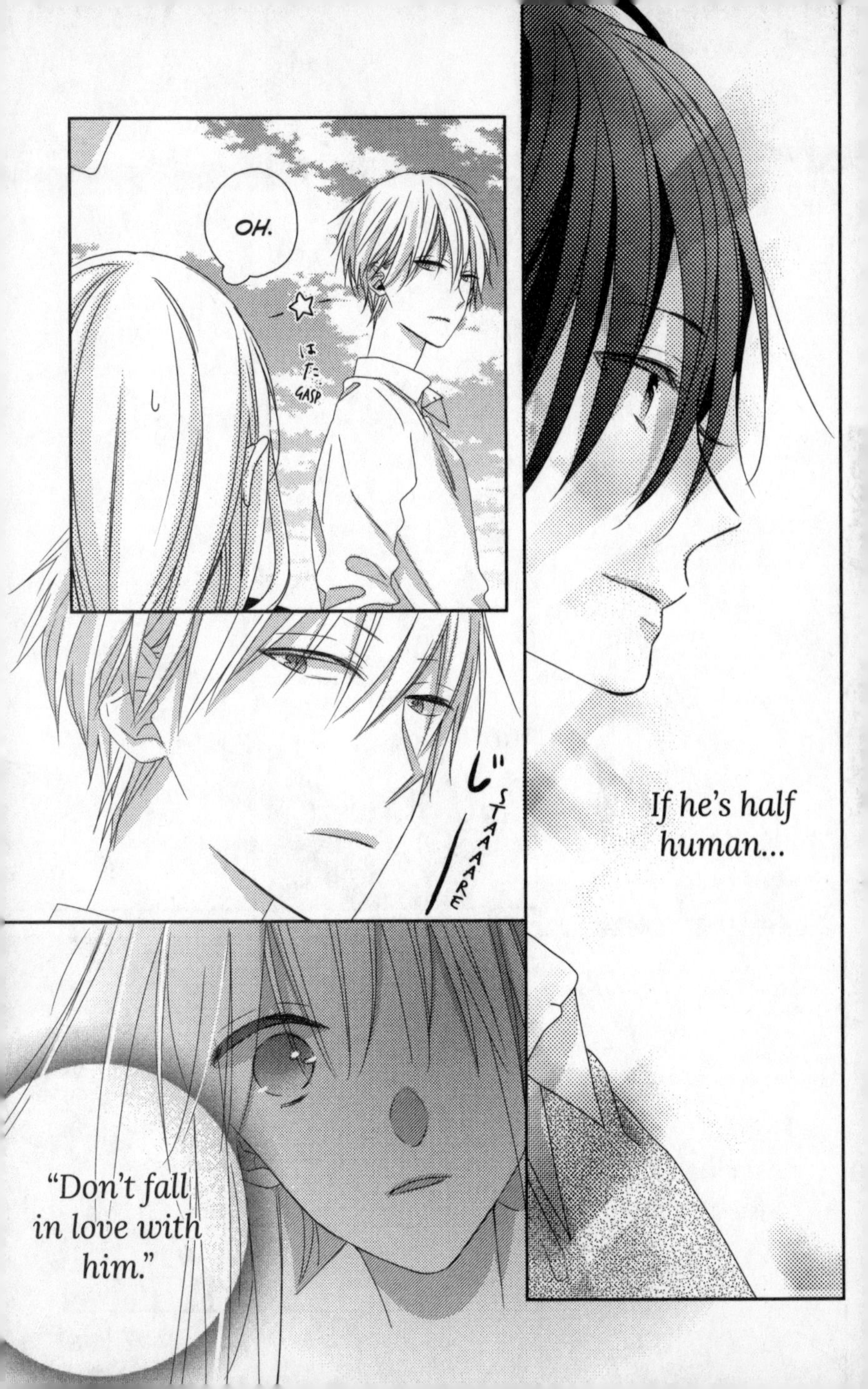
If he's half human...
OH.
はた
GASP
じ
STAAAARE
"Don't fall in love with him."

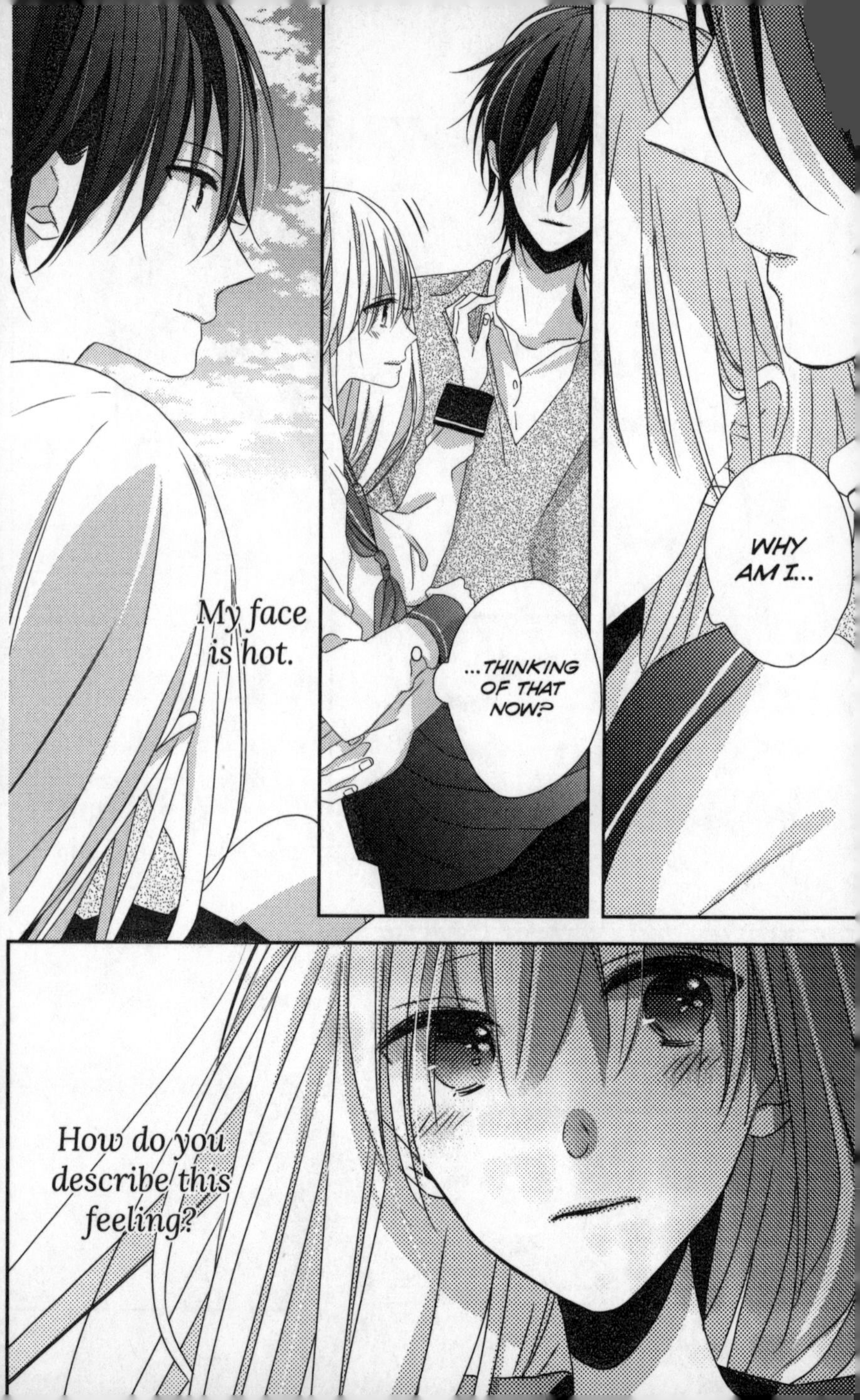
WHY AM I...
...THINKING OF THAT NOW?
My face is hot.
How do you describe this feeling?

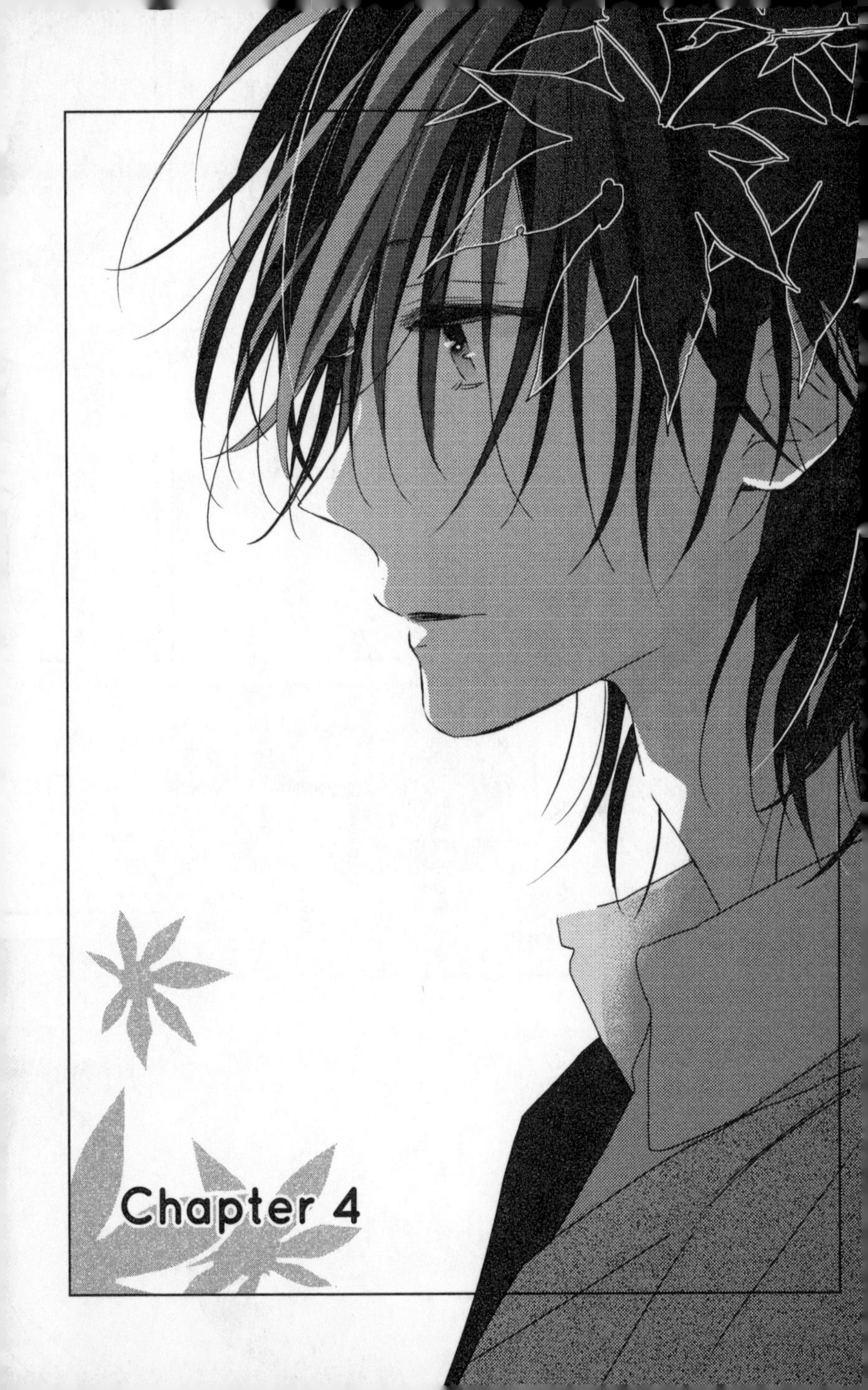
Chapter 4

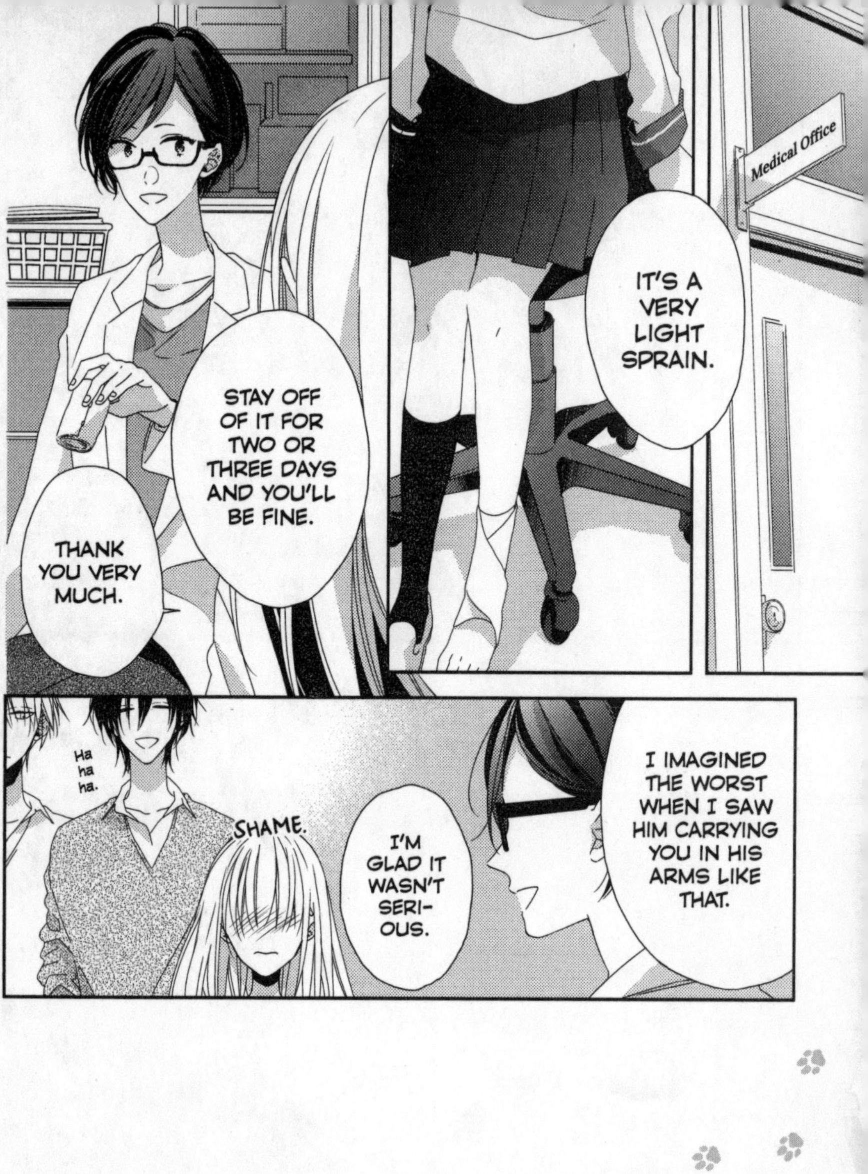
Medical Office
IT'S A VERY LIGHT SPRAIN.
STAY OFF OF IT FOR TWO OR THREE DAYS AND YOU'LL BE FINE.
THANK YOU VERY MUCH.
I IMAGINED THE WORST WHEN I SAW HIM CARRYING YOU IN HIS ARMS LIKE THAT.
I'M GLAD IT WASN'T SERI-OUS.
SHAME.
Ha ha ha.

That Wolf-Boy is Mine!

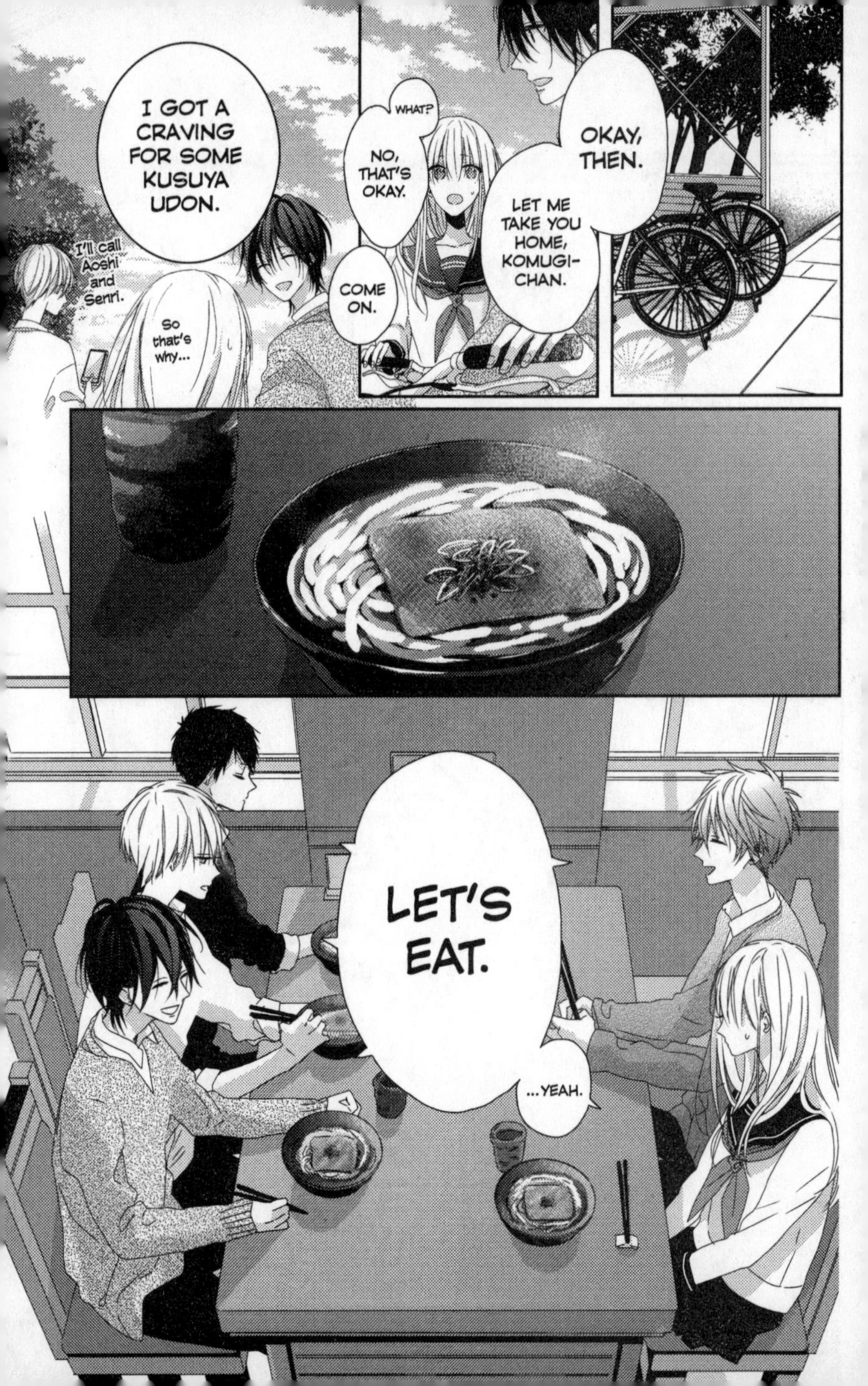
OKAY, THEN.
LET ME TAKE YOU HOME, KOMUGI-CHAN.
WHAT?
NO, THAT'S OKAY.
COME ON.
I GOT A CRAVING FOR SOME KUSUYA UDON.
I'll call Aoshi and Senri.
So that's why...
LET'S EAT.
...YEAH.

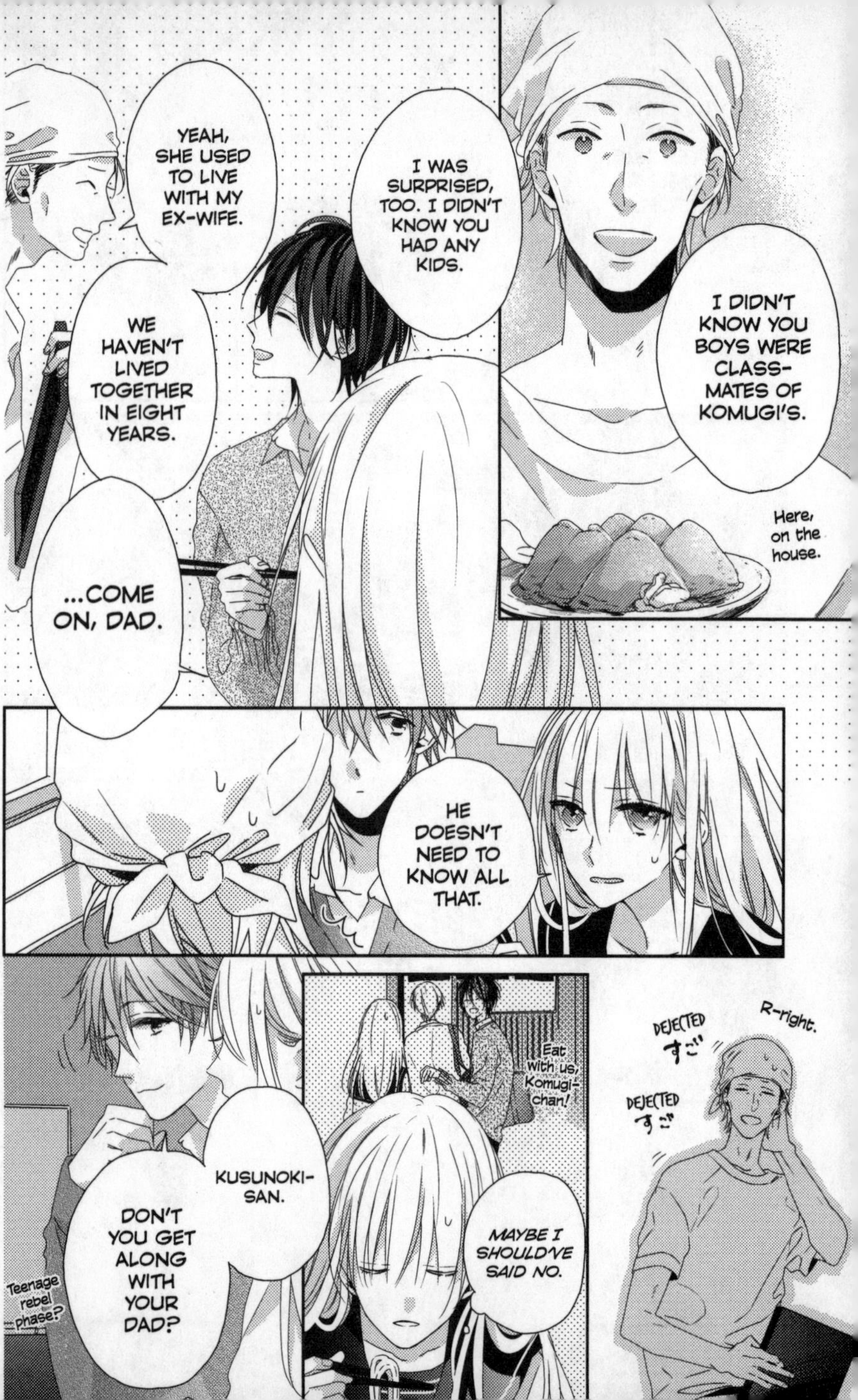
I DIDN'T KNOW YOU BOYS WERE CLASS-MATES OF KOMUGI'S.
Here, on the house.
I WAS SURPRISED, TOO. I DIDN'T KNOW YOU HAD ANY KIDS.
YEAH, SHE USED TO LIVE WITH MY EX-WIFE.
WE HAVEN'T LIVED TOGETHER IN EIGHT YEARS.
...COME ON, DAD.
HE DOESN'T NEED TO KNOW ALL THAT.
R-right.
DEJECTED すご
DEJECTED すご
Eat with us, Komugi-chan!
MAYBE I SHOULD'VE SAID NO.
KUSUNOKI-SAN.
DON'T YOU GET ALONG WITH YOUR DAD?
Teenage rebel phase?

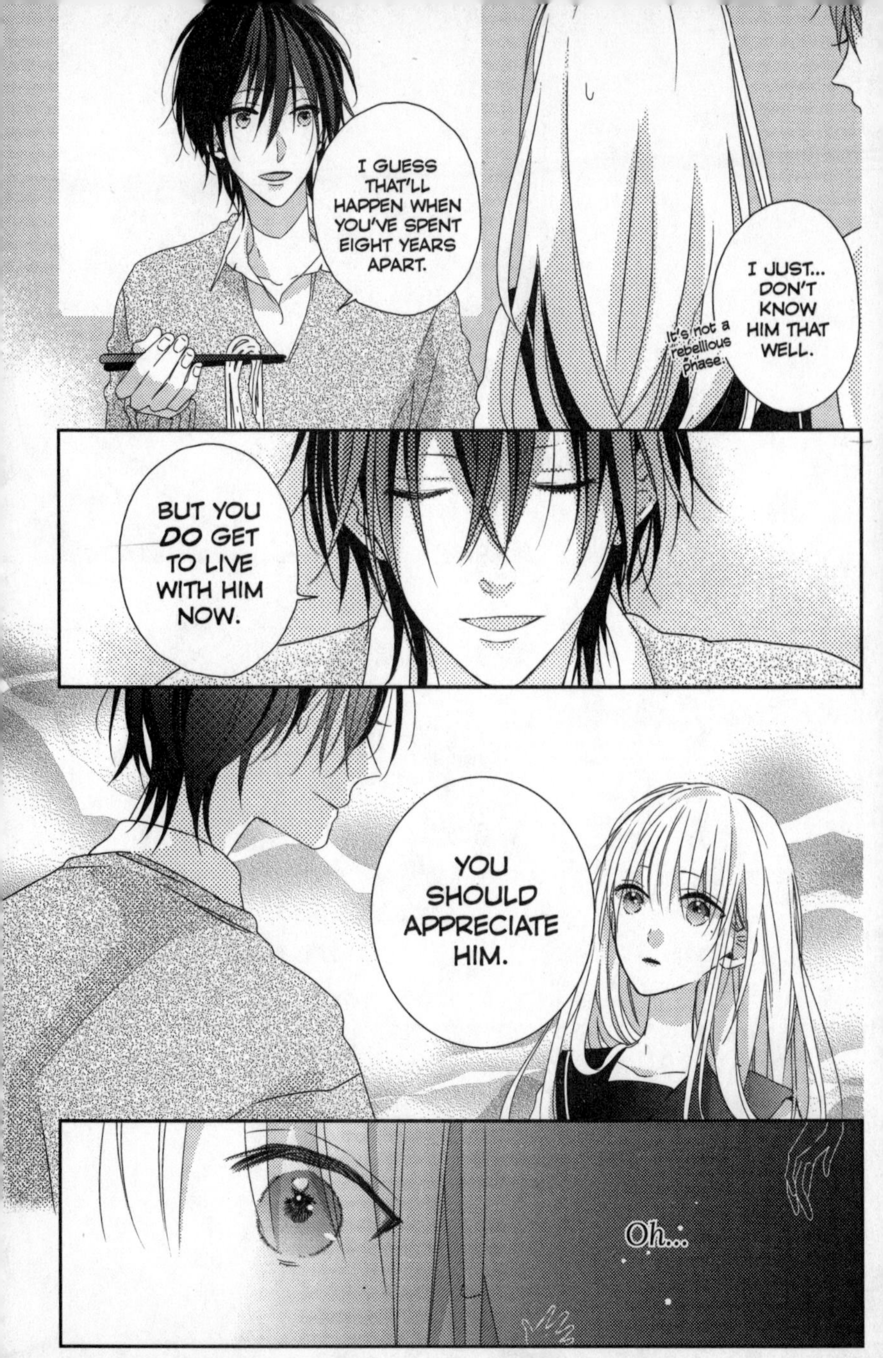
I JUST... DON'T KNOW HIM THAT WELL.
It's not a rebellious phase.
I GUESS THAT'LL HAPPEN WHEN YOU'VE SPENT EIGHT YEARS APART.
BUT YOU *DO* GET TO LIVE WITH HIM NOW.
YOU SHOULD APPRECIATE HIM.
Oh...

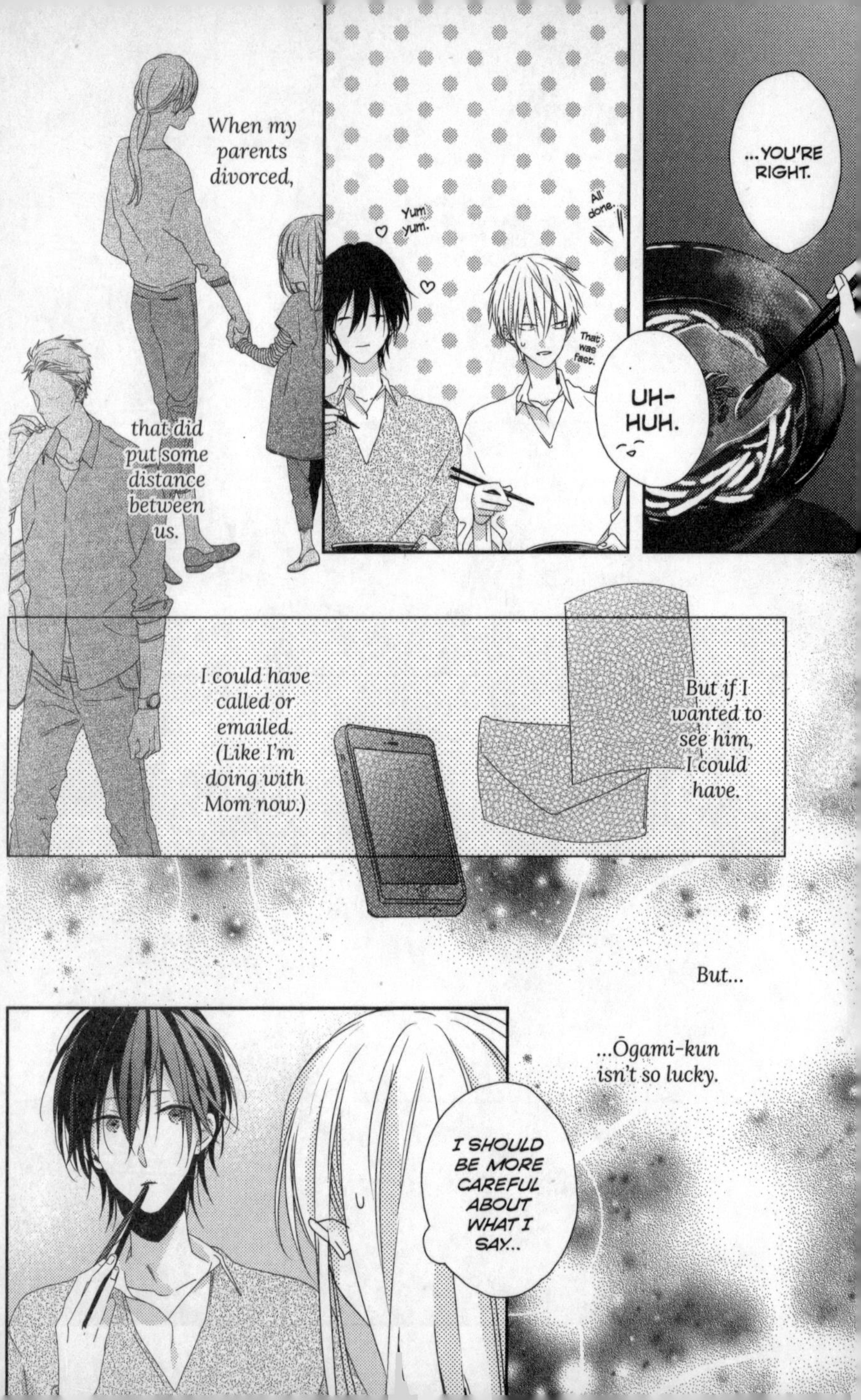
...YOU'RE RIGHT.
UH-HUH.
All done.
Yum yum.
That was fast.
When my parents divorced,
that did put some distance between us.
But if I wanted to see him, I could have.
I could have called or emailed. (Like I'm doing with Mom now.)
But...
...Ōgami-kun isn't so lucky.
I SHOULD BE MORE CAREFUL ABOUT WHAT I SAY...

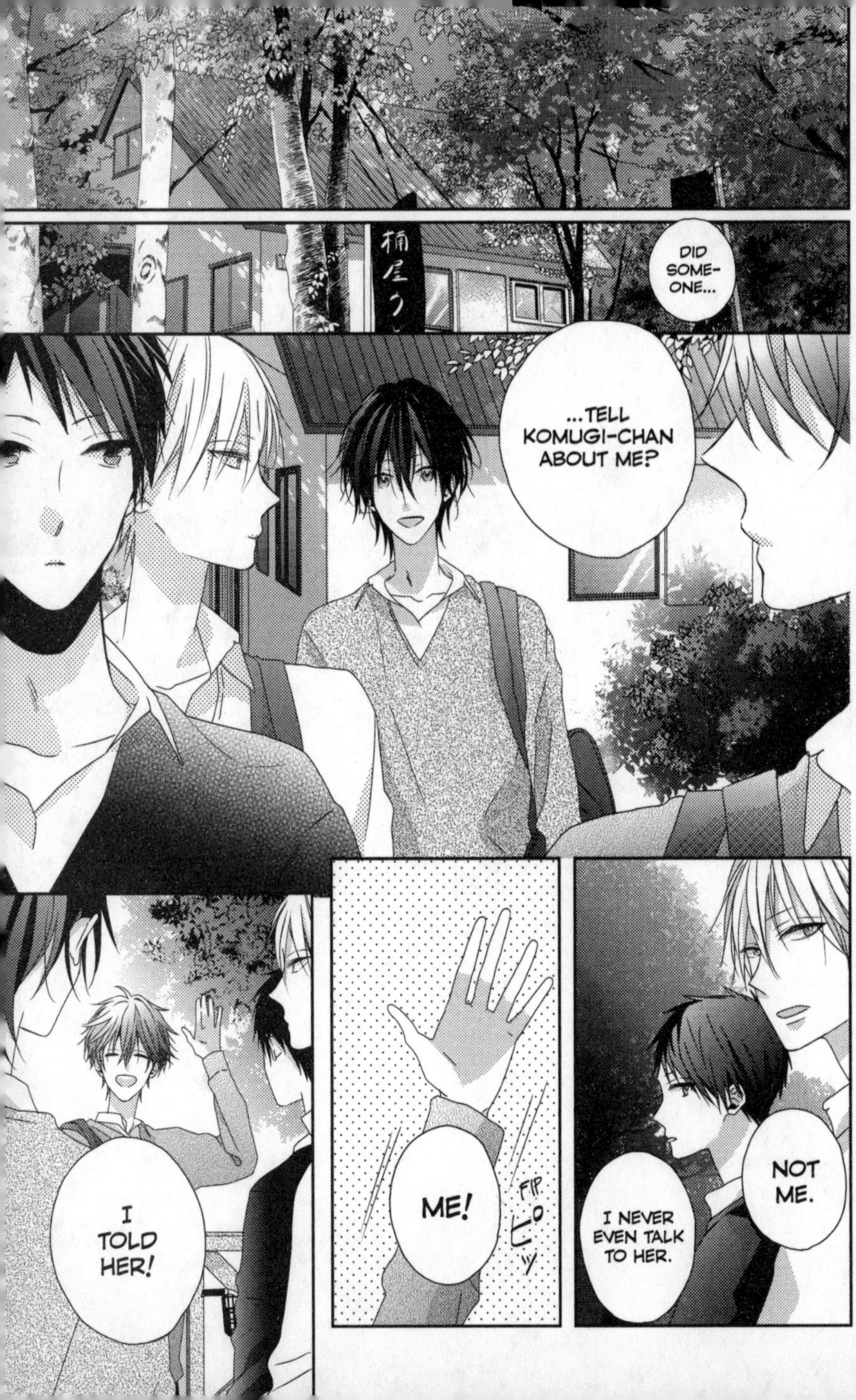
DID SOME-ONE...
...TELL KOMUGI-CHAN ABOUT ME?
NOT ME.
I NEVER EVEN TALK TO HER.
FIP
ピッ
ME!
I TOLD HER!

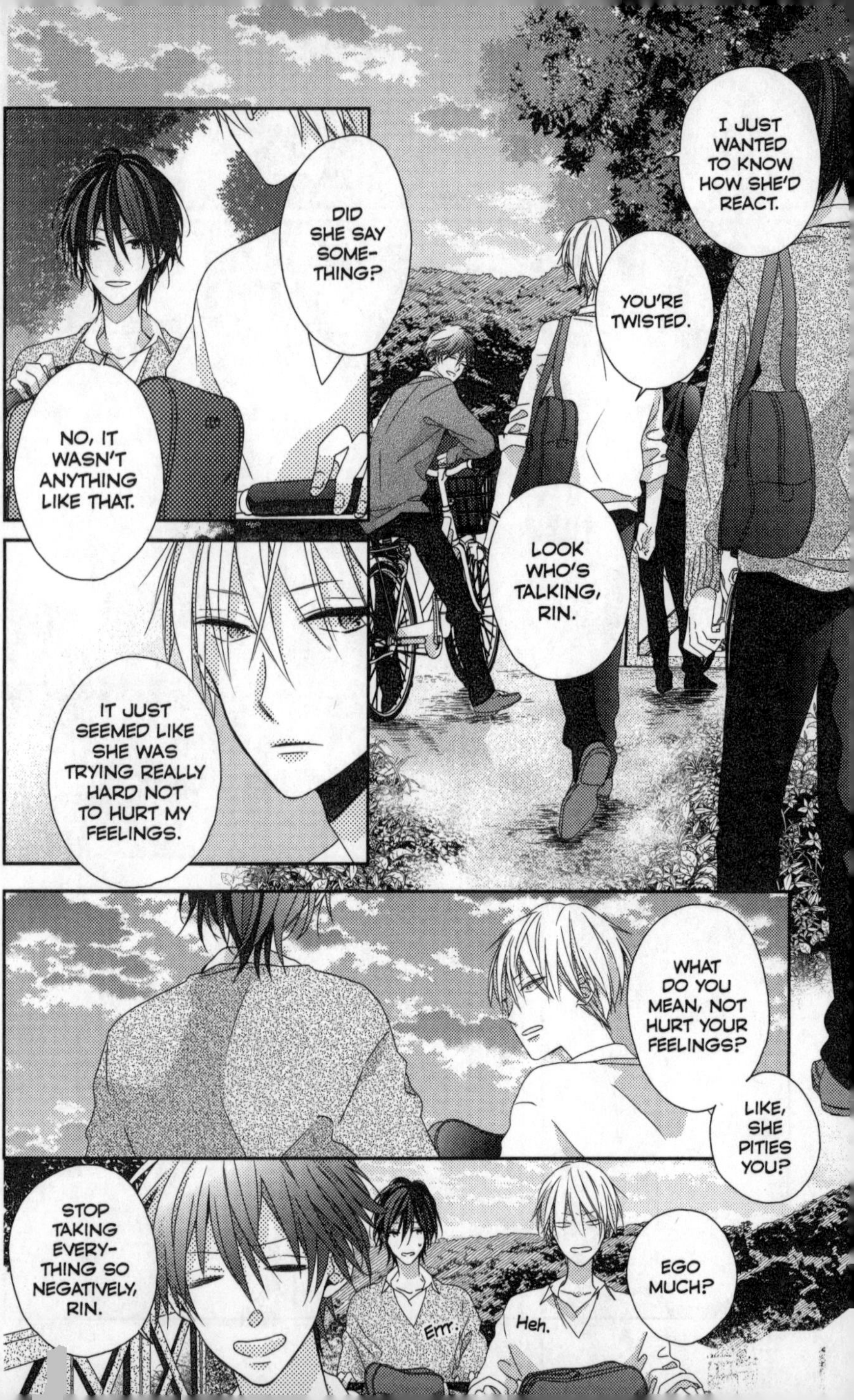
I JUST WANTED TO KNOW HOW SHE'D REACT.
YOU'RE TWISTED.
LOOK WHO'S TALKING, RIN.
DID SHE SAY SOME-THING?
NO, IT WASN'T ANYTHING LIKE THAT.
IT JUST SEEMED LIKE SHE WAS TRYING REALLY HARD NOT TO HURT MY FEELINGS.
WHAT DO YOU MEAN, NOT HURT YOUR FEELINGS?
LIKE, SHE PITIES YOU?
EGO MUCH?
Heh.
Errr.
STOP TAKING EVERY-THING SO NEGATIVELY, RIN.

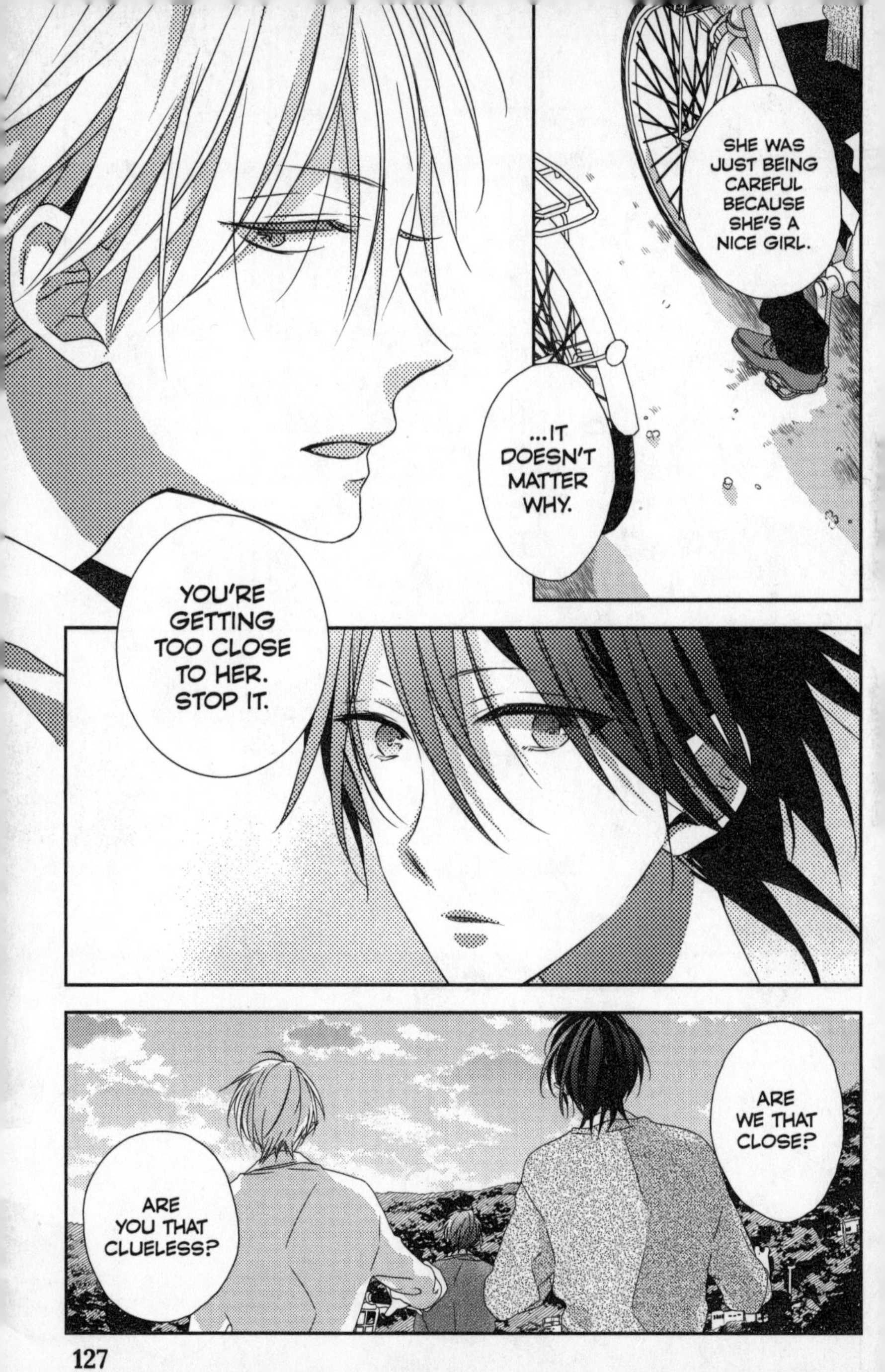
SHE WAS JUST BEING CAREFUL BECAUSE SHE'S A NICE GIRL.
...IT DOESN'T MATTER WHY.
YOU'RE GETTING TOO CLOSE TO HER. STOP IT.
ARE WE THAT CLOSE?
ARE YOU THAT CLUELESS?

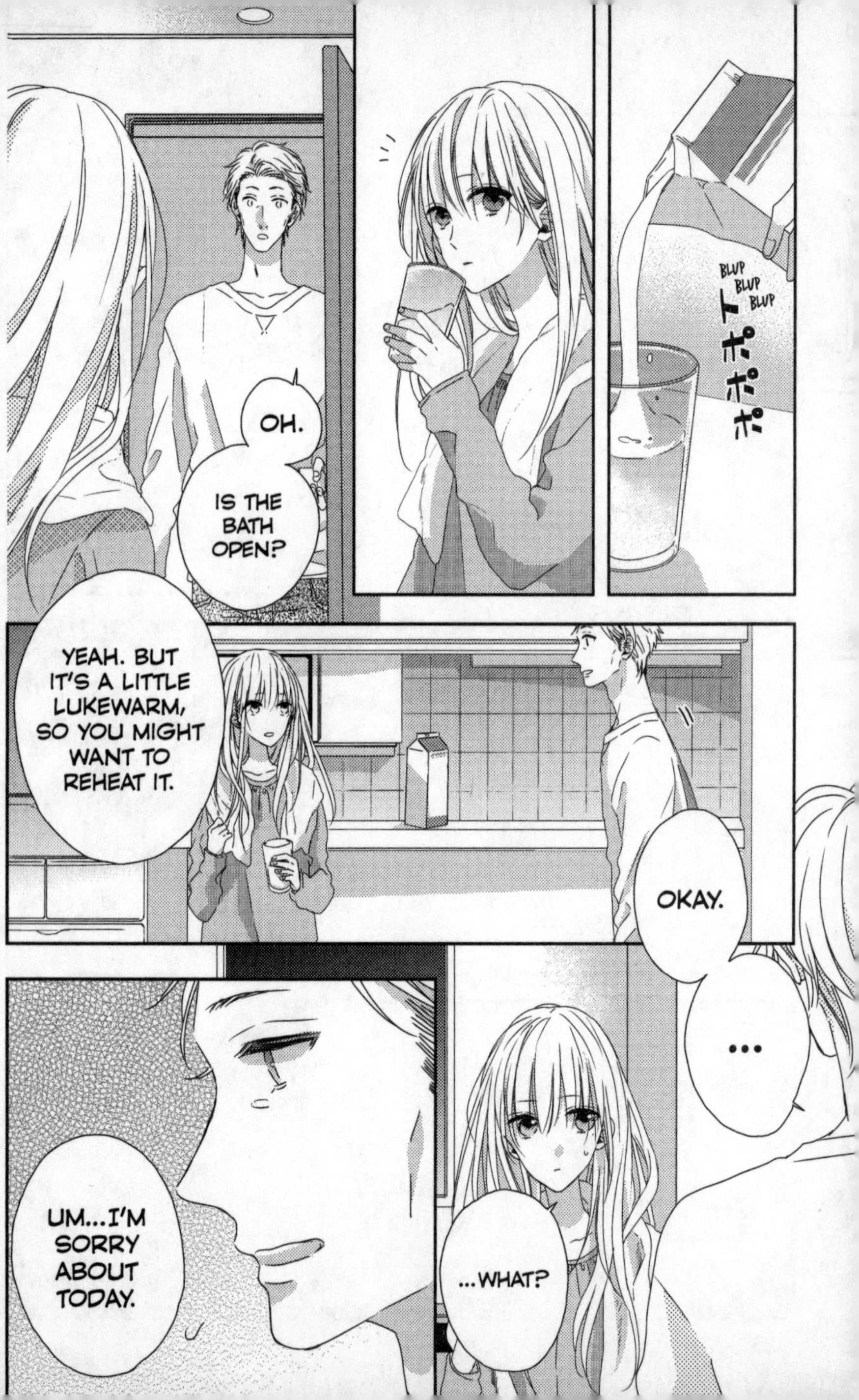
BLUP BLUP BLUP
トポポポ
OH.
IS THE BATH OPEN?
YEAH. BUT IT'S A LITTLE LUKEWARM, SO YOU MIGHT WANT TO REHEAT IT.
OKAY.
...
UM...I'M SORRY ABOUT TODAY.
...WHAT?

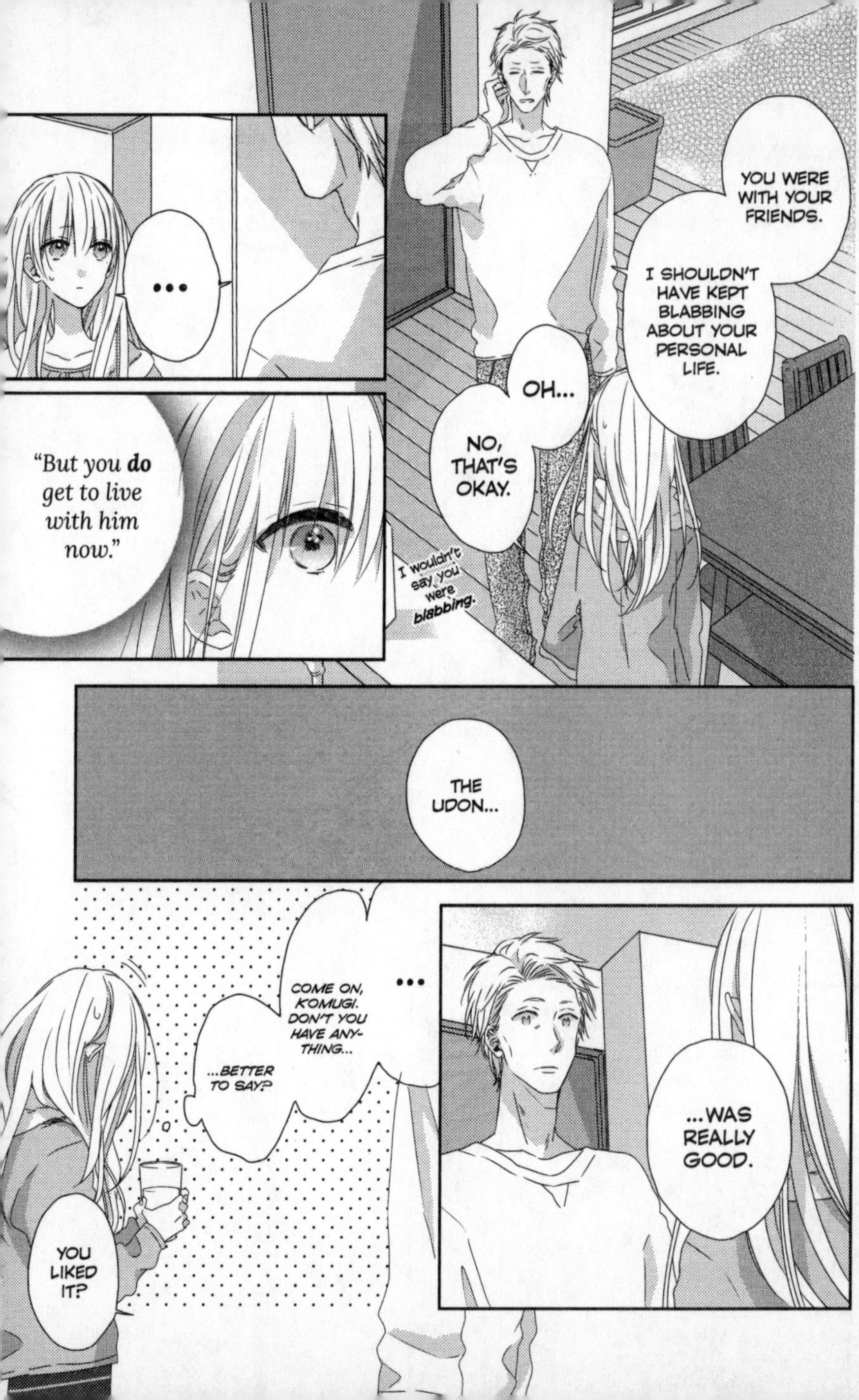
YOU WERE WITH YOUR FRIENDS.
I SHOULDN'T HAVE KEPT BLABBING ABOUT YOUR PERSONAL LIFE.
OH...
NO, THAT'S OKAY.
I wouldn't say you were blabbing.
...
"But you do get to live with him now."
THE UDON...
...WAS REALLY GOOD.
...
COME ON, KOMUGI. DON'T YOU HAVE ANY-THING...
...BETTER TO SAY?
YOU LIKED IT?

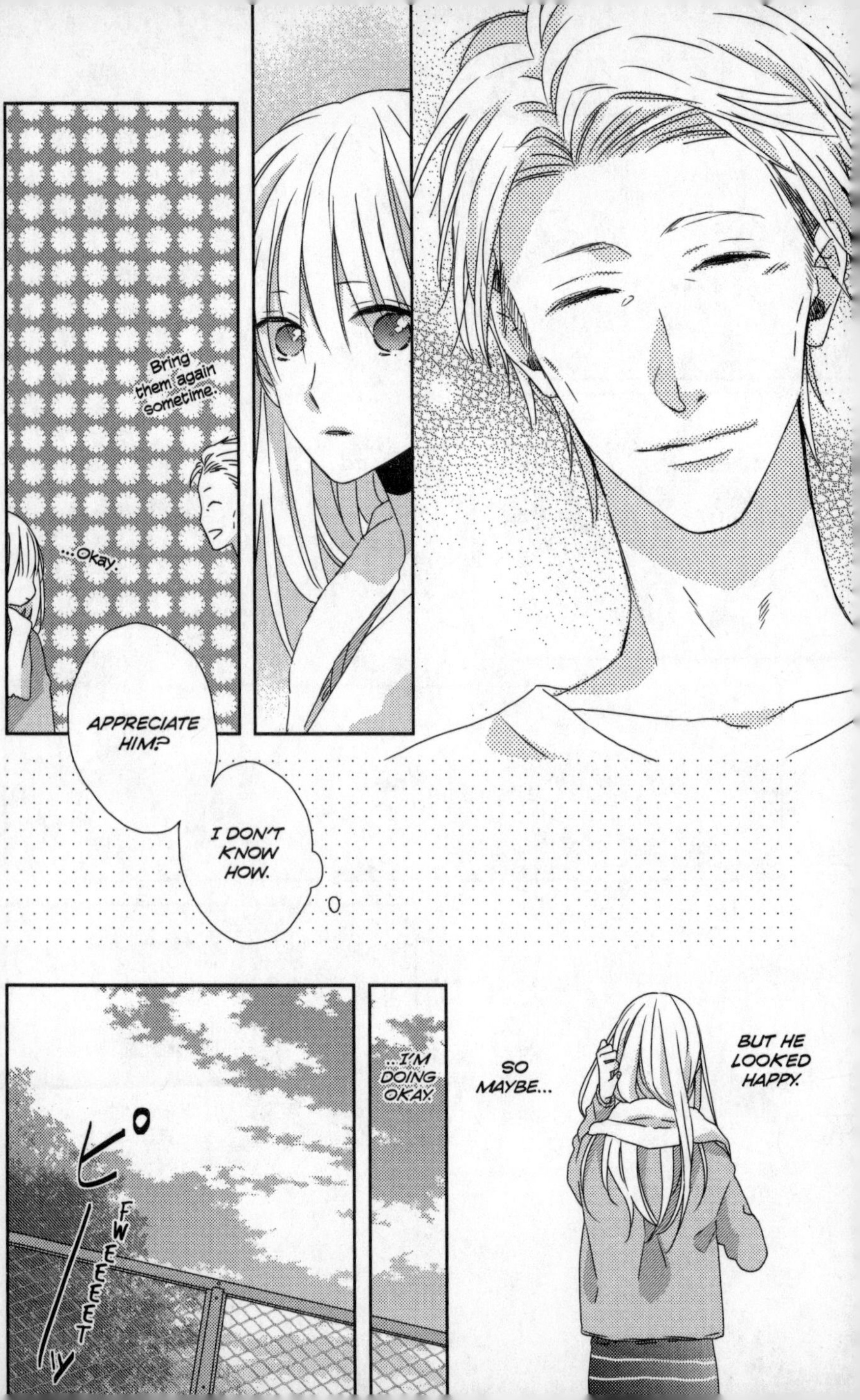
Bring them again sometime.
...Okay.
APPRECIATE HIM?
I DON'T KNOW HOW.
BUT HE LOOKED HAPPY.
SO MAYBE...
...I'M DOING OKAY.
FWEEEET

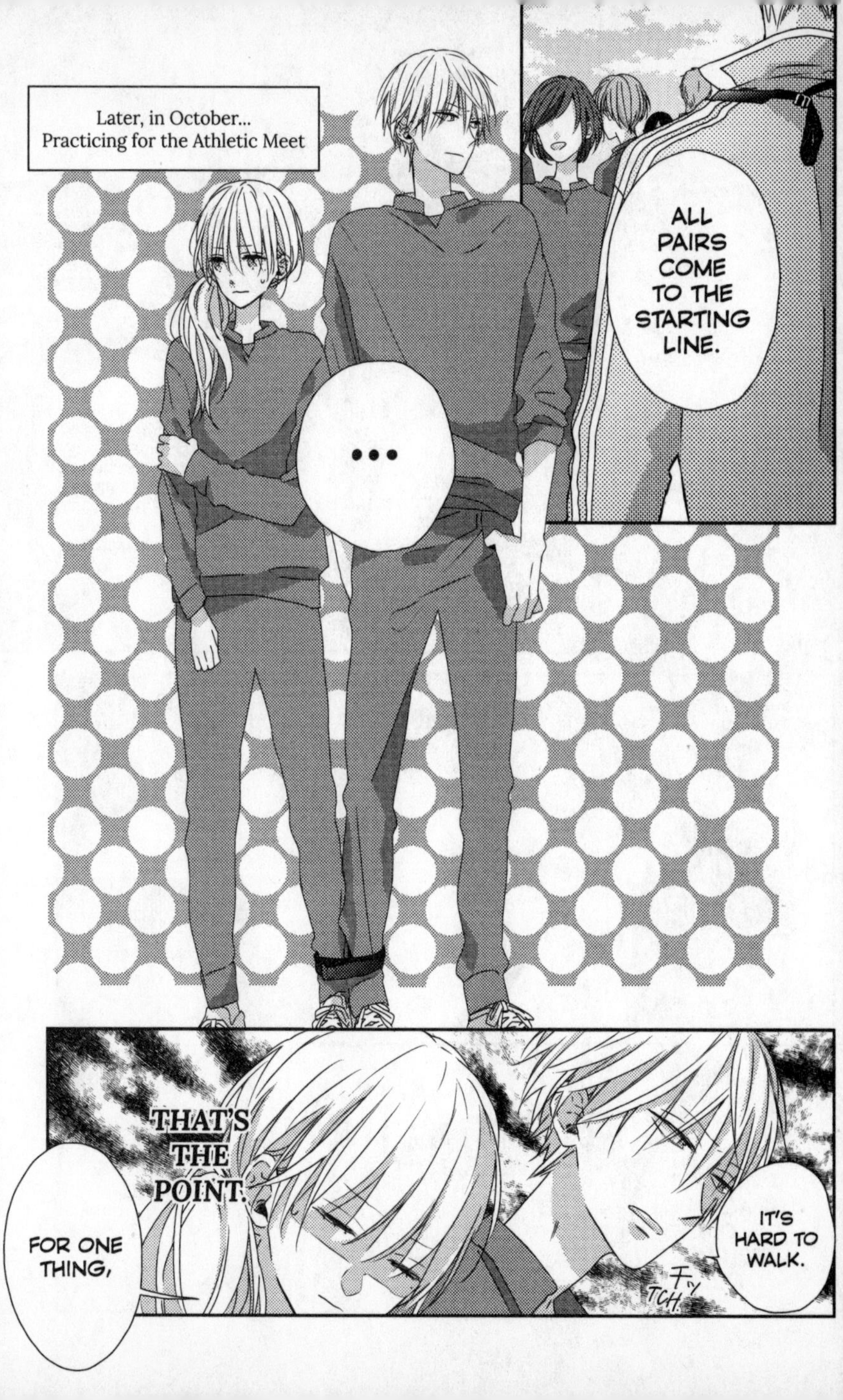
ALL PAIRS COME TO THE STARTING LINE.
Later, in October...
Practicing for the Athletic Meet
...
IT'S HARD TO WALK.
チッ TCH
THAT'S THE POINT.
FOR ONE THING,

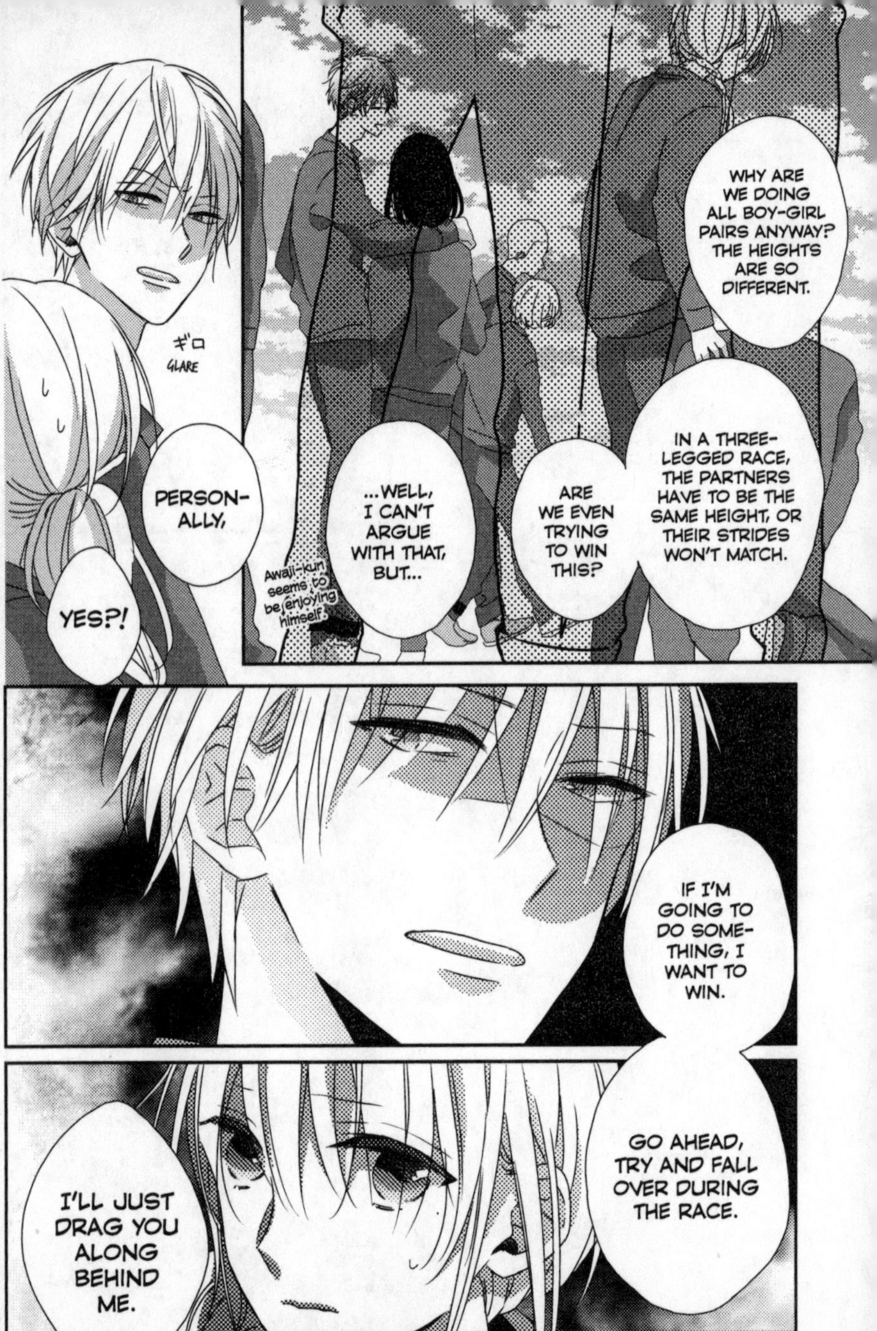
WHY ARE WE DOING ALL BOY-GIRL PAIRS ANYWAY? THE HEIGHTS ARE SO DIFFERENT.
IN A THREE-LEGGED RACE, THE PARTNERS HAVE TO BE THE SAME HEIGHT, OR THEIR STRIDES WON'T MATCH.
ARE WE EVEN TRYING TO WIN THIS?
...WELL, I CAN'T ARGUE WITH THAT, BUT...
Awaji-kun seems to be enjoying himself.
ギロ
GLARE
PERSON-ALLY,
YES?!
IF I'M GOING TO DO SOME-THING, I WANT TO WIN.
GO AHEAD, TRY AND FALL OVER DURING THE RACE.
I'LL JUST DRAG YOU ALONG BEHIND ME.

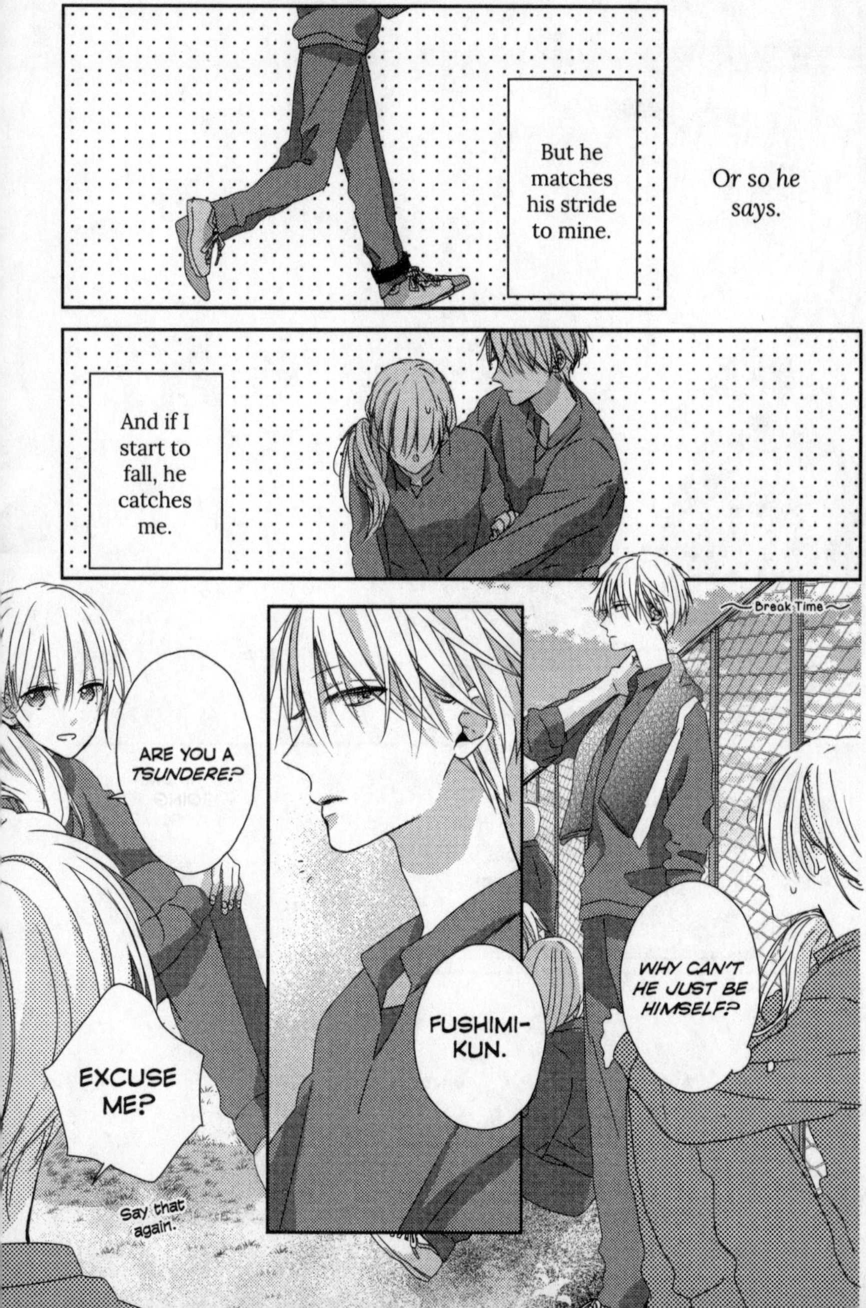
Or so he says.
But he matches his stride to mine.
And if I start to fall, he catches me.
Break Time
WHY CAN'T HE JUST BE HIMSELF?
FUSHIMI-KUN.
ARE YOU A TSUNDERE?
EXCUSE ME?
Say that again.

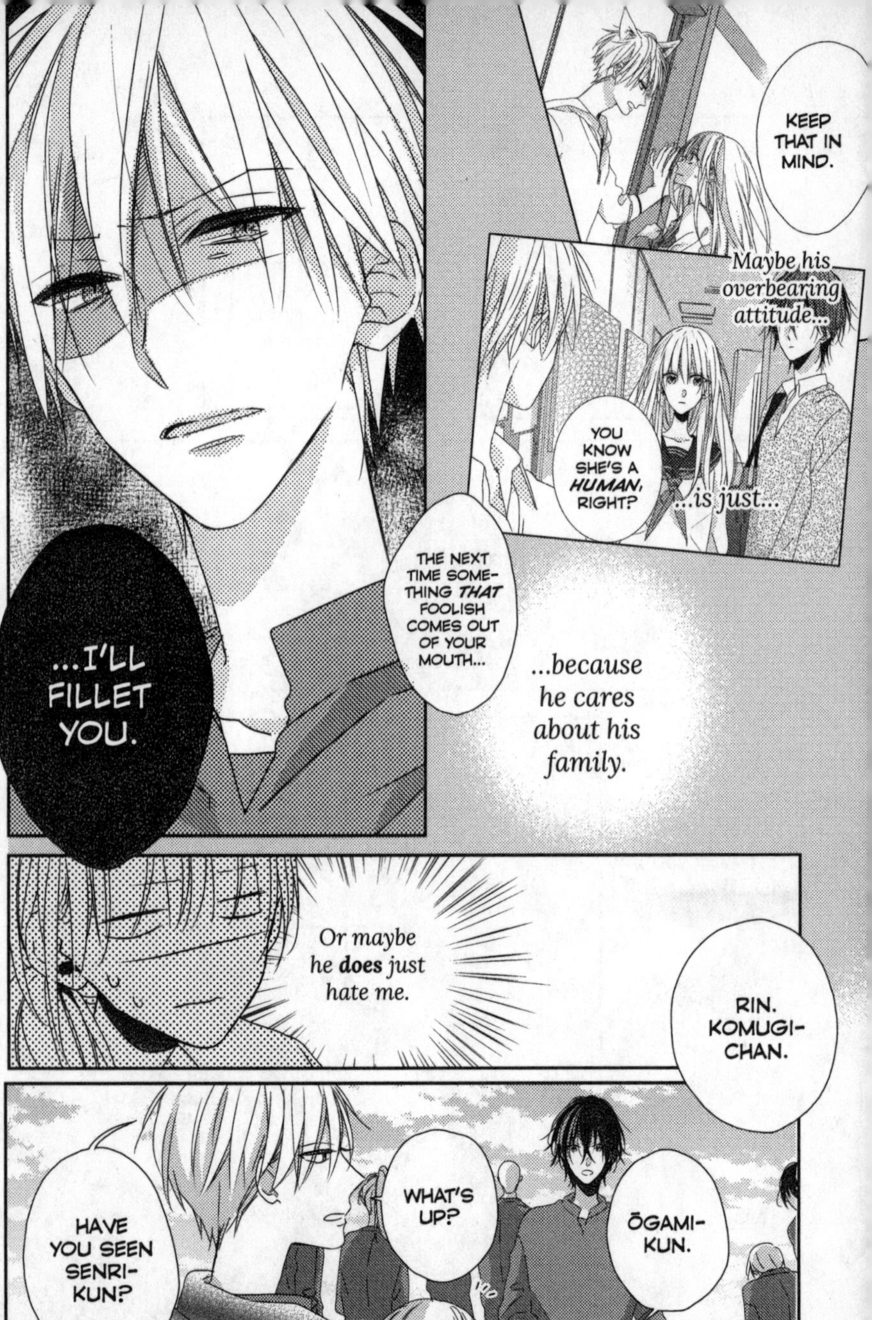
KEEP THAT IN MIND.
Maybe his overbearing attitude...
YOU KNOW SHE'S A *HUMAN*, RIGHT?
...is just...
THE NEXT TIME SOME-THING *THAT* FOOLISH COMES OUT OF YOUR MOUTH...
...I'LL FILLET YOU.
...because he cares about his family.
Or maybe he **does** just hate me.
RIN. KOMUGI-CHAN.
ŌGAMI-KUN.
WHAT'S UP?
HAVE YOU SEEN SENRI-KUN?

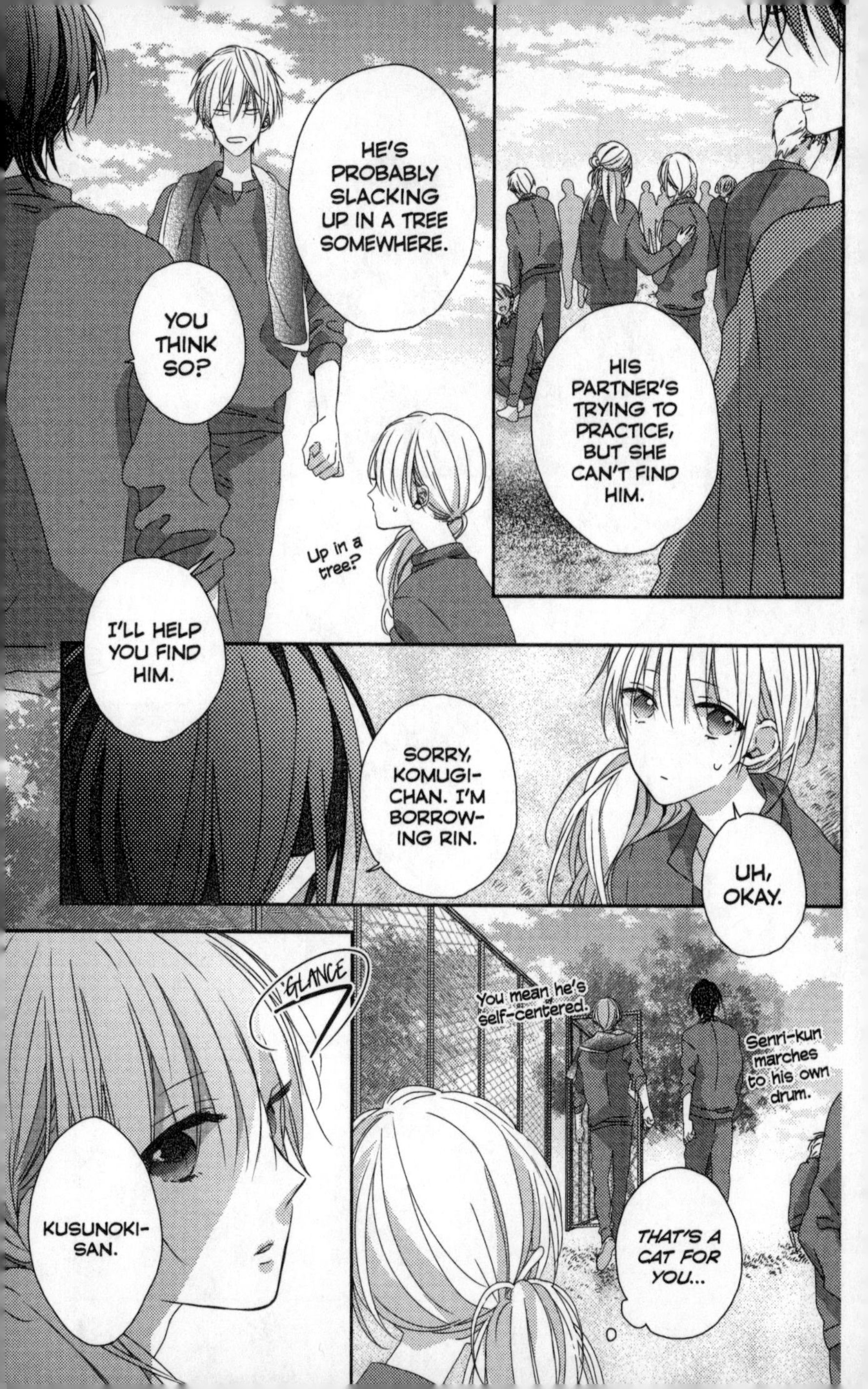
HIS PARTNER'S TRYING TO PRACTICE, BUT SHE CAN'T FIND HIM.
HE'S PROBABLY SLACKING UP IN A TREE SOMEWHERE.
YOU THINK SO?
Up in a tree?
I'LL HELP YOU FIND HIM.
SORRY, KOMUGI-CHAN. I'M BORROWING RIN.
UH, OKAY.
Senri-kun marches to his own drum.
You mean he's self-centered.
THAT'S A CAT FOR YOU...
GLANCE
KUSUNOKI-SAN.

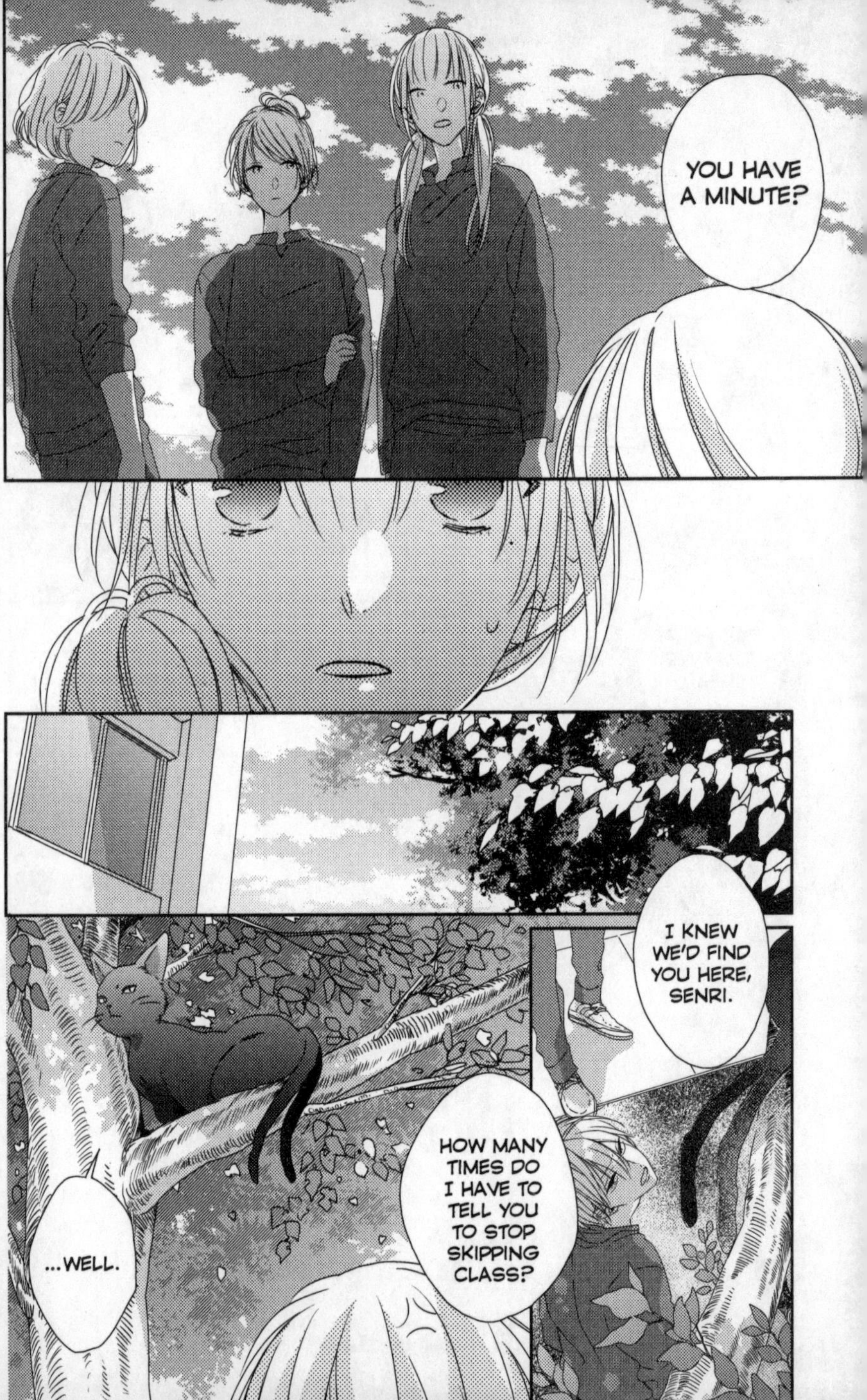
YOU HAVE A MINUTE?
I KNEW WE'D FIND YOU HERE, SENRI.
HOW MANY TIMES DO I HAVE TO TELL YOU TO STOP SKIPPING CLASS?
...WELL.

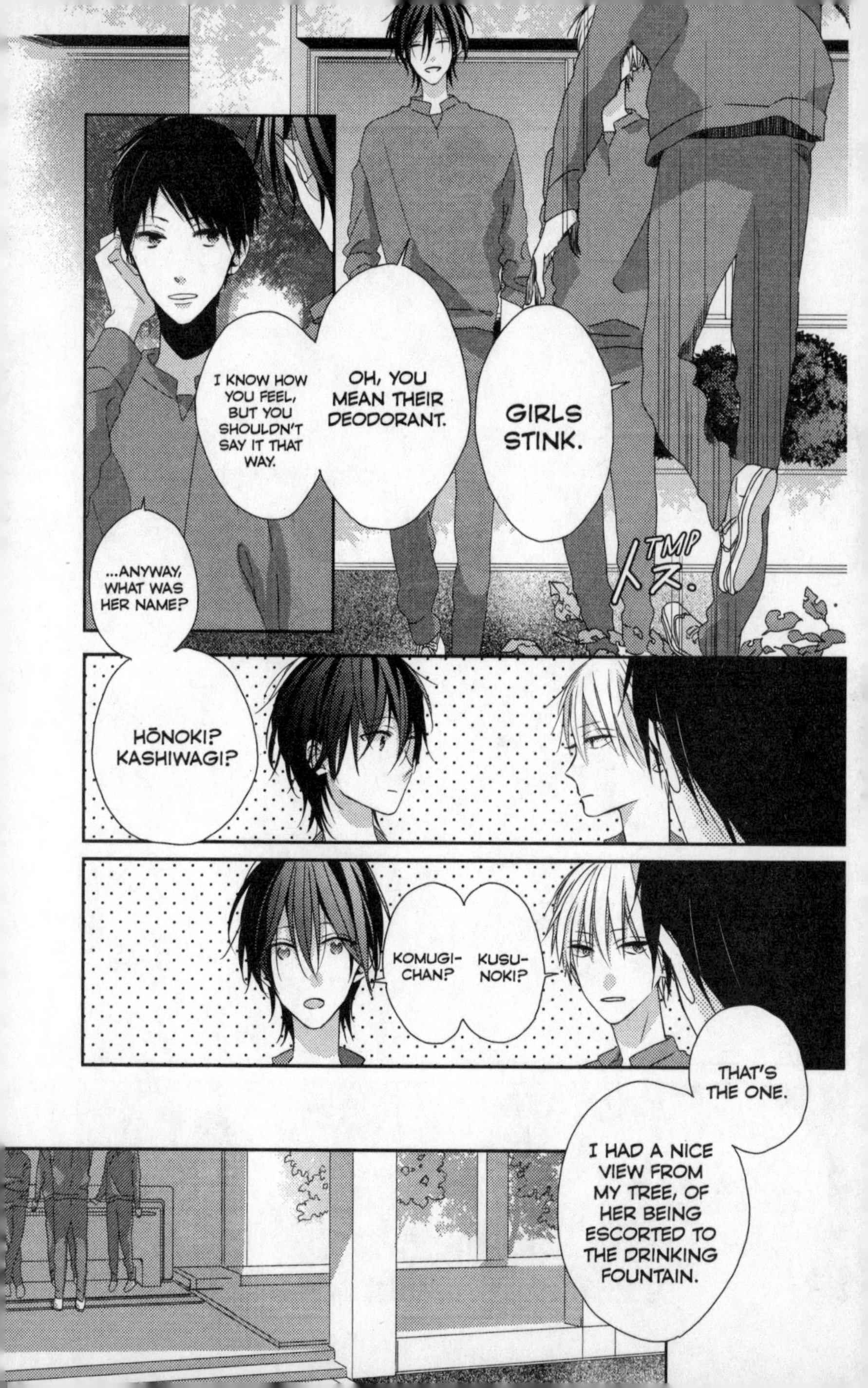
GIRLS STINK.
OH, YOU MEAN THEIR DEODORANT.
TMP
トス。
I KNOW HOW YOU FEEL, BUT YOU SHOULDN'T SAY IT THAT WAY.
...ANYWAY, WHAT WAS HER NAME?
HŌNOKI? KASHIWAGI?
KUSU-NOKI?
KOMUGI-CHAN?
THAT'S THE ONE.
I HAD A NICE VIEW FROM MY TREE, OF HER BEING ESCORTED TO THE DRINKING FOUNTAIN.

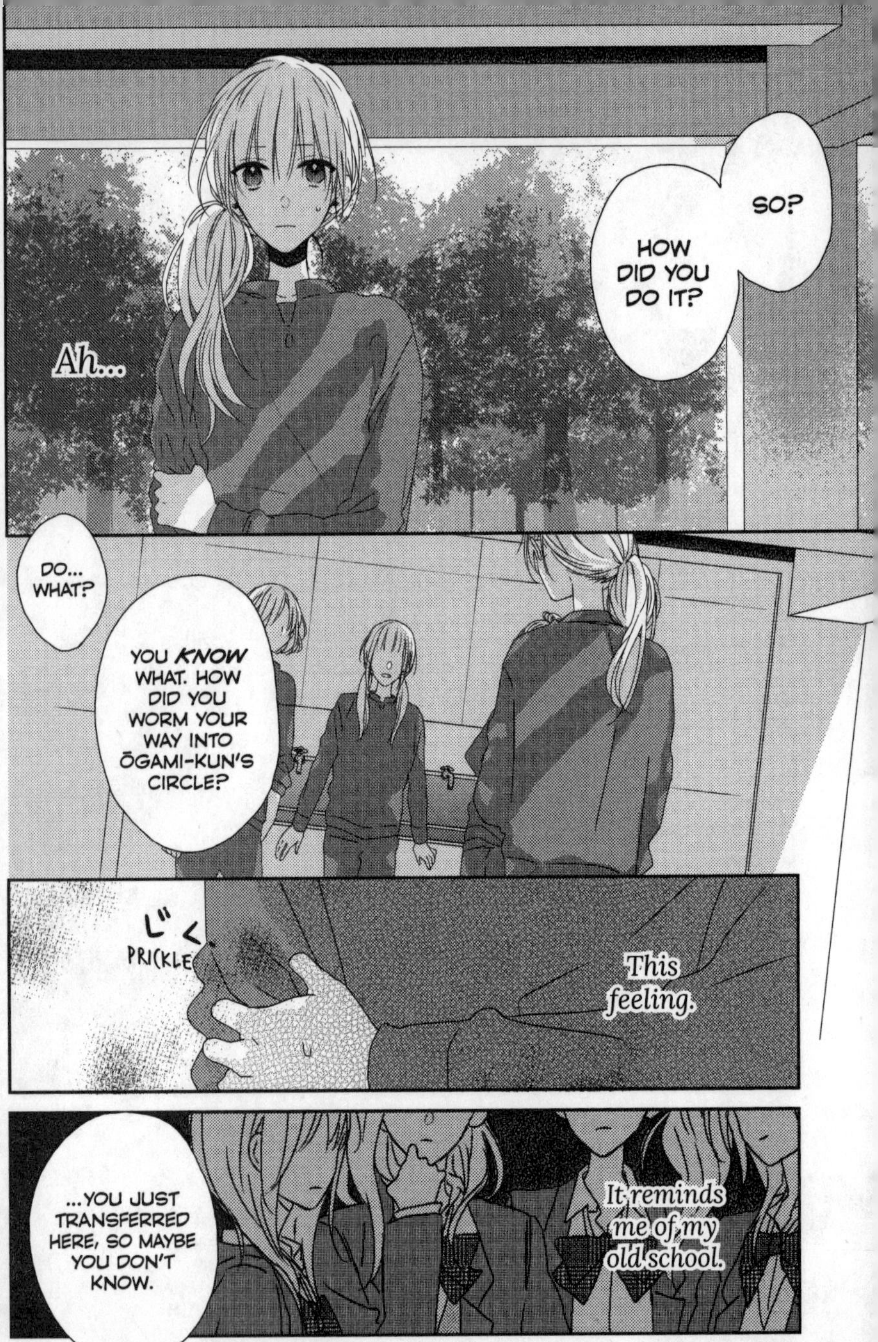
SO?
HOW DID YOU DO IT?
Ah...
DO... WHAT?
YOU KNOW WHAT. HOW DID YOU WORM YOUR WAY INTO ŌGAMI-KUN'S CIRCLE?
じく
PRICKLE
This feeling.
It reminds me of my old school.
...YOU JUST TRANSFERRED HERE, SO MAYBE YOU DON'T KNOW.

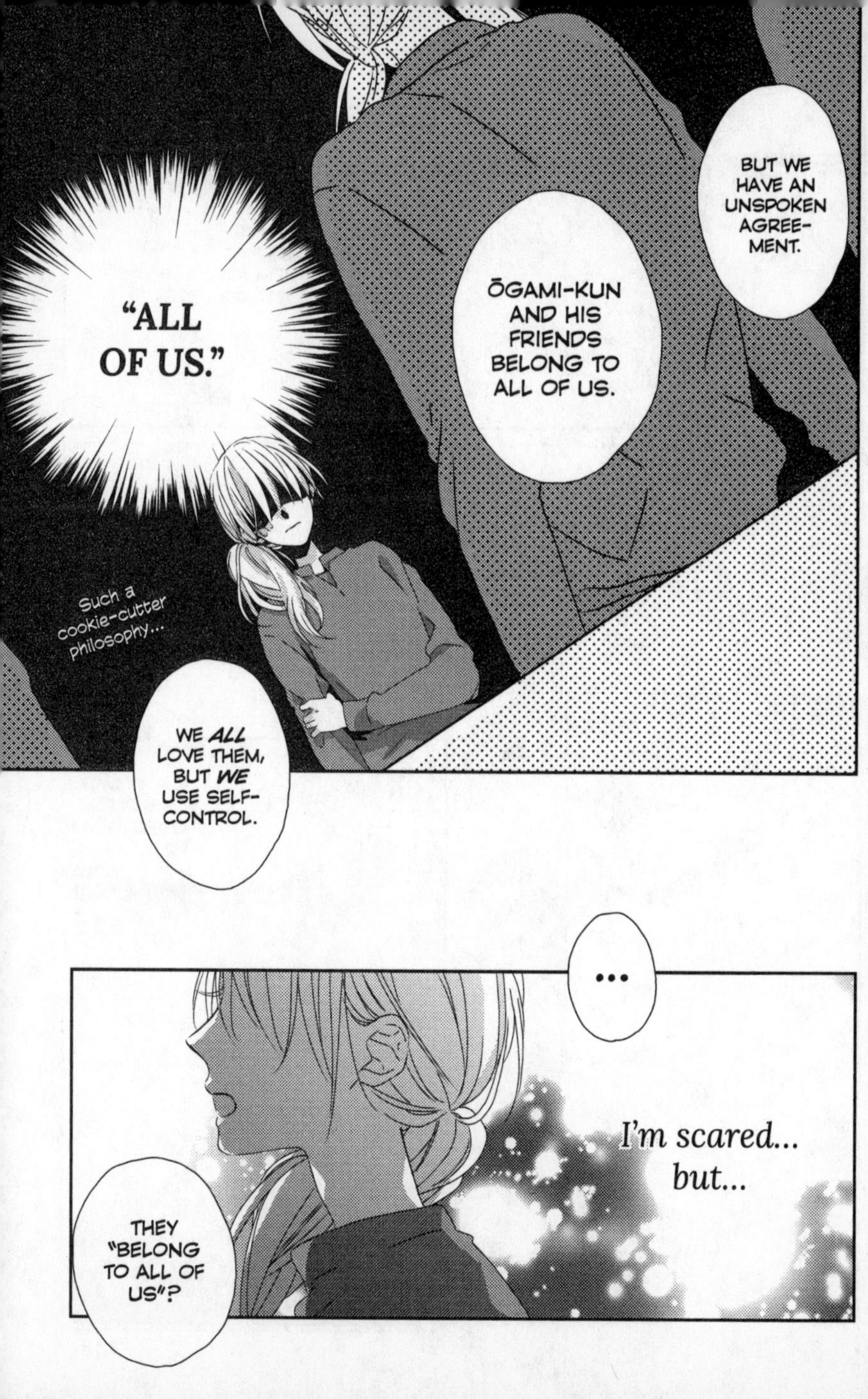
BUT WE HAVE AN UNSPOKEN AGREEMENT.
ŌGAMI-KUN AND HIS FRIENDS BELONG TO ALL OF US.
"ALL OF US."
Such a cookie-cutter philosophy...
WE *ALL* LOVE THEM, BUT *WE* USE SELF-CONTROL.
...
I'm scared... but...
THEY "BELONG TO ALL OF US"?

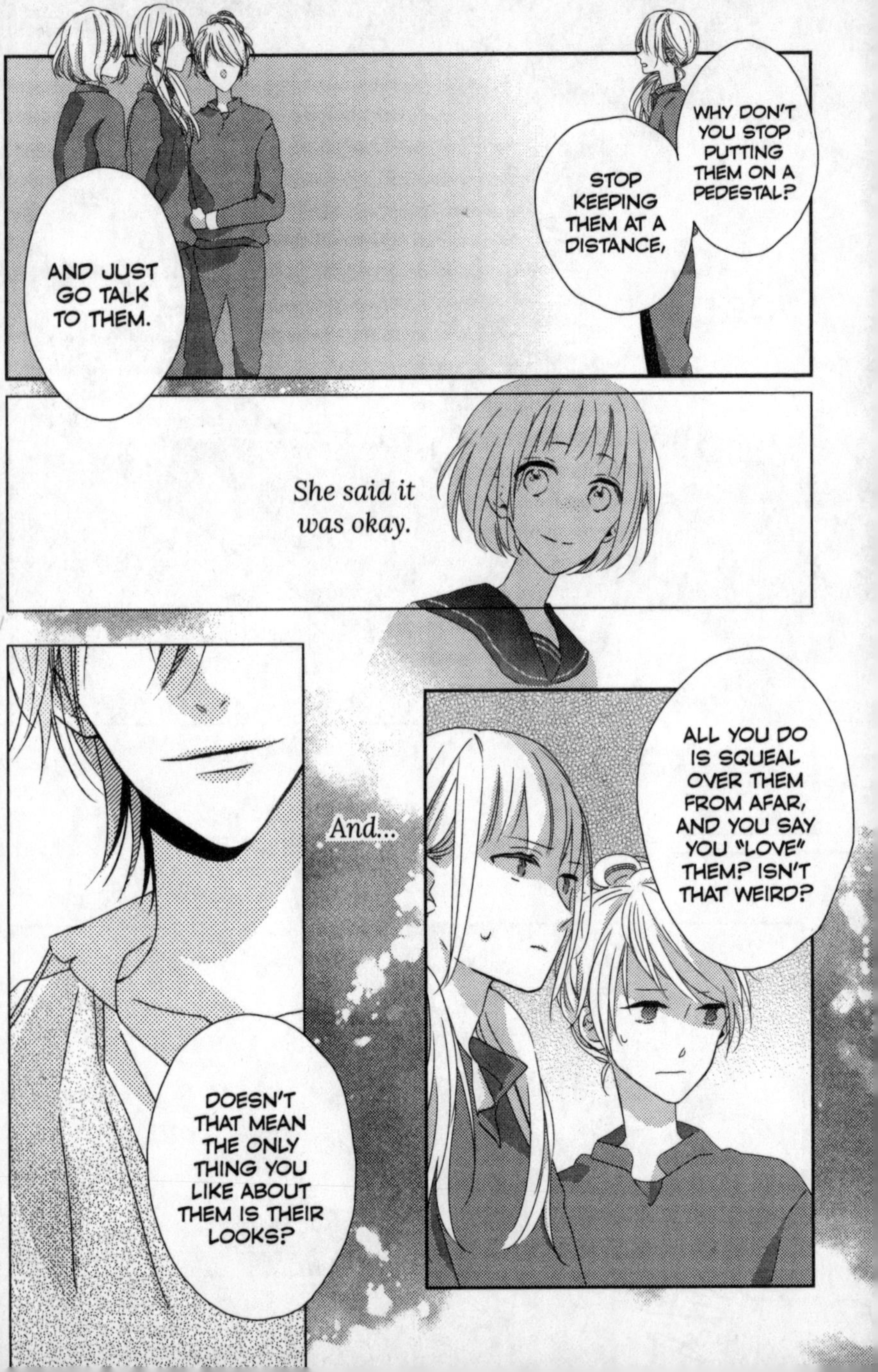
WHY DON'T YOU STOP PUTTING THEM ON A PEDESTAL?
STOP KEEPING THEM AT A DISTANCE,
AND JUST GO TALK TO THEM.
She said it was okay.
ALL YOU DO IS SQUEAL OVER THEM FROM AFAR, AND YOU SAY YOU "LOVE" THEM? ISN'T THAT WEIRD?
And...
DOESN'T THAT MEAN THE ONLY THING YOU LIKE ABOUT THEM IS THEIR LOOKS?

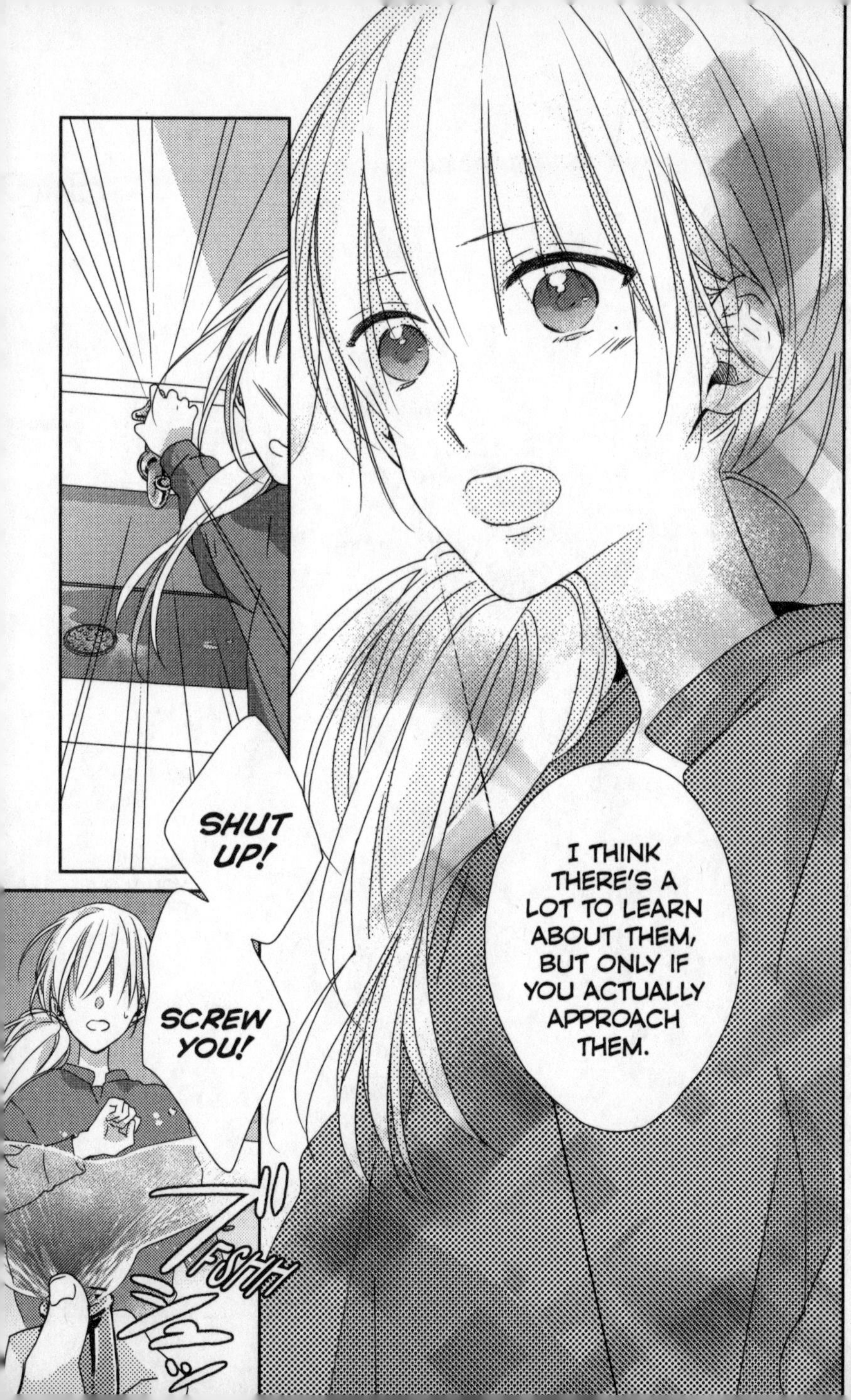
I THINK THERE'S A LOT TO LEARN ABOUT THEM, BUT ONLY IF YOU ACTUALLY APPROACH THEM.
SHUT UP!
SCREW YOU!
FSHH

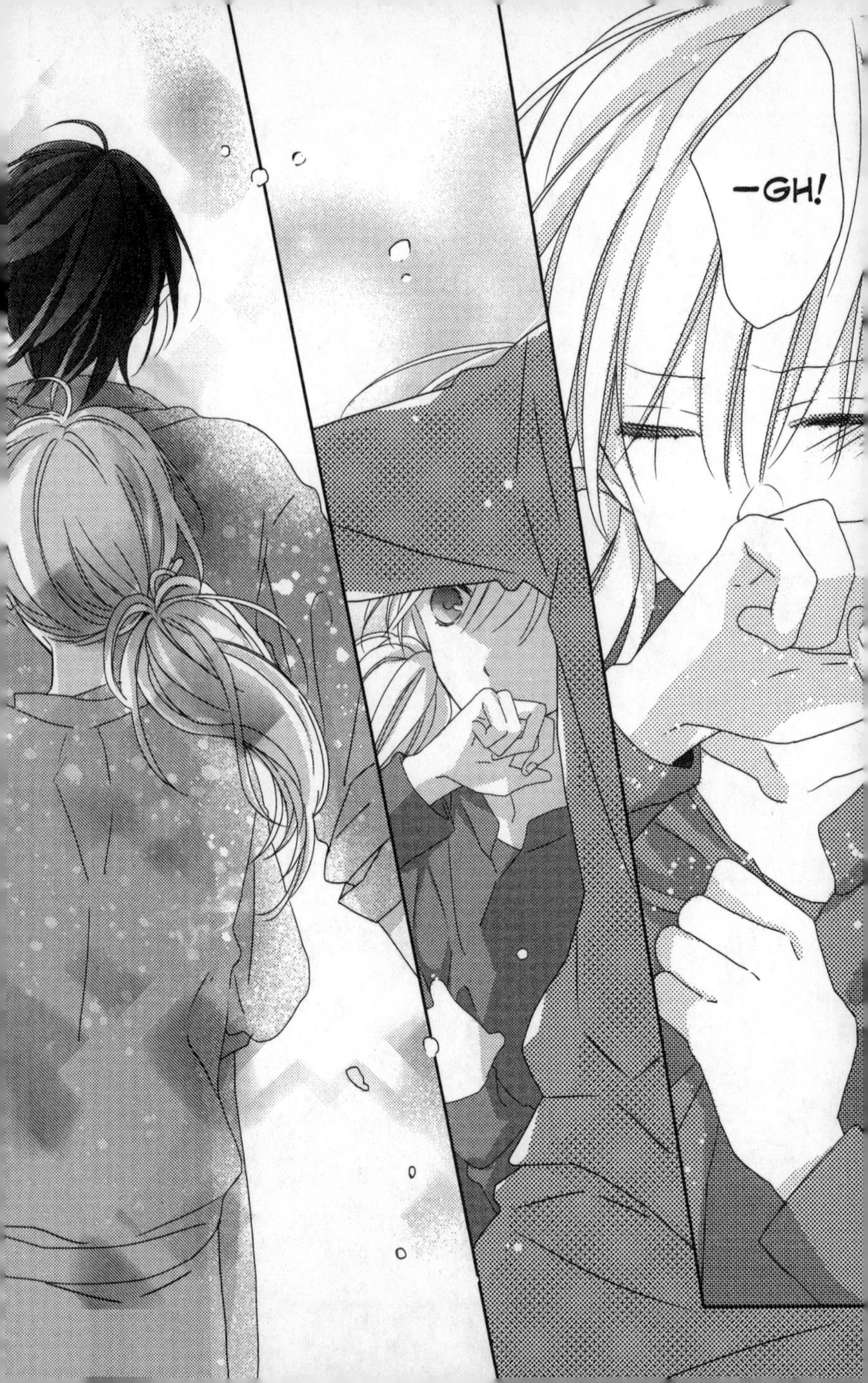
—GH!

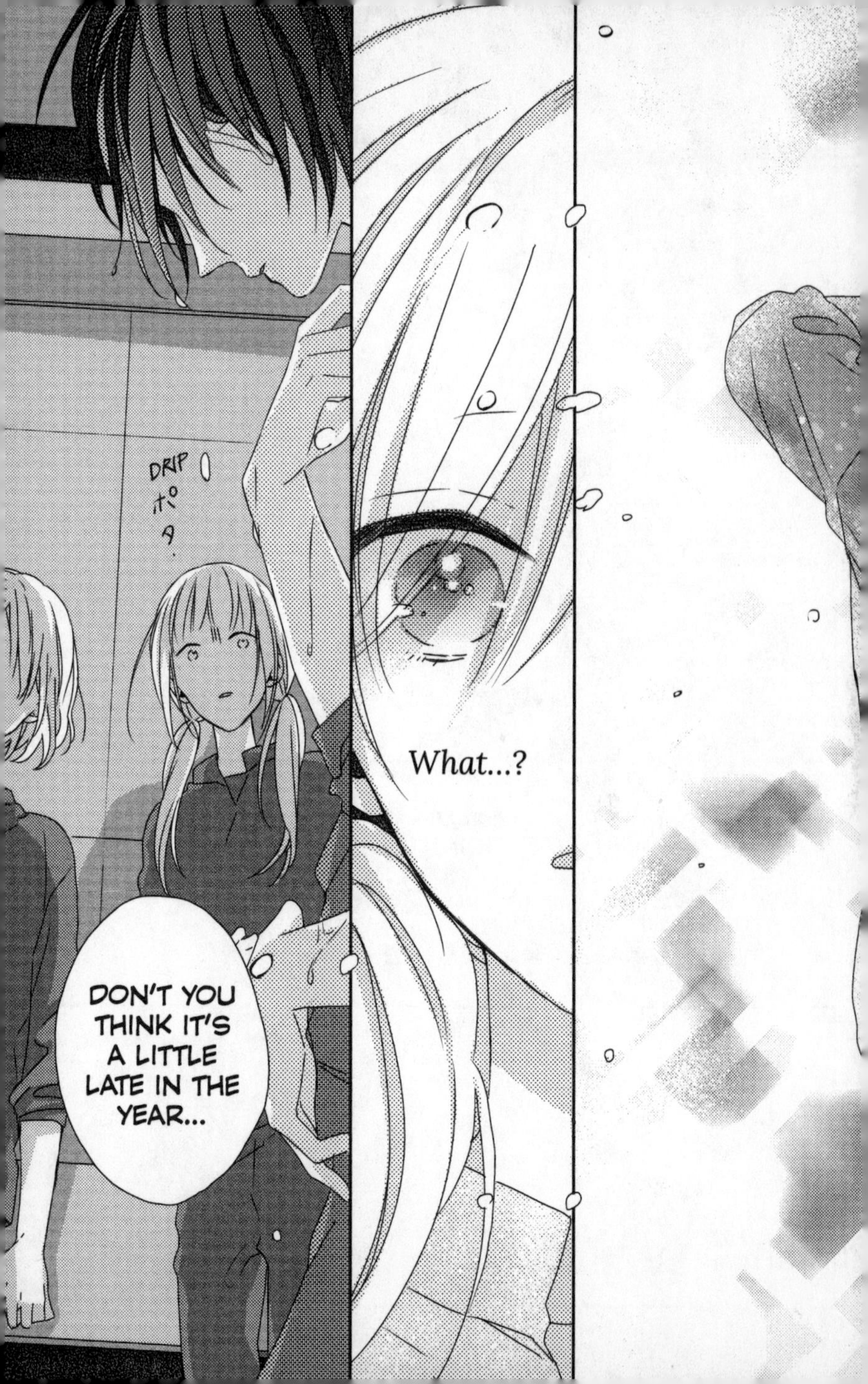
What...?
DRIP
ポタ
DON'T YOU THINK IT'S A LITTLE LATE IN THE YEAR...

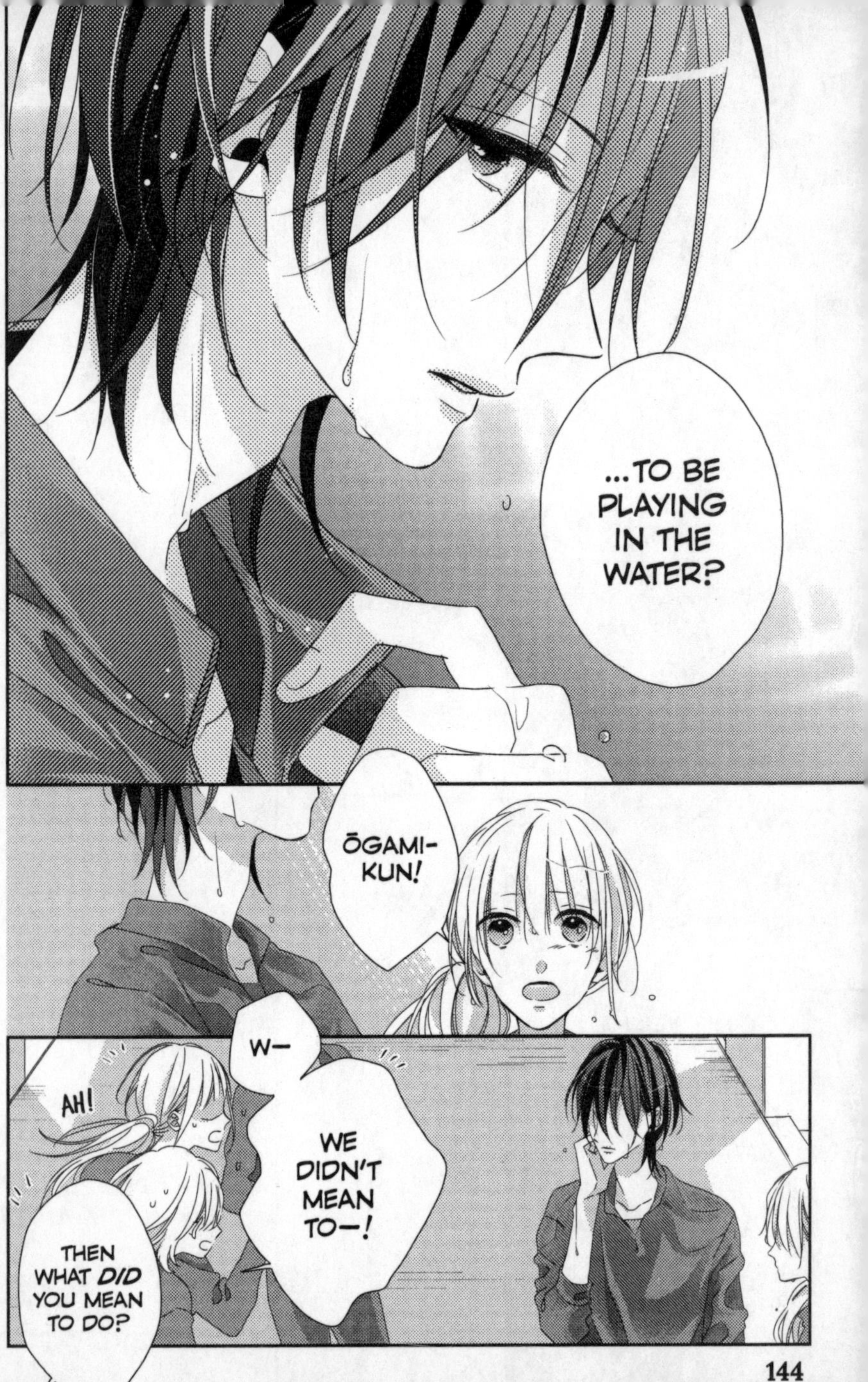
...TO BE PLAYING IN THE WATER?
ŌGAMI-KUN!
W—
AH!
WE DIDN'T MEAN TO—!
THEN WHAT *DID* YOU MEAN TO DO?

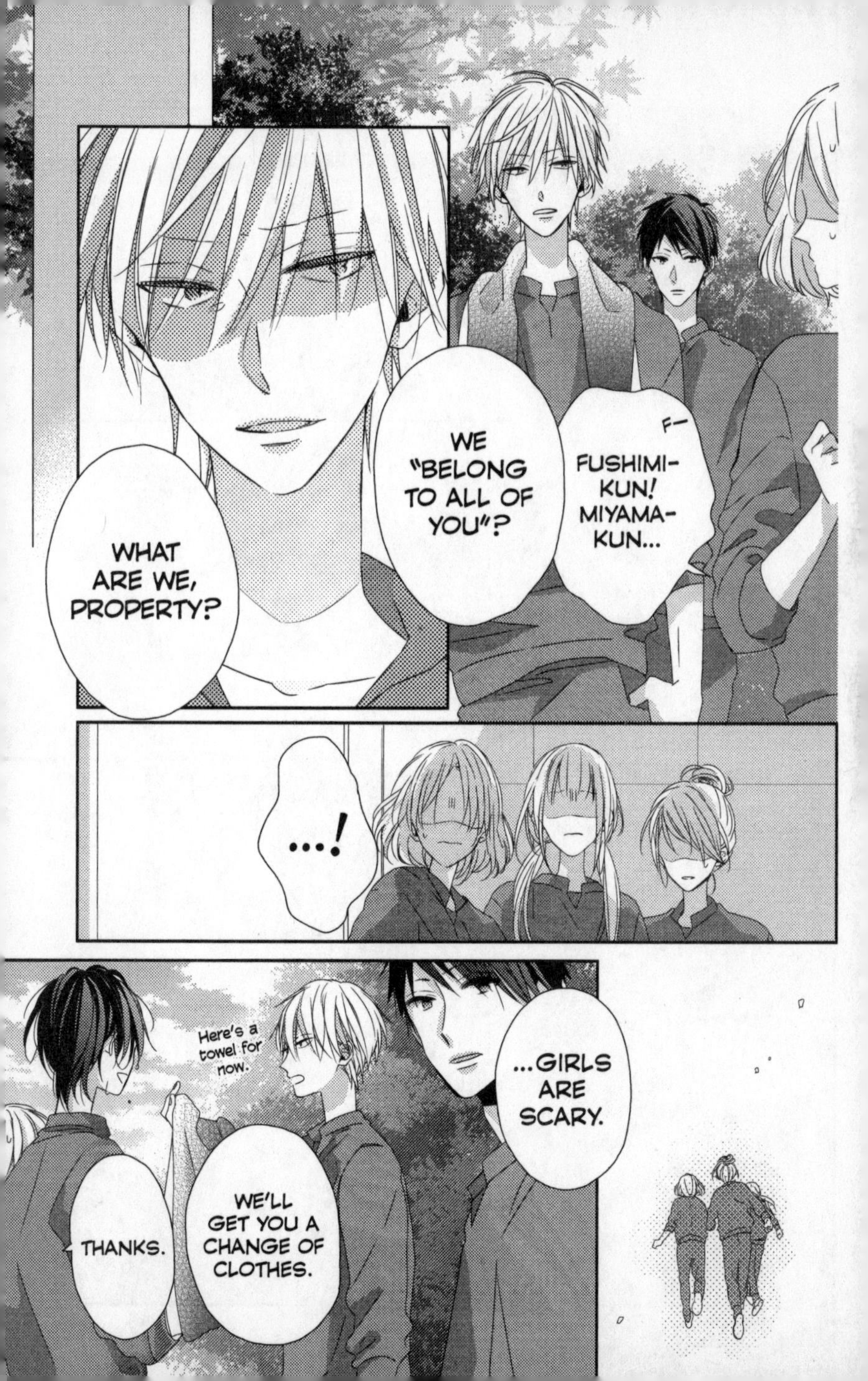
F— FUSHIMI-KUN! MIYAMA-KUN...
WE "BELONG TO ALL OF YOU"?
WHAT ARE WE, PROPERTY?
...!
...GIRLS ARE SCARY.
Here's a towel for now.
WE'LL GET YOU A CHANGE OF CLOTHES.
THANKS.

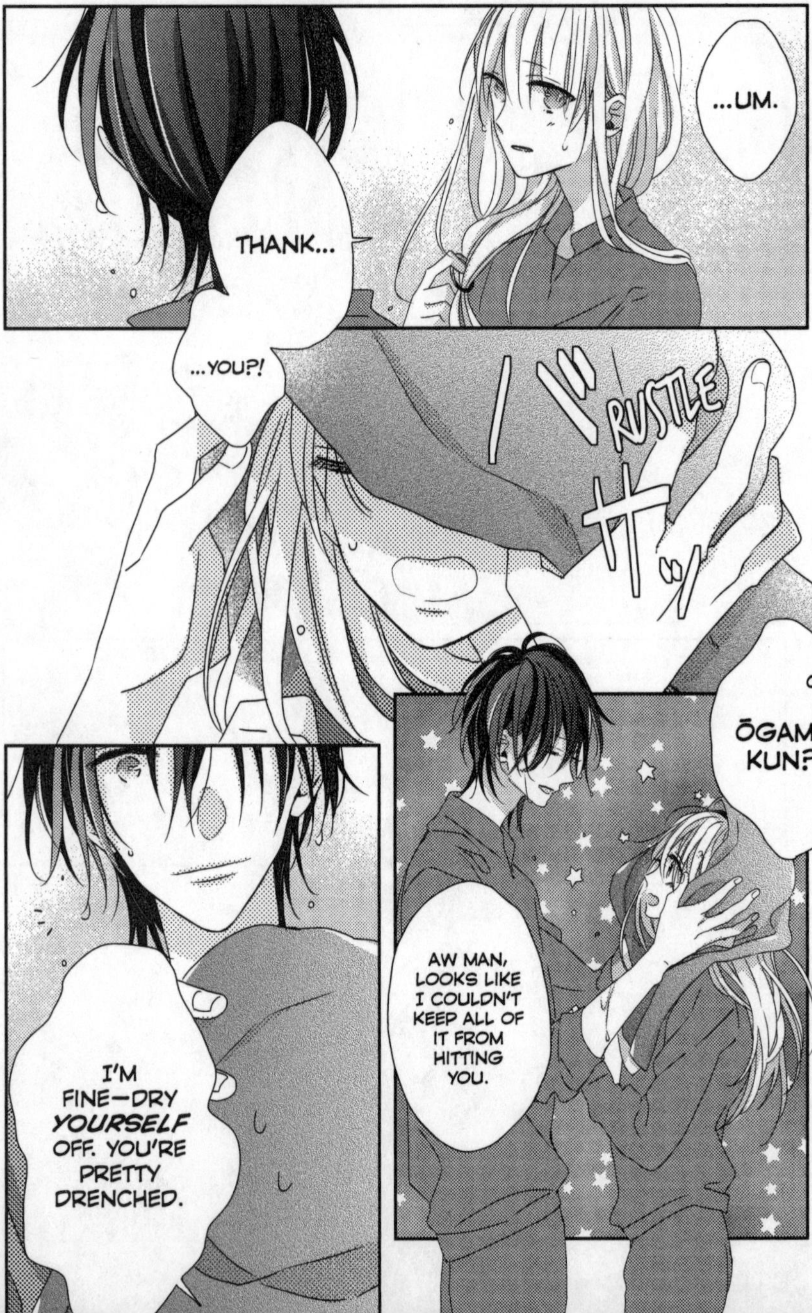
...UM.
THANK...
...YOU?!
RUSTLE
O-
ŌGAMI-KUN?!
AW MAN, LOOKS LIKE I COULDN'T KEEP ALL OF IT FROM HITTING YOU.
I'M FINE—DRY ***YOURSELF*** OFF. YOU'RE PRETTY DRENCHED.

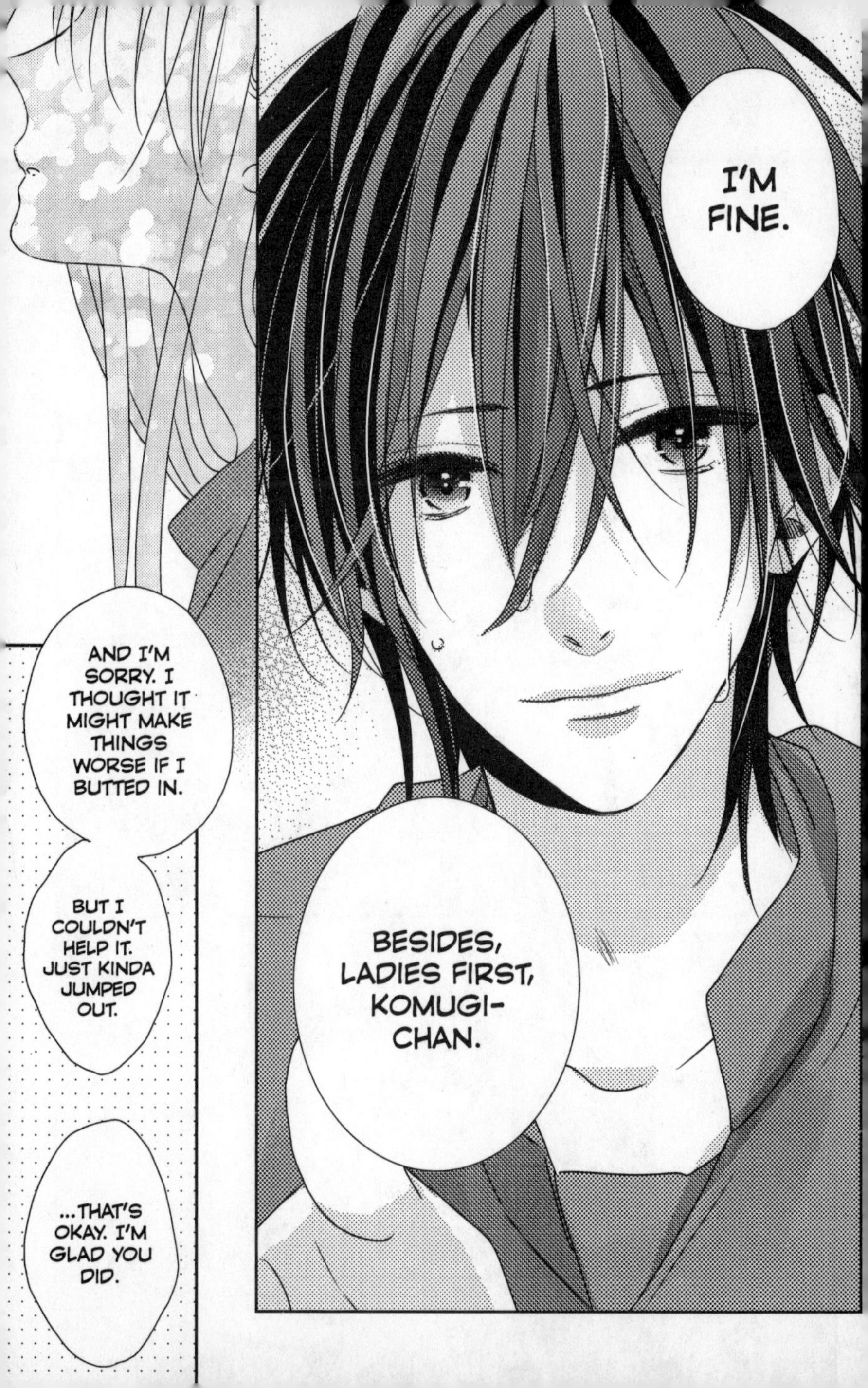
I'M FINE.
BESIDES, LADIES FIRST, KOMUGI-CHAN.
AND I'M SORRY. I THOUGHT IT MIGHT MAKE THINGS WORSE IF I BUTTED IN.
BUT I COULDN'T HELP IT. JUST KINDA JUMPED OUT.
...THAT'S OKAY. I'M GLAD YOU DID.

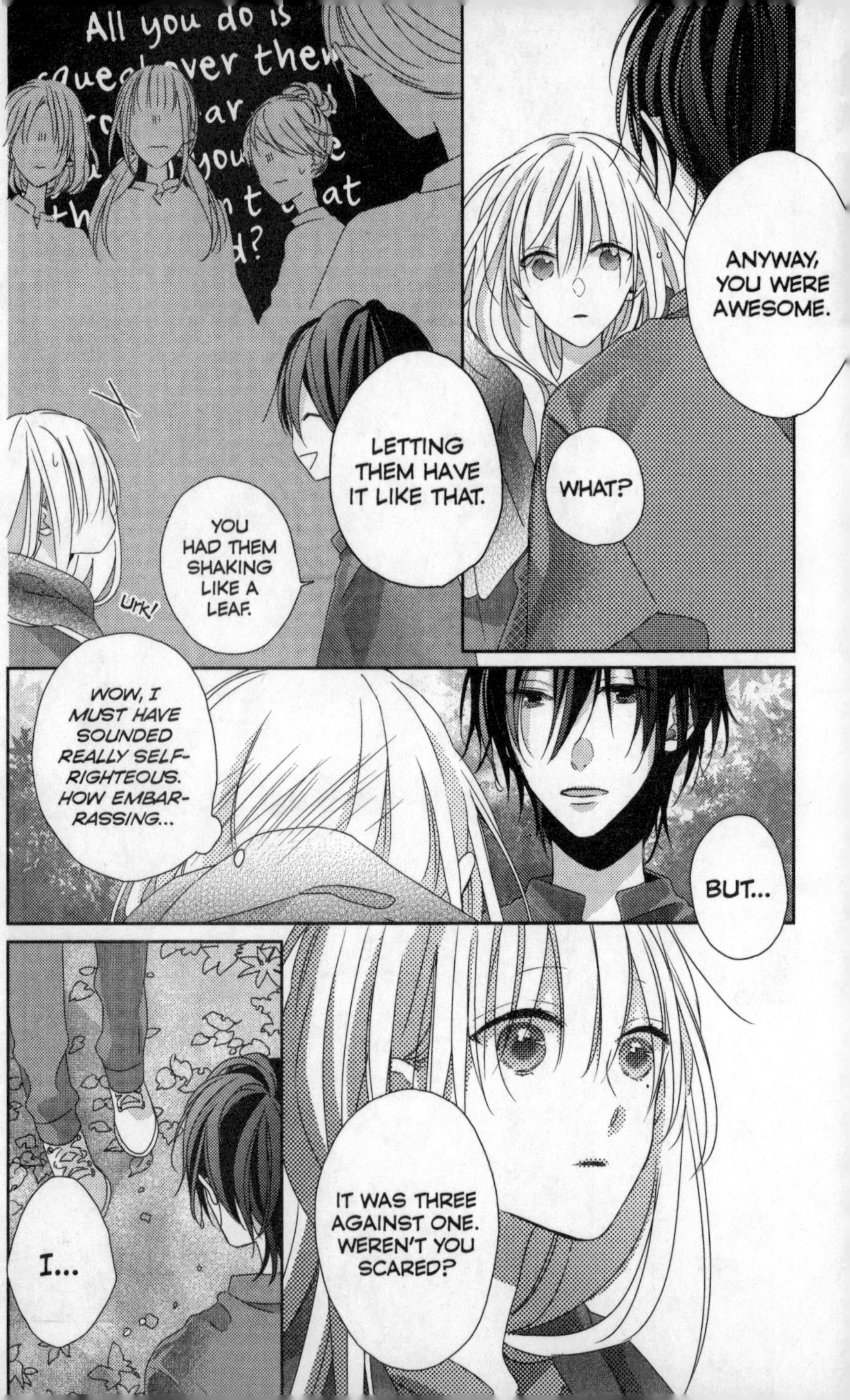
ANYWAY, YOU WERE AWESOME.
WHAT?
All you do is
LETTING THEM HAVE IT LIKE THAT.
YOU HAD THEM SHAKING LIKE A LEAF.
Urk!
WOW, I MUST HAVE SOUNDED REALLY SELF-RIGHTEOUS. HOW EMBARRASSING...
BUT...
IT WAS THREE AGAINST ONE. WEREN'T YOU SCARED?
I...

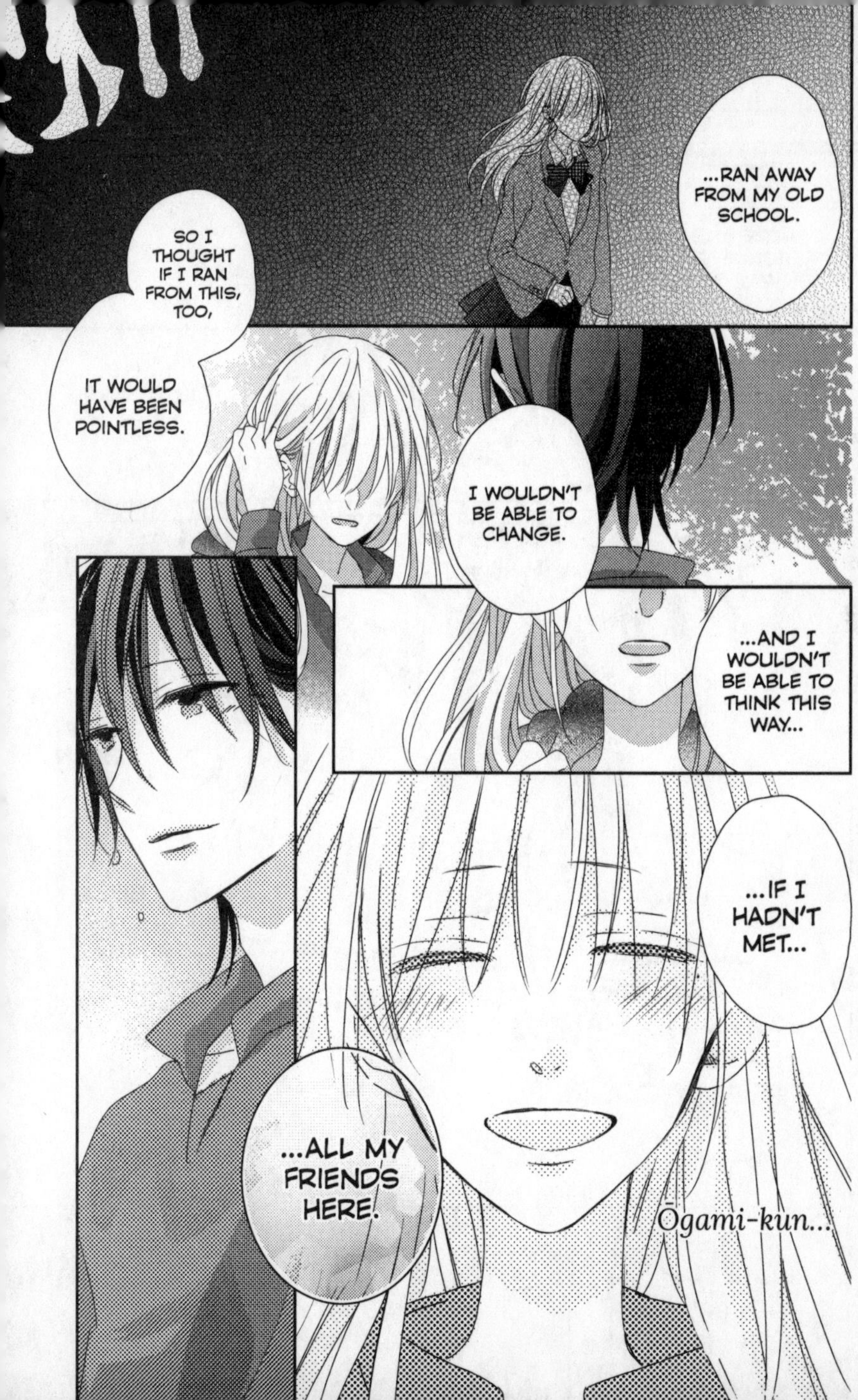
...RAN AWAY FROM MY OLD SCHOOL.
SO I THOUGHT IF I RAN FROM THIS, TOO,
IT WOULD HAVE BEEN POINTLESS.
I WOULDN'T BE ABLE TO CHANGE.
...AND I WOULDN'T BE ABLE TO THINK THIS WAY...
...IF I HADN'T MET...
...ALL MY FRIENDS HERE.
Ōgami-kun...

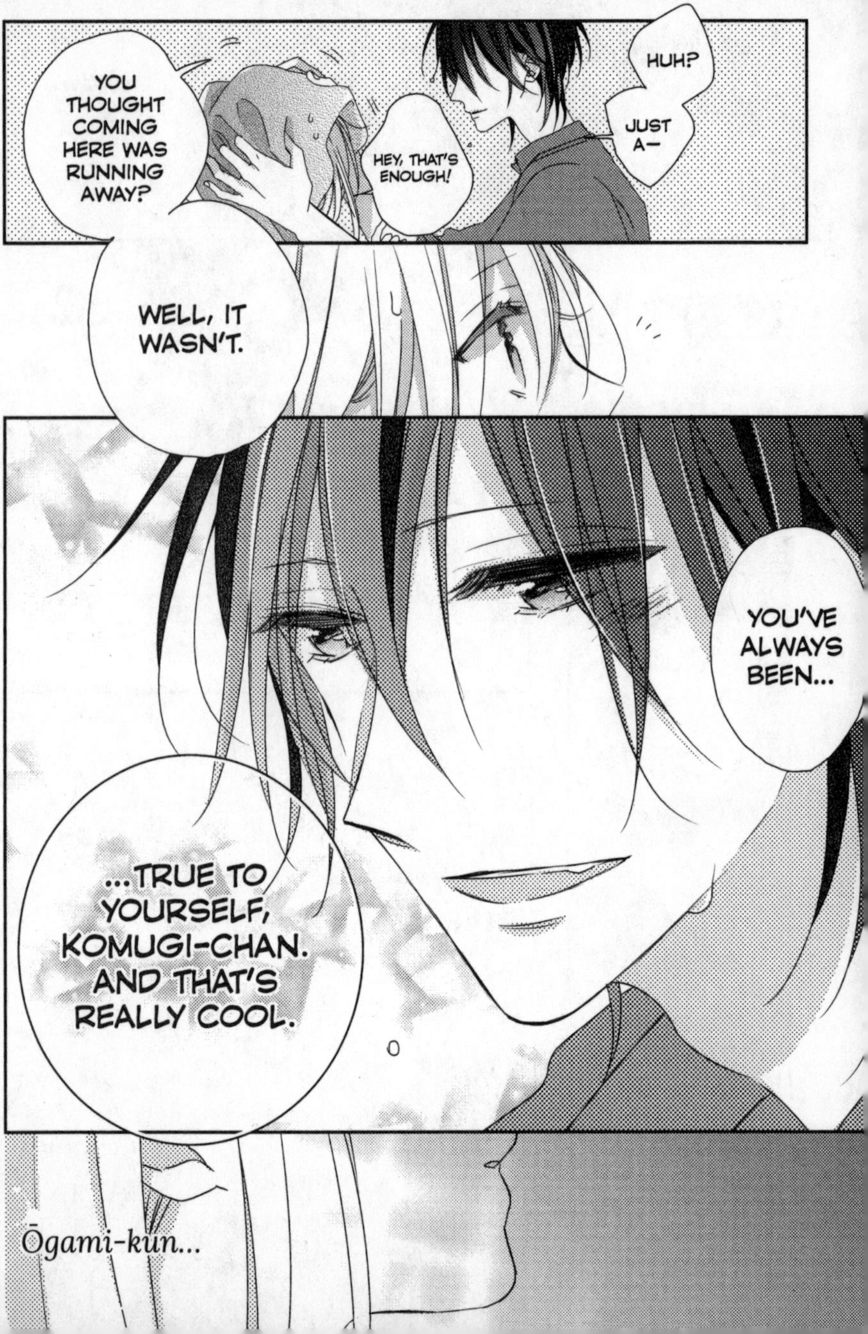
HUH?
JUST A—
HEY, THAT'S ENOUGH!
YOU THOUGHT COMING HERE WAS RUNNING AWAY?
WELL, IT WASN'T.
YOU'VE ALWAYS BEEN...
...TRUE TO YOURSELF, KOMUGI-CHAN. AND THAT'S REALLY COOL.
Ōgami-kun...

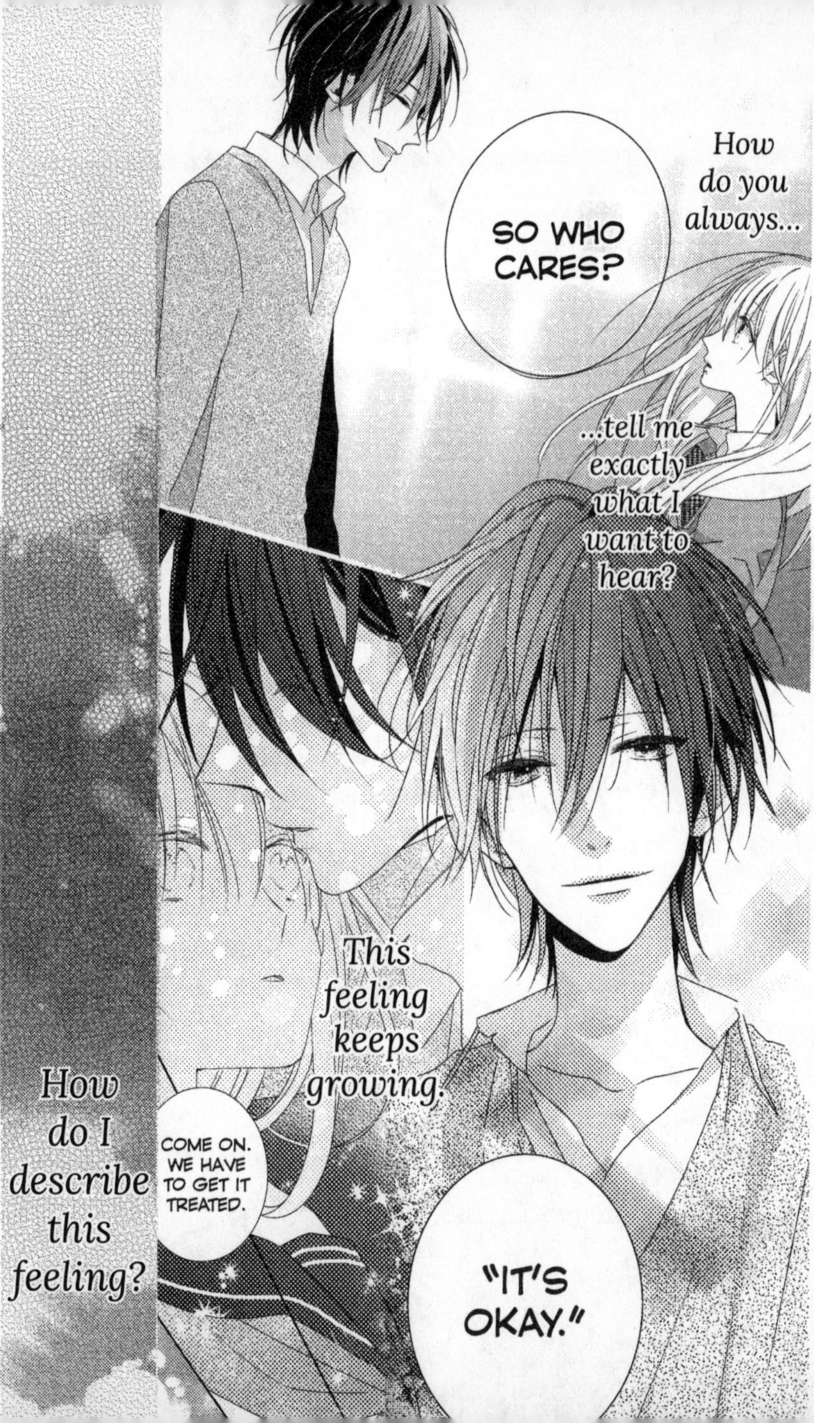
How do you always...
SO WHO CARES?
...tell me exactly what I want to hear?
This feeling keeps growing.
"IT'S OKAY."
COME ON. WE HAVE TO GET IT TREATED.
How do I describe this feeling?

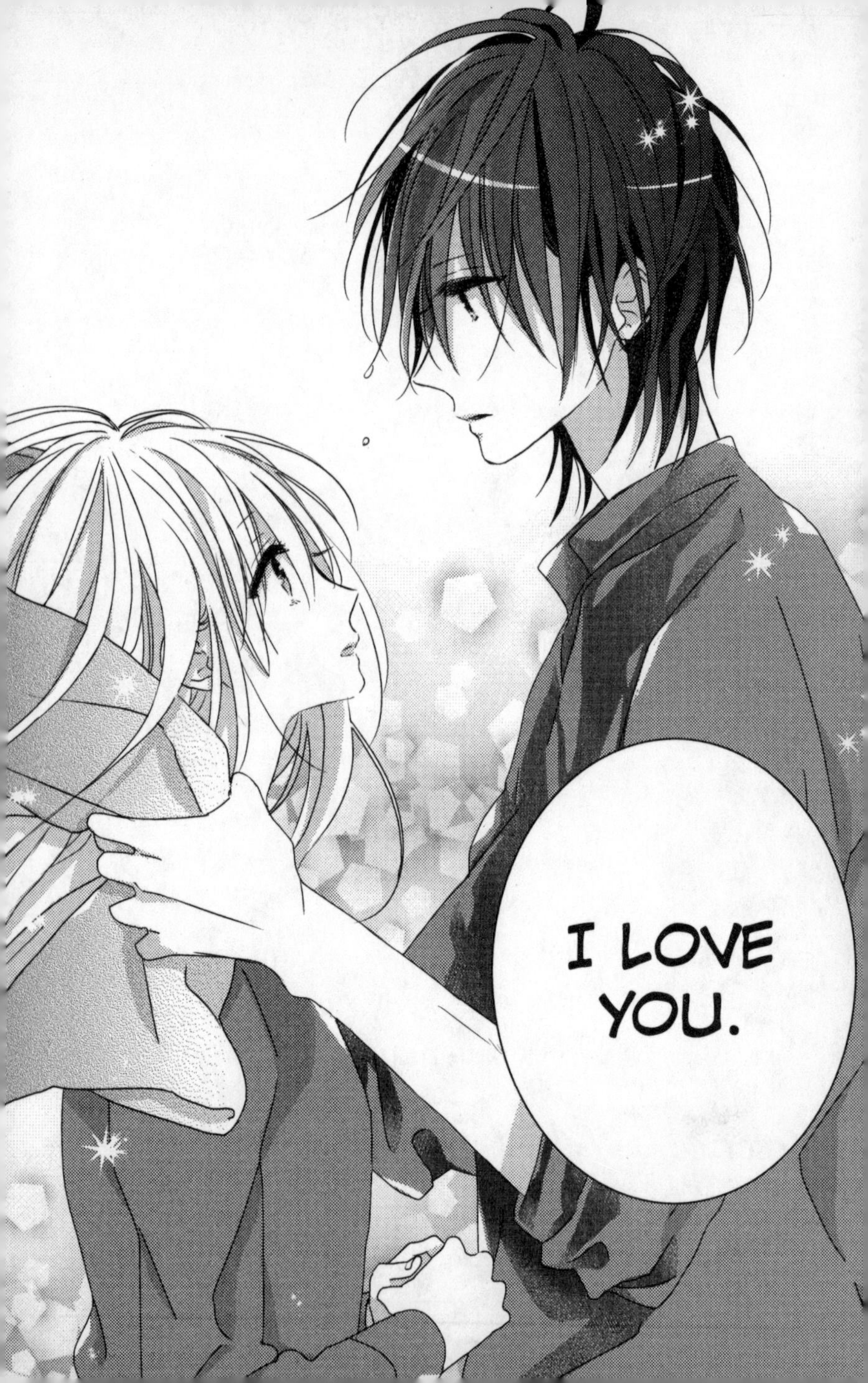
I LOVE YOU.

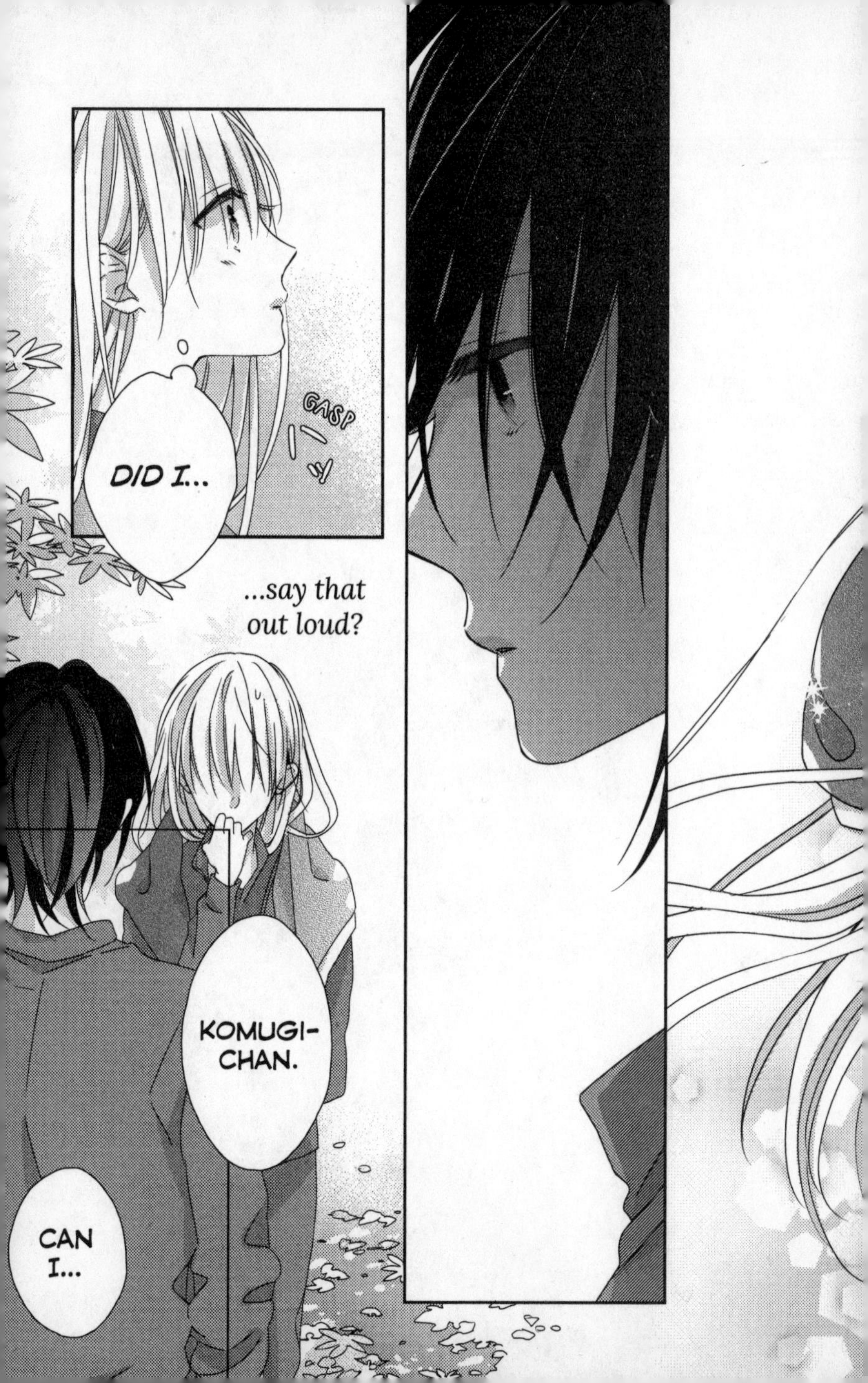
GASP
DID I...
...say that out loud?
KOMUGI-CHAN.
CAN I...

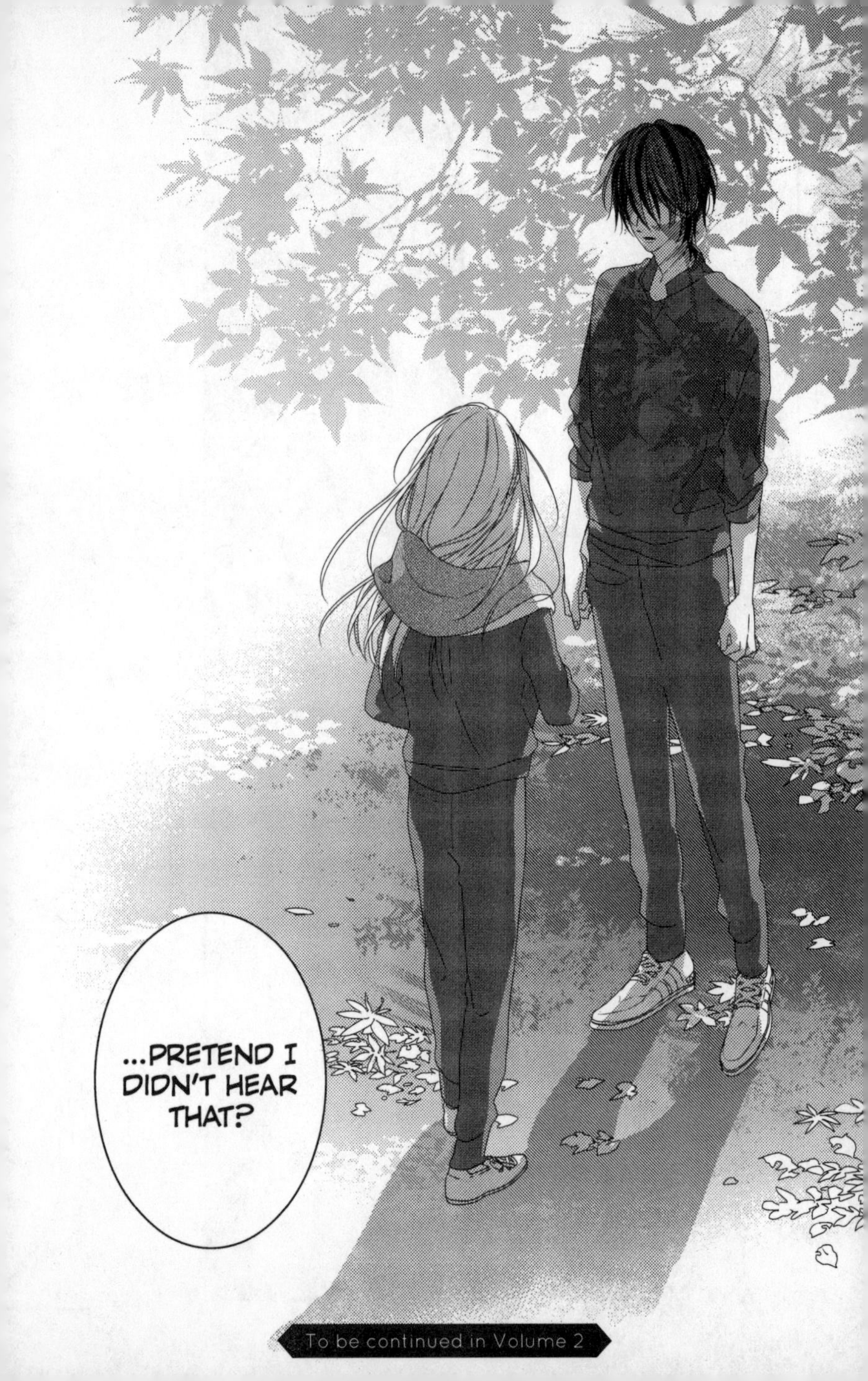
...PRETEND I DIDN'T HEAR THAT?
To be continued in Volume 2

That Wolf-Boy is Mine!

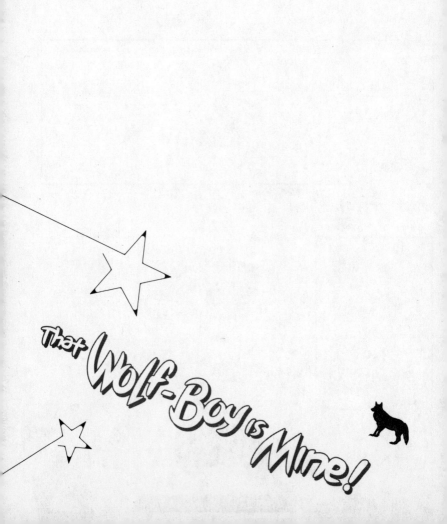

That Wolf-Boy is Mine! Volume 1 Bonus Pages

At Ōgami-kun and his friends' temporary residence,

Ayashi Inn,

Kita-san the kita-kitsune* (cop-out name)...

*Japanese for Red fox

...is the live-in maid.

(Cleaning the Bath)

SQUIK
SQUIK

But when there's no school, the boys take turns doing the chores.

	Meals	Cleaning	Laundry	Of
First Sunday	Yū	Aoshi	Rin	S
Second	Senri	Yū	Aoshi	R
Third	Rin	Senri	Yū	A
		Senri	Yū	

FLIP

HEY, HEY.

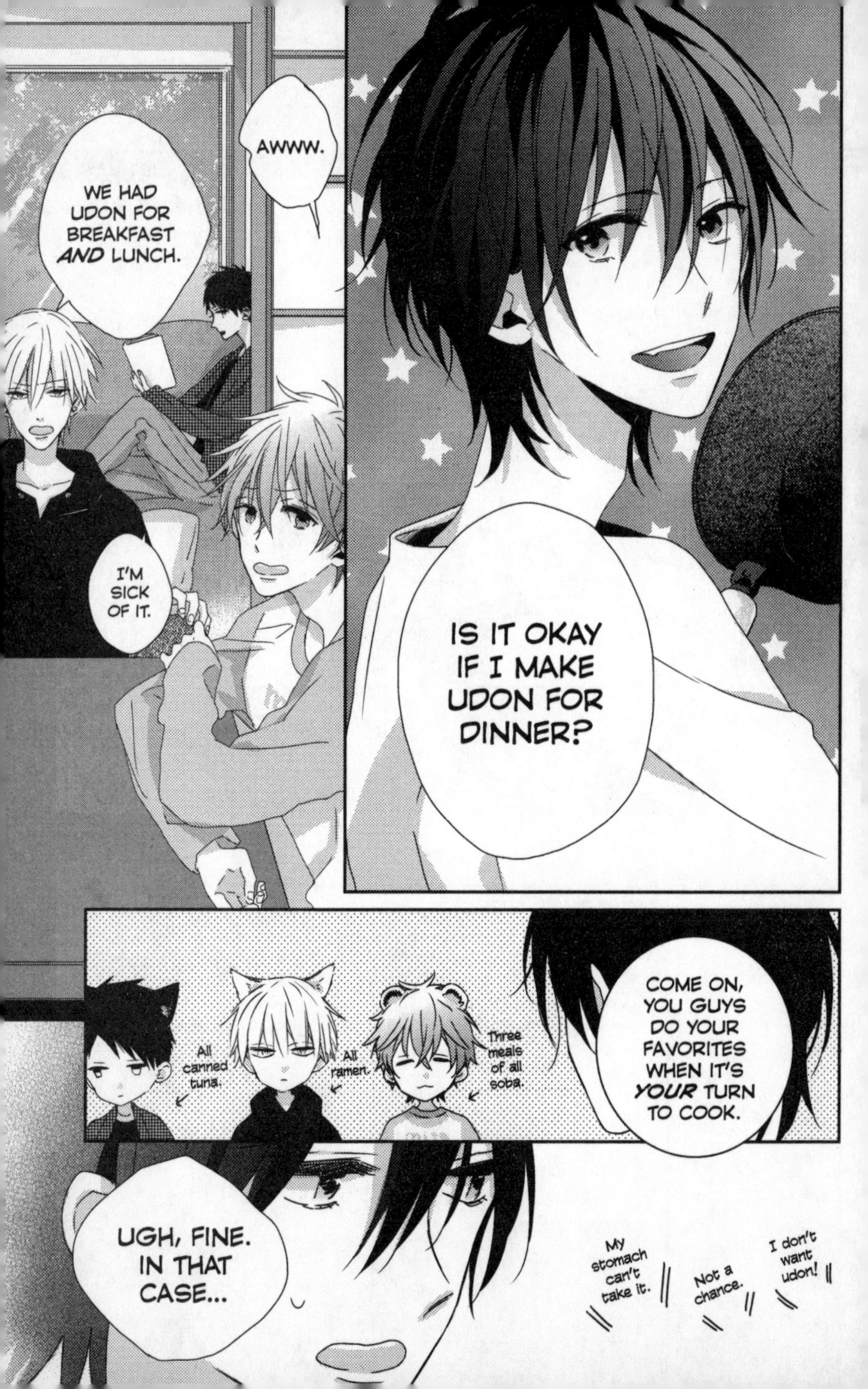
IS IT OKAY IF I MAKE UDON FOR DINNER?
AWWW.
WE HAD UDON FOR BREAKFAST *AND* LUNCH.
I'M SICK OF IT.
COME ON, YOU GUYS DO YOUR FAVORITES WHEN IT'S *YOUR* TURN TO COOK.
Three meals of all soba.
All ramen.
All canned tuna.
I don't want udon!
Not a chance.
My stomach can't take it.
UGH, FINE. IN THAT CASE...

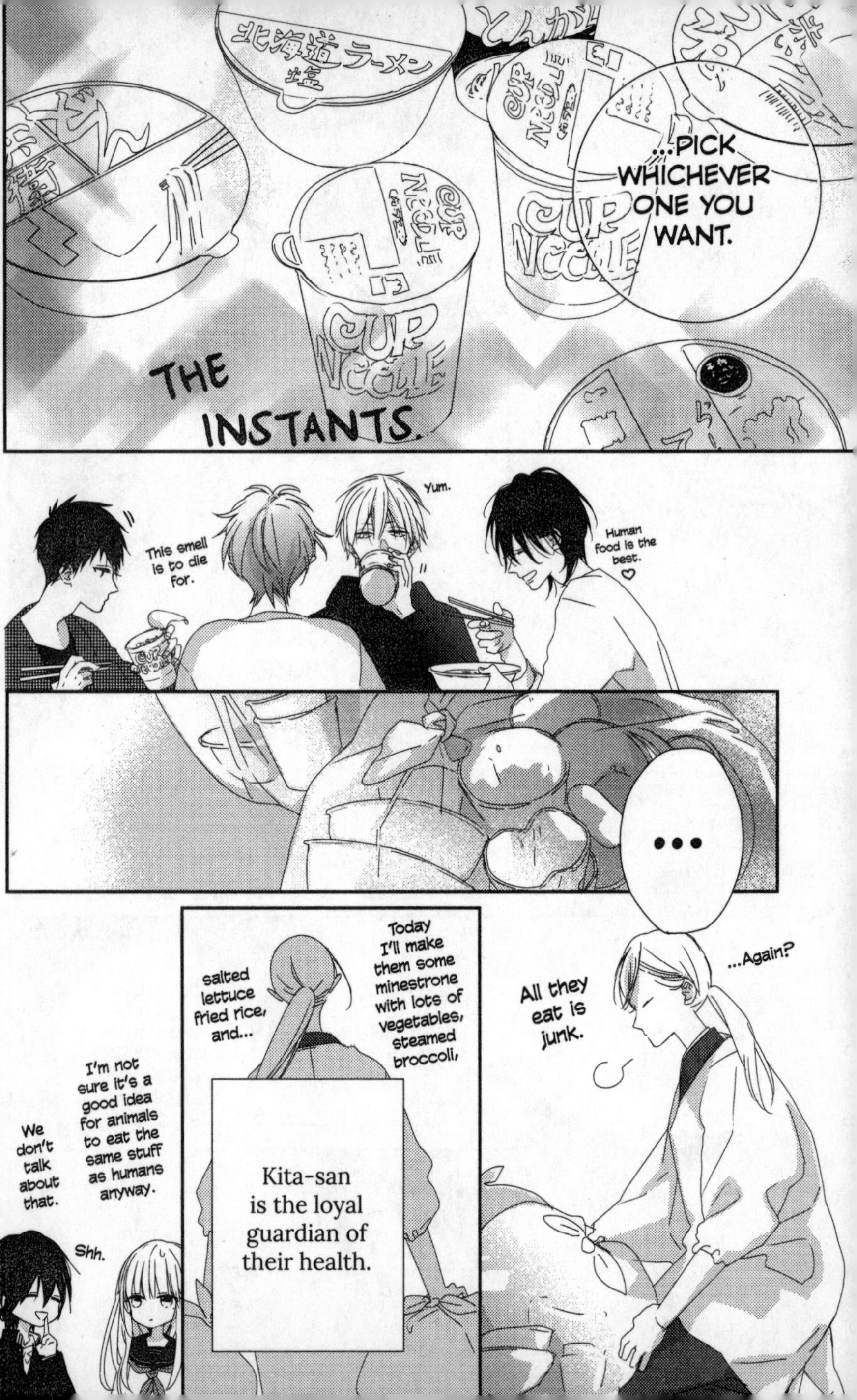
北海道ラーメン
塩
...PICK WHICHEVER ONE YOU WANT.
THE INSTANTS.
Human food is the best.
Yum.
This smell is to die for.
...
...Again?
All they eat is junk.
Today I'll make them some minestrone with lots of vegetables, steamed broccoli,
salted lettuce fried rice, and...
Kita-san is the loyal guardian of their health.
I'm not sure it's a good idea for animals to eat the same stuff as humans anyway.
We don't talk about that.
Shh.

Afterword

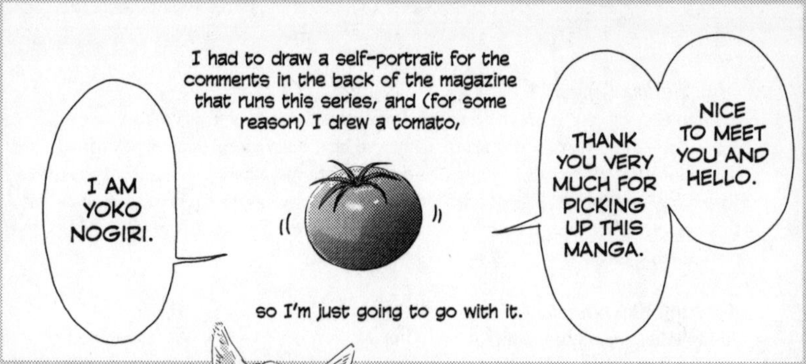
NICE TO MEET YOU AND HELLO.
THANK YOU VERY MUCH FOR PICKING UP THIS MANGA.
I had to draw a self-portrait for the comments in the back of the magazine that runs this series, and (for some reason) I drew a tomato,
I AM YOKO NOGIRI.
so I'm just going to go with it.

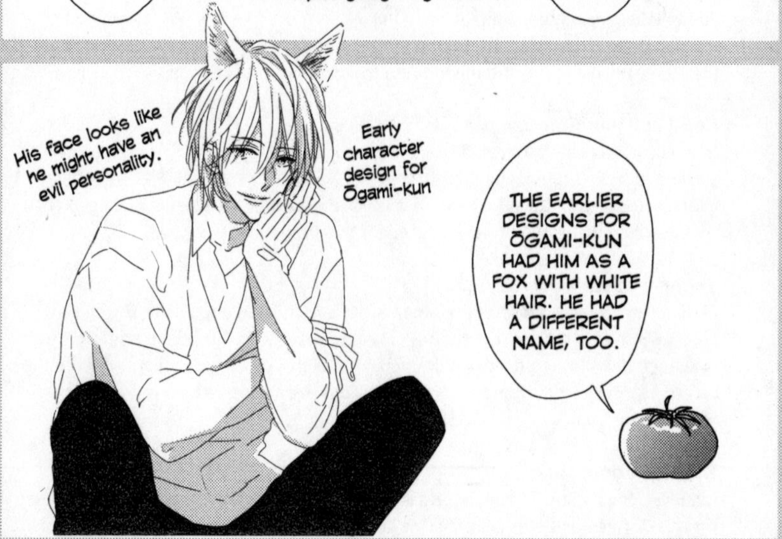
THE EARLIER DESIGNS FOR ŌGAMI-KUN HAD HIM AS A FOX WITH WHITE HAIR. HE HAD A DIFFERENT NAME, TOO.
Early character design for Ōgami-kun
His face looks like he might have an evil personality.

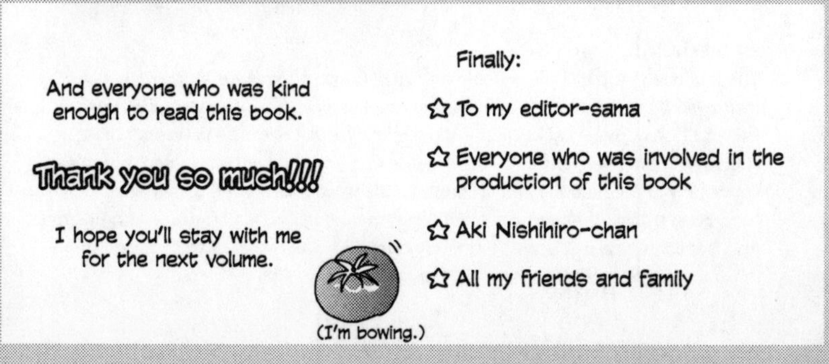
Finally:
☆ To my editor-sama
☆ Everyone who was involved in the production of this book
☆ Aki Nishihiro-chan
☆ All my friends and family
And everyone who was kind enough to read this book.
Thank you so much!!!
I hope you'll stay with me for the next volume.
(I'm bowing.)

Translation Notes

Ooh, a blazer, page 12

In Japanese schools, there are basically two types of uniforms. At Komugi's new school, the girls wear sailor collars, while the boys wear jackets called *gakuran*. At her old school, the girls wore blazers. Generally speaking, sailor collars and *gakuran* are associated with public schools, while blazers are associated with private schools. In this case, the fact that Komugi wears a blazer adds to the chicness of her having come from the big city.

Komugi, like wheat, page 15

Food names are not uncommon in Japan, and they're especially not uncommon in manga. As Yū kindly explains, *komugi* is the Japanese word for wheat. The name is fitting for the daughter of someone who makes *udon* wheat noodles for a living.

Can I call you Komugi, page 16

In Japan, even in high school, if you don't know someone very well, it can be considered rude to call them by their first name. Normally, Kana would be expected to address Komugi as "Kusunoki-san", but since she wants to be friends, she just asks if they can skip that formality and go straight to a first-name basis.

Tsune-jiichan, page 25

Jiichan translates roughly to "grandpa," and is a friendly title to add to the name of an elderly man, whether or not the speaker is related. Considering that they are still at school, the other students would probably call this gentleman *sensei*, which is the proper title for teachers and other faculty. Thus, we see that Yū considers everyone to be a close friend.

Kitsune udon, page 35

Kitsune udon means "fox udon," and is named after the fox because the main topping for this dish of noodles is *aburaage*, or deep-fried tofu. According to Japanese folklore, *aburaage* is a favorite food of foxes.

Ayakashi Inn, page 68

The name of this particular inn already gave Komugi cause for concern, because *ayashi-sō* (Ayashi Inn) can also mean "seems suspicious" in Japanese. But now, with the addition of the syllable *ka*, the inn becomes a place for the gathering of beings such as Yū and his friends. *Ayakashi* is one of a few blanket terms used to describe supernatural phenomena and creatures. This word and related terms (such as *yōkai*) have been translated many different ways, including ghost, phantom, demon, ghoul, etc., but in this case, it seems to mainly refer to animals that have acquired supernatural powers, including the ability to take a human shape.

Translation Notes

Oinari-san, page 70
Named after a Japanese god of rice and agriculture who is strongly associated with foxes, Oinari-san, or *inarizushi*, is a dish consisting of seasoned rice stuffed inside a pouch of *aburaage* fried tofu.

Animals living among humans, page 71
The stories referenced here are actual parts of Japanese folklore. Though it can't be proven that his mother was the white fox Kuzunoha, Abe no Seimei is a real person who served as an *onmyōji* (practitioner of *onmyōdō* cosmology) for emperors about a thousand years ago. Sōko Tanuki is a tanuki that took human form and worked as a Buddhist priest. His identity was discovered just like Yū's was—while he was napping. But because of his hard work, the priests at the temple made him a page and let him continue to work there.

Two-tailed cat, page 78
According to Japanese folklore, if a cat lives long enough, its tail will split into two and it will become an *ayakashi* known as a *nekomata*.

Otome games, page 98
An otome game is a video game made for *otome*, or "maidens," to simulate fantasies geared for the female gaze. In addition to playing through the main story as the leading lady, the player can also make choices that lead to a romantic ending with one of many male, and sometimes female, characters. Clearly Kana believes that the men in these games are much more worth her while than any real man.

Tsundere, page 133
For readers unfamiliar with Japanese anime and manga tropes, *tsundere* comes from *tsun-tsun* (meaning prickly) and *dere-dere* (meaning lovestruck). A *tsundere* is a character whose first reaction to other people is prickly and mean, but because they care deep down, sometimes those ooey-gooey emotions will show through.

A Kodansha Comics Trade Paperback Original
That Wolf-Boy is Mine! volume 1 copyright © 2015 Yoko Nogiri
English translation copyright © 2016 Yoko Nogiri

Published in the United States by Kodansha Comics, an imprint of
Kodansha USA Publishing, LLC, New York.

Publication rights for this English edition arranged through
Kodansha Ltd, Tokyo.

ISBN 978-1-63236-373-2

Printed in the United States of America.

www.kodansha.us

4th Printing
Translation: Alethea and Athena Nibley
Lettering: Sara Linsley
Editing: Haruko Hashimoto
Kodansha Comics edition cover design by Phil Balsman